Indispensable Counsel

INDISPENSABLE COUNSEL

The Chief Legal Officer in the New Reality

E. Norman Veasey

Christine T. Di Guglielmo

OXFORD
UNIVERSITY PRESS

Oxford University Press, Inc., publishes works that further Oxford University's objective of excellence
in research, scholarship, and education.

Oxford   New York
Auckland   Cape Town   Dar es Salaam   Hong Kong   Karachi   Kuala Lumpur
Madrid   Melbourne   Mexico City   Nairobi   New Delhi   Shanghai   Taipei   Toronto

With offices in
Argentina   Austria   Brazil   Chile   Czech Republic   France   Greece   Guatemala
Hungary   Italy   Japan   Poland   Portugal   Singapore   South Korea   Switzerland
Thailand   Turkey   Ukraine   Vietnam

Published by Oxford University Press, Inc.
198 Madison Avenue, New York, New York 10016

Oxford is a registered trademark of Oxford University Press
Oxford University Press is a registered trademark of Oxford University Press, Inc.

Library of Congress Cataloging-in-Publication Data

Veasey, E. Norman.
Indispensable counsel : the chief legal officer in the new reality / E. Norman Veasey,
Christine T. Di Guglielmo.
    p. cm.
Includes bibliographical references and index.
ISBN 978-0-19-539492-4 (hardback)
1. Corporate lawyers—United States. I. Di Guglielmo, Christine T. II. Title.
KF1425.V43 2012
346.73'06642—dc23
                                        2011039608

1 2 3 4 5 6 7 8 9
Printed in the United States of America on acid-free paper

Note to Readers
This publication is designed to provide accurate and authoritative information in regard to the subject
matter covered. It is based upon sources believed to be accurate and reliable and is intended to be
current as of the time it was written. It is sold with the understanding that the publisher is not
engaged in rendering legal, accounting, or other professional services. If legal advice or other expert
assistance is required, the services of a competent professional person should be sought. Also, to
confirm that the information has not been affected or changed by recent developments, traditional
legal research techniques should be used, including checking primary sources where appropriate.

*(Based on the Declaration of Principles jointly adopted by a Committee of the
American Bar Association and a Committee of Publishers and Associations.)*

You may order this or any other Oxford University Press publication by
visiting the Oxford University Press website at www.oup.com

CONTENTS

ABOUT THE AUTHORS

E. Norman Veasey is a senior partner at Weil, Gotshal & Manges LLP. He serves as a strategic adviser to the firm's roster of prominent global clients on a wide range of issues related to mergers & acquisitions, restructuring, and litigation. Additionally, he advises on corporate governance issues involving the responsibilities and fiduciary duties of corporate directors and officers in complex financial transactions, litigation, and crisis management.

Chief Justice Veasey is the former Chief Justice of Delaware, having stepped down from the Delaware Supreme Court in May 2004, after serving a 12-year term as the top judicial officer and administrator of that state's judicial branch. During his tenure as chief justice and beyond, the US Chamber of Commerce ranked Delaware's courts first in the nation for their fair, reasonable, and efficient litigation environment. Veasey has also been credited with leading nationwide programs to restore professionalism to the practice of law and adopt best practices in the running of America's courts. Delaware Governor Ruth Ann Minner awarded him the Order of the First State, the highest honor for meritorious service the state's governor can grant.

A graduate of Dartmouth College (AB 1954) and the University of Pennsylvania Law School (LLB 1957), he was Senior Editor of *The University of Pennsylvania Law Review*. After graduation from law school, from 1957 until he took office as chief justice in 1992, Veasey practiced law with the Wilmington, Delaware law firm Richards, Layton and Finger, where he concentrated on business law, corporate transactions, litigation, and counseling. He served at various times as managing partner and the chief executive officer of the firm. During 1961-63, he was Deputy Attorney General and Chief Deputy Attorney of the State of Delaware. In 1982-83, he was president of the Delaware State Bar Association. He served as Legal Officer of the Delaware Air National Guard, being honorably discharged in 1963 as a Captain in the Air Force Reserve.

Veasey was president of the Conference of Chief Justices, chair of the Board of the National Center for State Courts, chair of the Section of Business Law of the American Bar Association, and chair of the American Bar Association's Special Committee on Evaluation of the Rules of Professional Conduct (Ethics 2000). He was awarded in 1996 the Lewis Powell Award for ethics and professionalism by the American Inns of Court and in 2005 the Michael Franck Award by the American Bar Association. He is a past chair of the Committee on Corporate Laws of the Section of Business Law of the American Bar Association. During 1992-93 he was the editor of Volume 48 of *The Business Lawyer*, the scholarly legal journal published by the Section of Business Law of the ABA.

Veasey serves on the ABA Standing Committee on Ethics and Professional Responsibility. He is a Fellow of the American College of Trial Lawyers. He is a director of the Institute for Law and Economics at the University of Pennsylvania and a member of the American Law Institute, the International Advisory Board of the Centre for Corporate Law and Securities Regulation, the Board of Directors of the National Association of Corporate Directors, and numerous other professional organizations. He is a frequent panelist and lecturer on the corporation law, corporate governance, ethics, and professionalism. He is an Adjunct Professor at the Deadman School of Law of Southern Methodist University, the University of Virginia School of Law, and Wake Forest University School of Law. In 2009 and 2010 he received the "Global Corporate Governance Lawyer of the Year" award from the "Who's Who Legal Awards" and has been named in "Best Lawyers in America" for corporate governance and compliance.

He is married to the former Suzanne Johnson. They live in Wilmington, Delaware, and have four married children and eleven grandchildren.

Christine T. Di Guglielmo is an associate in the litigation department of Weil, Gotshal & Manges LLP, where she is a member of the securities litigation group. She is a member of the Delaware bar, practicing in Weil's Wilmington, Delaware, office. Ms. Di Guglielmo focuses on corporate governance matters, frequently representing boards of directors, senior management, and other constituents in shareholder derivative and class action litigation and counseling on corporate governance and fiduciary duty issues. She is also actively involved in pro bono work.

Ms. Di Guglielmo serves on the Delaware Board on the Unauthorized Practice of Law and on the Delaware Child Placement Review Board. She is active in the Women and the Law Section of the Delaware State Bar Association and in various community organizations and activities.

Ms. Di Guglielmo is a 1998 graduate of Brown University. She graduated, *summa cum laude*, from the University of Pennsylvania Law School in 2003, where she was executive editor of *The University of Pennsylvania Law Review*. Before joining Weil, Ms. Di Guglielmo served as a judicial clerk to Chief Justice Veasey. Ms. Di Guglielmo frequently writes with Chief Justice Veasey articles concerning corporate law and governance, corporate litigation, and the role of legal counsel with corporations.

She lives in Wilmington, Delaware, with her husband, Matthew Di Guglielmo, M.D., Ph.D., and their two children.

ACKNOWLEDGMENTS

We are so very grateful to numerous people for their support and assistance throughout the many months of work devoted to the preparation and writing of this book that it is impossible to name all of them or to thank them adequately. First, we must give the highest order of thanks to the members of our families for their unceasing and loving support, not to mention their tolerance of the many days, nights, weekends, and holidays that we were glued to the research, writing, and editing necessary for this effort, which, at times, seemed insurmountable to us.

High on our list of persons and institutions to thank for supporting and encouraging this project is our law firm, Weil, Gotshal & Manges LLP, and the many Weil partners, associates, clients, and staff who have shared their insights, wisdom, and skills with us. Our highest praise and thanks go to Carol Miller, our Wilmington assistant. And we owe, as well, many thanks to the other members of the Weil staff who provided us with invaluable assistance, especially Celeste Wright and Eleni Thomas, as well as research assistants Gregory Dodge and Jordan Schneider.

We are particularly grateful to Ben W. Heineman, Jr., and Ira M. Millstein for preparing their very gracious forewords to this text. To Ben, the quintessential general counsel, we owe a huge debt of gratitude for his sharing with us, along the way, his many cogent and thoughtful analyses of the expectations and challenges of the chief legal officer as "lawyer-statesman" in the pursuit of "high performance with high integrity." To Ira, our wise counselor, mentor, and senior partner, we are deeply grateful for his extraordinary and well-articulated insights into the necessity for the highest levels of professional skills, hard work, and personal integrity that must characterize all corporate lawyers, especially the general counsel, in navigating the challenges of corporate lawyering, especially in what he terms The New Normal.

We could not have carried out this task without the many clients and friends in the general counsel community who graciously and unselfishly took the time to share their wise thoughts and talents with us in many ways, especially in the interviewing process. As we have said in the Introduction, these interviews were essential to deepening our understanding of the world of the general counsel. There are well over thirty of these extraordinary interviewees whose quotes are liberally sprinkled throughout the book. They are listed, with their corporate affiliations, in the Introduction, *infra*. In addition to their interviews, many of these general counsel and other friends, particularly including Professor Stephen Bainbridge, Kenneth Fredeen, and Kim Rucker, took the time to provide us with additional comments on the text.

It has been said that "it takes a village" to do many grand and worthwhile things. We have tried to single out here just some of the "villagers" among the extraordinary community that was essential in producing this work.

FOREWORD
BY BEN W. HEINEMAN, JR.

This outstanding book explores with incisive detail and broad vision the "practical ideal" of the modern general counsel. Norman Veasey and Christine Di Guglielmo have written a comprehensive account of the varying roles and responsibilities of the corporation's top lawyer.

The foundational goals of the modern corporation should be the fusion of high performance with high integrity. The ideal of the modern general counsel is a lawyer-statesman who is adept at three distinct legal roles: an acute lawyer, a wise counselor, and a company leader. The contemporary general counsel, in carrying out those roles, plays a major part in assisting the corporation to achieve that fundamental fusion of performance with integrity which should be the foundation of global capitalism.

I believe that this concept of general counsel as lawyer-statesman has strong roots in major American companies, is growing in the UK and elsewhere in the EU, and has adherents in some companies elsewhere in the world. Trends over the past twenty-five years have made possible a powerful, affirmative leadership role for the general counsel, at least in large transnational enterprises, which is now on par in importance and status with the role of chief financial officer.

High performance means strong, sustained economic growth through provision of superior goods and services, which in turn provide durable benefits for shareholders and other stakeholders upon whom the company's health depends. Such performance entails an essential balance between risk taking (the creativity and innovation so essential to economic growth) and economic risk management (the financial, commercial, and operational disciplines so essential to the soundness and durability of business institutions).

High integrity means robust adherence to the letter and spirit of formal rules, both legal and financial; voluntary adoption of global ethical standards that bind the company and its employees; and an employee commitment to core values of honesty, candor, fairness, trustworthiness, and reliability. It involves understanding, and mitigating, other types of risk—beyond direct economic risk—which can cause a company catastrophic harm: legal, ethical, reputational, communications, public policy, and country-geopolitical.

But the fusion of high performance with high integrity is not just about risk mitigation. It is about creating affirmative benefits in the company, in the marketplace, and in the broader global society. Ultimately, high performance with high integrity is about the role of business in society—about corporate citizenship. High performance with high integrity creates fundamental trust among shareholders, creditors, employees, recruits, customers, suppliers, regulators, communities, the media, and the general public. This trust is essential to sustaining the corporate power and freedom that drives the economy with widespread economic and social benefits—trust which, in the past ten years, has dramatically eroded due to stark corporate scandals and unthinkable business failures.

The core task of the CEO and of top senior executives like the general counsel is to build a performance-with-integrity culture that permeates the corporation. Such a culture entails shared principles (values, policies, and attitudes) and shared practices (norms, systems, and processes). Although this culture must include elements of deterrence against legal, financial, and ethical wrongdoing, it must, at the end of the day, be affirmative. An underlying tenet of this culture should be that people want to do the right thing because leaders—starting with the CEO and led, importantly, by the general counsel—make it a company imperative and live it themselves. Clear expectations must be driven down into the company, and there must be a uniform global culture that applies in every nation and cannot be bent by corrupt local practices, regardless of short-term business costs.

This conception of the core mission of the corporation has evolved over the past twenty-five years due to a number of developments: the drumbeat of scandals with ever-greater financial and institutional harms, often approaching the catastrophic; a heightened concern among a growing number of non-governmental institutions who are corporate watchdogs with access to the global media; the swing of the political pendulum from deregulation to increasing regulation; the challenges of developing a uniform company culture on the core functions of law and finance, which are the nervous system of great transnational companies; the great challenges of doing business in emerging markets plagued by corruption and lacking rule of law; and, most important, the recognition by CEOs and boards, in light of these developments and in light of their own values, of the need for strong corporate citizenship. This strong corporate citizenship entails making and selling great goods and services the right way and, in doing so, serving local, regional, national, and global communities in order to engender the crucial trust that is so necessary to sustained economic growth, brand power, and strong reputation with both internal and external constituencies.

The essence of being a lawyer-statesman is to move beyond the first question—"is it legal?"—to the ultimate question—"is it right?" Such a role involves leadership, or shared responsibility, not just for the corporation's legal matters but also for its positions on ethics, reputation, public policy, communications, corporate citizenship, country, and geopolitical trends. The lawyer-statesman role involves not just dealing with past problems, but charting future courses; not just playing defense, but playing offense; not just providing legal advice, broadly defined, but being part of the business team and offering business advice. Even more broadly, it involves the wise counseling and leadership roles that stem from practical wisdom, not just technical mastery; that require broad judgment based on knowledge of history, culture, human nature, and institutions, not just a sharp tactical sense; that flow from the ability to understand long-term implications, not just achieve short-term advantage; and that are founded on a deep concern for the public interest, not just the private good.

In aspiring to be a lawyer-statesman, the general counsel, and inside lawyers, must be skilled in asking "what ought to be" questions; in articulating systematic and constructive options that expose and explore the value tensions inherent in most decisions; in assessing risk, but not being paralyzed by its existence; in understanding how to make rules realities and develop strategies for meaningful implementation of policies; in understanding the hurly burly world of politics, media, and power outside the corporation and how to navigate with principle and purpose in that domain; in leading and building organizations, creating the vision, the values, the priorities, the strategies, the people, the systems, the resources, and the motivation; in having understanding, intuition, perspective, and respect relating to different cultures around the globe; in, ultimately, having the quintessential quality of the great generalist to envision and understand the multiple dimensions of issues—to define the problem properly—and the ability to comprehensively integrate those dimensions in decision-making.

Increasingly, CEOs and boards of directors have recognized the value of a sophisticated general counsel who can fill this capacious lawyer-statesman role. They have hired as general counsel—and other key inside lawyers whether generalist or specialist—highly accomplished lawyers from the bar, from government, and from other corporations. They have recognized that meeting or exceeding market rates, especially for lawyers coming from private practice or other companies, is a small price to pay for creation of an inside legal group that can truly partner on a day-to-day basis with business leaders. Both CEOs and boards of directors increasingly want independent, courageous general counsel who can, ultimately, be guardians of the corporation, even as they work effectively on business teams. Increasingly, CEOs and boards recognize that they must provide strong support for the general counsel so that he or she can resolve the partner-guardian tension that is at the core of being a chief legal officer.

In sum, in the course of a generation, general counsels' prestige, status, compensation, power, and position at the core of major transnational corporations have been transformed. The general counsel has become, in many cases, the chief legal advisor to the CEO and to the board of directors, replacing the venerable senior partner from the great law firm. This is so because the general counsel in many companies has, as noted, broad responsibilities, as leader or top team participant, for law; ethics; reputation, commercial, and integrity risk; country and geopolitical risk; and, ultimately, for corporate citizenship, often leading or co-leading not just the legal organization but corporate units responsible for compliance, environment, trade, taxes, public policy, and corporate citizenship.

In this book, the authors make a timely argument, with which I wholeheartedly agree, that one important step for corporations to take—in order to regain corporate trust eroded by persistent scandals and catastrophic business failures—is to define, hire, and support a general counsel as lawyer-statesman. Despite strong trends toward an enhanced general counsel role, not all medium and large corporations are doing this. All should.

Ben W. Heineman, Jr.
Former Senior Vice President-General Counsel and Senior Vice President
    Law and Public Affairs General Electric Company
Distinguished Senior Fellow
Program on the Legal Profession
Harvard Law School
Senior Fellow
Program on Corporate Governance
Harvard Law School
Senior Fellow
Belfer Center for Science and International Affairs
John F. Kennedy School of Government
Harvard University
July 2011

FOREWORD

BY IRA M. MILLSTEIN

I have a strong bias in adding my introduction to this path-breaking book on the modern life and evolution of the role of the corporate general counsel, written by Judge Norman Veasey and Christine Di Guglielmo.

I have known Judge Veasey for many years, beginning with his career as a preeminent Delaware lawyer, when Delaware was earning the role of the place for equal justice for all constituents of the corporate community. In those days, Norman Veasey's demeanor as "outside" counsel, as well as his being the choice of local counsel by law firms all over the country, was based on his unique capacity for sensitivity to the role of the profession, in general.

When he became Chief Justice of the Supreme Court, he was a leader in shaping Delaware law to fit the exciting new times of takeovers and other corporate events. Many of Judge Veasey's decisions are landmarks, shaping formerly uncharted territories. Good enough, but more importantly, he regularly saw and heard the best and worst of our profession up close and personal, both from inside and outside the corporation. I never heard of Judge Veasey being intemperate, but rather he was patient, instructive, and non-judgmental about our behavior. It rounded further his vast understanding of the evolution of our responsibilities as, again, both inside and outside counsel. There wasn't very much he didn't see and hear about counsel's responsibilities and behavior from his perch on that Court.

After he left the Bench, I had the good luck, based on our long friendship outside the courtroom, to convince him to join our firm. Not simply because of his total understanding of the law and the role of counsel, but also because of his unquestioned integrity, my partners and I believed he would be a role model as a true professional. He is everything we expected and more, and is turned to regularly by our lawyers for counsel on everything from the mundane to the sticky.

I firmly believe that this book, thus, is not just an academic primer. It is, rather, the accumulated experience of a true "lawyer" who has seen and ingested just about everything our profession, inside and outside, faces today in what he terms The New Reality, but which is, in my terms, The New Normal. These are, and will be, very challenging times for the whole profession. And where else can one find such accumulated wisdom than in this comprehensive work?

Then there is the foreword by my former client and my now very good friend and compatriot in moving the world of corporate governance forward, Ben Heineman. I would have liked better the opportunity to write what Ben said, placing in context the role and responsibilities of the general counsel. Ben, however, got there first in this book, and I would only echo every word, so I won't. Ben's advice, which he has and will develop in his writing and lectures, centers on the core of the corporation: "High Performance with High Integrity." This excellent new book by Judge Veasey and our colleague, Christine Di Guglielmo, fills in the implementation. Perfect harmony, in my judgment, for all of us.

My contribution, granting my bias, is simply to contribute more than sixty years of experience with judges, regulators, academics, and outside and many inside counsel. I intend that experience to convince readers to dig deeply into the collective wisdom of the authors and their interviewees in this book.

I have had the opportunity to participate in the evolution of the role, and hence quality, of the men and women who are assuming the now more and more challenging role of general counsel. As the book notes, I started representing major corporations at a time when outside counsel were most frequently being chosen by a CEO, or board of directors, directly. Then, one met the general counsel of a corporate client as a courtesy; it was not made known that outside counsel reported to the general counsel, rather that the CEO or board was to be the client and contact. But, as time wore on, corporations became larger and more complex, and the notion that executives might hire friends and acquaintances wore thin. Because the choices were not always based on quality, but rather contacts of one kind or another, this became problematic as companies went truly national and international. Less than full quality advice, away from home base, often led to disastrous results.

Corporations began to seek control over all the advice they were being given, from anywhere. This need, to make a long evolution shorter, ultimately led to the general counsel being given the responsibility to control the choice of outside counsel from wherever and for whatever.

For me, and other firms, this was a welcome development. We believed we were more likely to see the newly empowered general counsel seek quality and retain it, and that turned out to be the case. My two principal mentors were the GCs of JC Penney and General Electric. They literally taught me that quality was the objective, and that if my firm was to be retained, we would have to have the quality expected, or lose out.

This was a sobering message for many outside counsel; I believe it caused us all to upgrade seriously, a good result for all of us.

Following this early development of the role of GC, at least in my experience, and as Judge Veasey, Christine, and Ben have noted, the GC increasingly became responsible for more and more. In my opinion, this has been a very welcome development for the profession in representing our key economic vehicle, the corporation. I believe it has provided the whole corporate community and the economy more certainty of "professional" services.

This book provides the guide to implementing all of the responsibilities of those representing Corporate America, not just the general counsel, but those who serve, or hope to serve, the corporation. Outside counsel can learn they have a corporate contact to work with, who, in all likelihood, is fully qualified to know and demand quality service. That wasn't the usual situation when I started!

Ira M. Millstein
Senior Partner
Weil, Gotshal & Manges LLP
Senior Associate Dean for Corporate Governance,
    Yale School of Management
July 2011

PREFACE

The title of this book, *Indispensable Counsel: The Chief Legal Officer in the New Reality*, is somewhat cryptic. Crafting a short title that captures in a meaningful way the complexities and challenges in the life of a modern general counsel[1] has proven difficult. But we have attempted to suggest in the title some of the themes that run throughout this book.

One of those themes relates to the many nuances and tensions that the chief legal officer must navigate nearly every day as the persuasive counselor to the corporation and its constituents. Another is our attempt to capture the relatively recent and revolutionary changes in the general counsel's role. In overview, the dynamic evolution of the role has intensified the indispensability of the general counsel to the corporate enterprise. The principal mission of this book is to explore, at least on an overarching level, some of the major challenges and trends that pervade the daily lives of corporate general counsel of U.S. public companies. We will also endeavor to conclude with some of our own opinions about best practices.

It is rather presumptuous of us to write about the life and work of a corporate chief legal officer when neither of us has ever been one. The reader will have to evaluate our shortcomings in that regard. We have, of course, worked—and continue to work—with many chief legal officers. To some extent, over the years, we have seen the good and not-so-good examples of general counsel lawyering, acumen, and conduct from observation, the cases, literature, and anecdotes. Of most importance, however, we have gained knowledge and enrichment from our professional interaction with general counsel over the years. These experiences have been enhanced immeasurably by the interviews of more than thirty general counsel that

---

1. Throughout the book we use interchangeably the title "general counsel" (abbreviated at times to GC) and "chief legal officer" (abbreviated at times to CLO).

we conducted in connection with writing this book. Thus, we hope that we bring an objective, outside perspective to an understanding of the role.

We are very grateful for the support and interest in this project of our firm and of the many talented general counsel we interviewed. Nevertheless, we must add this important caveat: The views expressed in this book are solely the views of the authors and they do not necessarily reflect the views of our interviewees, Weil, Gotshal & Manges LLP, or the firm's clients, partners, and associates.

INTRODUCTION

The chief legal officer straddles the world of business and law, and thus occupies a status that is unique among both lawyers and business people. First, it is unique among other leaders in the corporation—the other senior officers and members of the board of directors. The general counsel possesses and employs unique skills and qualities of mind that help the executive team and the directors to guide the corporate enterprise to desired and ethical business results. The CLO undertakes to accomplish this while keeping in the front of the minds of the principal corporate actors the myriad ethical, legal, policy, political, and risk considerations that may be implicated by a particular business strategy. Indeed, the indispensability of the properly functioning and ethical CLO has been dramatically elevated in recent years to rival in importance that of the chief executive officer (CEO) and the chief financial officer (CFO) in many organizations.

Second, the CLO's role is unique in comparison with that of other lawyers—including those practicing corporate law, either as subordinate in-house counsel or outside corporate counsel. That is because of the unique relationship of trust and confidence that the CLO develops with the other members of the senior business team, and the unique view and understanding she develops as a lawyer, trusted advisor, and business partner inside the corporation.

The role is distinctive because of the CLO's dual role as both (a) the "business partner" with the CEO, CFO, and other members of the senior management "C-suite" in dealing with the company's strategy, opportunity, and risk; and (b) the "guardian of the corporate integrity" in the C-suite and in the boardroom by seeking to ensure that the corporation and its constituents adhere to the highest legal and ethical principles. These responsibilities are of critical importance to the corporation on many levels. Ben Heineman, the legendary former general counsel of General Electric (who has graciously written a foreword to this book), has succinctly captured these concepts in his use of the terms "partner/guardian" and "statesman" to describe the embodiment of the quintessential general counsel.[1]

Our focus on the "New Reality" is an attempt to connote the continual evolution of the challenging legal and business landscape in which the CLO operates. "New Reality" can mean different things to different people. To us, it denotes three primary phenomena: (a) the dynamic escalation of the difficulties and tensions being regularly experienced by general counsel of public companies over the past few years; (b) the dramatic and ongoing changes during the same period in the complexities of the law, business, investor activism, litigation, regulation, politics, and the media; and (c) the considerable impact of globalization on business realities.

In doing our research for this book we consulted not only the literature and our various experiences as practitioner or judge, as the case may be, but also—and this is of paramount significance—we conducted extensive interviews of more than thirty general counsel of major entities in the United States and Canada. We are very grateful to the following incumbent or former general counsel who kindly consented to our in-depth interviews (listed with the organization with which they are currently or were most recently affiliated as general counsel): Alan Braverman, The Walt Disney Company; Louis J. Briskman, CBS Corporation; Kristin Campbell, Staples, Inc.; Adam Ciongoli, Willis Group Holdings, Ltd; Daniel Cooperman, Apple Inc.; Brackett B. Denniston III, General Electric Company; Daniel Desjardins, Bombardier, Inc.; Simon A. Fish, BMO Financial Group; Kenneth J. Fredeen, Deloitte & Touche LLP (Canada); J. Alberto Gonzalez-Pita, HCP, Inc.; Susan Hackett, Association of Corporate Counsel; Douglas Hagerman, Rockwell Automation, Inc.; Patricia R. Hatler, Nationwide Mutual Insurance Company; Ben W. Heineman, Jr., General Electric Company; Michael J. Holston, Hewlett-Packard Company; Charles J. Kalil,

---

1. *See, e.g.*, Ben W. Heineman, Jr., *The General Counsel as Lawyer-Statesman*, Harv. L. School Program on the Legal Profession Blue Paper (Sept. 5, 2010), *available at* http://blogs.law.harvard.edu/corpgov/2010/09/05/the-general-counsel-as-lawyer-statesman/ (discussing the general counsel's role as lawyer-statesman) [hereinafter Heineman, *Lawyer-Statesman*]; Ben W. Heineman, Jr., *Caught in the Middle*, Corp. Counsel, Apr. 2007, http://www.law.harvard.edu/programs/olin_center/corporate_governance/articles/Heineman-CC-Caught-in-the-Middle-April07.pdf ("The greatest challenge for general counsel and other inside lawyers is to reconcile the dual—and at times contradictory—roles of being both a partner to the business leaders and a guardian of the corporation's integrity and reputation."); *see also* E. Norman Veasey, Chief Justice of Delaware, Law Day Reflections on Lawyers' Fees, Address to the Corpus Christi Texas Bar and Business Community (May 4, 1995) [hereinafter Veasey, Lawyers' Fees], and Address to the Wilmington Delaware Rotary Club (May 18, 1995) (noting the role of the "lawyer statesman" or "lawyer statesperson," in which lawyers are "highly visible" as "leaders of the community") (on file with authors).

The Dow Chemical Company; Stasia Kelly, American International Group, Inc.; Gary F. Kennedy, American Airlines, Inc.; E. Julia Lambeth, Reynolds American, Inc.; David Leitch, Ford Motor Company; Charles W. Matthews, Exxon Mobil Corporation; Michele Mayes, Allstate Insurance Company; Sara E. Moss, The Estée Lauder Companies, Inc.; Robert H. Mundheim, Salomon Smith Barney Holdings, Inc.; Louise Parent, American Express Company; Kim K.W. Rucker, Avon Products, Inc.; Thomas L. Sager, E. I. du Pont de Nemours and Company; Amy Schulman, Pfizer, Inc.; Bruce Sewell, Apple Inc; Deirdre Stanley, Thomson Reuters Corporation; Laura Stein, The Clorox Company; Larry D. Thompson, PepsiCo, Inc. In addition, we interviewed other general counsel who asked that we not identify them by name.

These interviewees painted vivid pictures of the challenges and significance of the role of general counsel, as well as how it has recently undergone a striking transformation. Many interviewees contrasted the role of the general counsel of today with that of a decade or longer ago, with some describing a "sea change" in the CLO's "day job" over the past five years or less. Many quotations from these interviews are sprinkled throughout the book.

So, the "New Reality" is perhaps in the eye of the beholder. To some, the most vexing complications and challenges lie in new laws, regulations, and attitudes of regulators, prosecutors, lawmakers, and activist investors. To others, the major changes are in the nature of corporate business today, including the globalization of the marketplace. To many, the *bête noire* is litigation. We hope that, as the book unfolds, the reader will pull from it what is most relevant and applicable to the reader's world.

WHO IS "THE" CHIEF LEGAL OFFICER?

We recognize that in-house legal departments vary widely in characteristics such as size, resources, culture, style, and the particular legal and business issues confronting their companies. Some in-house legal departments of large, multinational corporations rival the size of many large, global law firms.[2] Moreover, they may employ lawyers with expertise as deep and varied as that which can be found in such firms.[3] Other in-house

---

2. *See, e.g.*, Ben W. Heineman, Jr., *Big Isn't Always Best*, OUTSIDE COUNSEL, Nov. 2008, at 94 (noting that General Electric's global law department consists of approximately 1,100 in-house lawyers).

3. *Id.*

law departments are smaller and rely more heavily on outside counsel. We focus primarily on public corporations with sizable in-house legal departments, but many of the issues discussed in this book may be relevant to the life of a general counsel of a non-corporate or non-public entity or a law department of more modest size, as well.

In short, there is no single, representative, or stereotypical chief legal officer. We describe a vision of the general counsel in the modern corporation that other general counsel or other constituents may wish to use to test their own understandings and visions of the general counsel's roles, responsibilities, and challenges.

WHO IS THE INTENDED AUDIENCE?

When we began the process of planning and writing, we thought that the audience for the book would most likely be confined to persons who hold the office of general counsel. Yet, we never intended—and still do not intend—that the book be a detailed, "how to" manual about "best practices" for the chief legal officer and other in-house counsel in carrying out specific functions or dealing with specific laws, regulations, or other challenges. Others have done that job well.[4]

As our themes and the text unfolded, however, we ultimately decided that chief legal officers should not be seen as our *exclusive* audience because it is important that those participating in, or interacting with, U.S. corporations in various other capacities understand the world of the corporate general counsel in the new reality. Thus, while one who is a general counsel may well benefit from the views of her peers as presented in the book, there are also other readers to whom the book might be meaningful. Moreover, an enhanced understanding among various constituencies of the general counsel's role might tend to improve corporate governance and management, generally.

The book aims to explore and analyze the role of the person occupying the position of chief legal officer, but also to help other stakeholders, particularly the senior officers, other in-house lawyers, outside counsel, directors, and investors gain an important understanding of the role as well as the challenges and tensions that arise for one in the position of general counsel. The text is designed to confront, on both a practical and

---

4. For example, an excellent "how to" work is JOHN K. VILLA'S two-volume treatise CORPORATE COUNSEL GUIDELINES (1999, Supp. 2010).

theoretical basis, some difficult and recurring questions facing general counsel in the new reality.

In addition, the book might be helpful to an even broader audience, including the media, regulators, lawmakers, prosecutors, academics, and the judiciary, who often see the work of, or come in contact with, the general counsel. We envision that this broader audience may well benefit from a more in-depth and holistic understanding of the unique role of the chief legal officer than they might acquire based only on sporadic contact or anecdotal evidence.

CHAPTER 1

The General Counsel's Challenges in the New Reality

General counsel deal with big problems and big opportunities.
—Louise M. Parent[1]

A. THE LANDSCAPE

Cataclysmic financial events and corporate misconduct scandals of the last decade have created a "new reality" that forms an unprecedented environment for corporate counsel and, in particular, the chief legal officer. In this new reality, general counsel face troubling challenges and new regulatory and legal worries. The new reality is, in part, a phenomenon of the post-Enron/Sarbanes-Oxley era and the financial "meltdown" era of 2008–2011. The events of those years, followed by the ensuing U.S. federal legislation embodied in the Dodd-Frank Act and the impending regulations, have ratcheted up the intensity of the tensions beyond what was already a very challenging environment for the general counsel.

With the 2010 passage of the Dodd-Frank Act and before it the 2002 Sarbanes-Oxley Act (SOX), the federal government has undertaken such an increased role in corporate governance and regulatory matters that these events are likely to alter significantly the traditional balance of state and federal government authority. Stockholder activism is increasing.

---

1. Interview with Louise M. Parent, Executive Vice President and General Counsel, American Express Company (Nov. 2, 2009).

Accordingly, the relative roles of, and balance of power among, management, directors, and stockholders are changing.

In his excellent book entitled *Corporate Governance After the Scandals and the Financial Crisis*,[2] Professor Bainbridge of UCLA Law School has put it succinctly as follows:

> The new economic crisis was far larger and infinitely more complex than the one that had motivated passage of The Sarbanes-Oxley Act. Because Sarbanes-Oxley was a response to a series of securities frauds rather than systemic market failures, the Act's focus was on various forms of fraud prevention. In contrast, the financial crisis that produced Dodd-Frank revealed massive systemic problems throughout the financial services industry and triggered such far-flung responses as the federal bailout of GM and Chrysler.
>
> In short order, a nearly universal consensus formed among legislators, regulators, and opinion makers that corporate governance was again at fault. . . .
>
> In fact, however, systemic flaws in the corporate governance of Main Street corporations were not a causal factor in the housing bubble, the bursting of that bubble, or the subsequent credit crunch. . . .
>
> . . . .
>
> Compared to some of the proposals floated in Congress following the 2007–2008 financial crisis, Dodd-Frank's corporate governance provisions are relatively modest. . . . Even so, however, the remaining provisions impose important new duties and expand the federal regulatory role in corporate governance.
>
> What do these provisions have to do with the causes and consequences of the financial crisis? In short, not much. . . .
>
> Are Dodd-Frank's governance provisions quackery, as were Sarbanes-Oxley's? In short, yes. Without exception, the proposals lack strong empirical or theoretical justification. . . .
>
> . . . . Only in response to major economic crises does corporate governance become a matter of national political concern. This recurrent pattern inherently tends to result in flawed legislation.[3]

We focus here on the general counsel's challenges in the new reality with the goal of enhancing the understanding among all relevant corporate constituencies of the complexities of the CLO's roles. The corporate general counsel is a key player—perhaps *the* key player—in this new reality. While navigating the demands and interests of the various constituencies,

2. STEPHEN M. BAINBRIDGE, CORPORATE GOVERNANCE AFTER THE SCANDALS AND THE FINANCIAL CRISIS (forthcoming 2011).
3. *Id.* manuscript at 14–15, 23, 24.

the chief legal officer must remain ever vigilant to serve the best interests of the client—the corporation itself. In light of the heightened spotlight on ethics, integrity, and skill within the corporate legal and business environment, we attempt in this book to scrutinize the complicated life of the independent, yet business-oriented, chief legal officer.

We begin with the obvious truism that the general counsel's only client is (or should be) the corporate entity. So, what does it really mean to represent the corporation? What interests does corporate counsel serve? The answers to these questions are complicated.

First, the company's chief executive officer, in conjunction or consultation with the board of directors, has usually hired the chief legal officer. Second, the CLO is a member of the senior management team, and maintains a close working relationship with the CEO, the CFO, and other members of senior management. Third, the CLO is the principal legal advisor to the board, while operating in an environment in which corporate counsel are expected by many regulators to be "gatekeepers" or "cops on the beat." In short, and to oversimplify, the general counsel must possess certain fundamental characteristics: (a) great technical skills as a lawyer, (b) wisdom and judgment as a counselor, (c) strong leadership ability, (d) independence, and (e) an unwavering moral compass.

There may be times when the CEO and some board members perceive the "best interests of the corporation" differently. If and when the CEO and the directors have differing visions of the corporation's best interests, an effort at harmonizing these differing visions is an important goal. This highlights an inherent tension in the role of CLO: The CEO relies on the CLO for practical, strategic, and legal advice, and boards expect the general counsel to be an independent legal advisor to the board. The general counsel needs not only to ensure that both senior management and the board keep those things in mind, but also to identify, understand, and manage any resulting tensions that may arise.

The ultimate determination by the directors and senior management of what is in the corporation's best interests requires careful and ongoing assessment and management of strategy, risks, operations, and compliance. Accordingly, the general counsel must possess strong personal characteristics such as wisdom, judgment, leadership, and a strong sense of ethics, as well as great legal skills. She has to be positioned to take, and should take, an active role in overseeing and guiding the design, direction, and monitoring of the corporation's business strategy, risk assessment, compliance, and operations. The general counsel therefore must be thoroughly grounded in all of these areas and be prepared to be independent, courageous, and assertive when necessary.

The general counsel is, most importantly, the "guardian of the corporate integrity" and should act as a persuasive counselor for the CEO and the board. Consider the following articulations by some of the general counsel we interviewed:

The general counsel is the guardian of the integrity of the company. That may have been the case 20 years ago, 10 years ago, 5 years ago, but now the general counsel is much more in a fishbowl, under a magnifying lens, as to how they're fulfilling that role.[4]

* * *

The general counsel's job is to be the champion of integrity and the champion of compliance. That's the way the organization looks upon the general counsel. That's a tremendously important role. It cannot be done effectively without buy-in from the CEO and the rest of the leadership.

One of the things the general counsel can help do is ensure that the CEO understands what's being done and is supportive.

I wouldn't say we're the conscience of the corporation. I think the CEO, the board, and all of the leadership are the conscience. But the general counsel is a champion for integrity, compliance, and the rule of law.[5]

* * *

I view the general counsel as, in many ways, a steward of the company's values. As such, general counsel occupy a unique position. I like to say that we have the Archimedean vantage point, because we observe many worlds but don't completely belong to any of them. We have commitments to our shareholders, and therefore to the commercial world. We have a unique viewpoint of the centrality of the commercial focus in any organization.

At a biopharmaceutical company like ours, we have a regulatory component that we don't own but that we are responsible for safeguarding. We have a communication element that we don't own, but clearly from a disclosure and corporate integrity point of view, we're very closely connected to communications.

Risk assessment and trend spotting are important parts of our job as well.[6]

* * *

For the GC, the partnership role arises as he or she helps the CEO understand that the law can be used affirmatively and strategically in a wide variety of ways, including achieving business goals as quickly and effectively as possible . . . .

---

4. Interview with Laura Stein, Senior Vice President—General Counsel, The Clorox Company (Dec. 22, 2009).

5. Interview with Brackett B. Denniston III, Senior Vice President and General Counsel, General Electric Company (Dec. 16, 2009).

6. Interview with Amy W. Schulman, Senior Vice President and General Counsel, Pfizer Inc. (Mar. 17, 2010).

[T]he CEO must also want both the CFO and the GC to be strong voices in raising issues relating both to performance risks and to integrity risks. With respect to the integrity risks, the CEO must recognize that both the CFO and the GC represent the corporation's interests—not the CEO's interests. In fact, to serve effectively as guardians, both the CFO and the GC should have strong independent relationships with the board. . . .

In their guardian role, the CFO and the GC have to resist giving the kinds of quick, simplistic answers that may seem necessary in fast-moving, complex situations . . . .

[M]ost mixed business-integrity issues come cloaked in shades of gray. The task of the CFO and the GC in such cases is to give the CEO options that—while all are lawful, and are all based on clearly articulated assumptions about the facts—entail varying degrees of legal, regulatory, ethical, and reputational risk. If more facts are needed, this has to be weighed against real-time pressures.[7]

We have used the term "persuasive counselor" to describe the CLO's role in guarding the corporate integrity while operating in the context of her position as part of the senior executive team.[8] The general counsel as persuasive counselor affirmatively, proactively, and courageously tries to persuade her client to follow the law, to go beyond mere compliance with the law, and to lead the client to "do the right thing" from a moral, ethical, and sensible business perspective. Indeed, to use a hockey analogy, the persuasive counselor needs to know not only where the puck *is* but also where it is *going*, in terms of both particular issues confronting the corporation and anticipation of developments in the law and regulatory environment more broadly.

The CLO, as the guardian of the integrity of the firm, seeks to ensure that the "tone at the top"—as well as below the top—is exemplary and that the best efforts of the board and management are devoted to "doing the right thing," while advancing business profitability, guarding against unintended consequences, and avoiding or mitigating nasty encounters with regulators, plaintiffs' lawyers, activist investors, media, and politicians.

Thus, the CLO must operate in the "New Reality," which is the post-Enron/Sarbanes-Oxley period that progressed into the era of the financial meltdown and the Dodd-Frank Act. No doubt another new reality may follow some future crisis, scandal, or other development. But for now,

---

7. BEN W. HEINEMAN, JR., HIGH PERFORMANCE WITH HIGH INTEGRITY 69–71 (2008).

8. *E. g.*, E. Norman Veasey & Christine T. Di Guglielmo, *The Tensions, Stresses, and Professional Responsibilities of the Lawyer for the Corporation*, 62 BUS. LAW. 1 (2006).

the CLO must get her arms around all the issues of this New Reality, which include (but are not limited to) this sampling, in no particular order:

- Maintaining a "tone at the top" and "tone in the middle" of high integrity
- Legal and other compliance issues in a multitude of fields
- Strategy, risk assessment, and risk management
- Massive regulatory and litigation concerns for the corporate entity, officers, and directors
- Understanding and helping to navigate diverse areas of law and business, such as M&A, intellectual property, employment, Foreign Corrupt Practices Act (FCPA), etc.
- Crisis management
- Internal investigations
- Board accountability, objectivity, level of understanding, and leadership
- Leading the board and management to consider penetrating questions, rather than check-the-box processes
- Director overload as a governance concern
- Tensions between the board and senior management
- Executive compensation as a governance and regulatory matter
- Transparency and disclosure issues
- Fiduciary duties of directors of companies in distress
- The CLO's own ethics and professional responsibility issues
- Stockholder activism and communication
- Corporate reputational concerns and media or political attacks
- Potential lawyer liability and SEC enforcement sanctions against in-house and outside lawyers
- Challenges raised by complex corporate and alternative entity structures

We focus on the general counsel's multiple roles in the corporation and the various sources of tension faced by the general counsel in fulfilling those roles. In particular, the text postulates a thesis of integrity, ethics, business acumen, courage, and independence, an understanding of which can guide the CLO as a persuasive counselor, business advisor, and guardian of corporate integrity.

B. KEY CHARACTERISTICS OF THE GENERAL COUNSEL POSITION

Upon even a cursory consideration of the challenges facing the general counsel in the new reality, one quickly grasps both the complexity and the rewards inherent in the general counsel position. Indeed, one overarching framework for categorizing the characteristics of the CLO position is that the job is:

- Interesting
- Multifaceted
- Lonely
- Perilous

1. The "Interesting" Aspect

CLOs have the opportunity to work as an integral part of senior management and also to counsel the board in shaping and furthering business strategy. This aspect of the job requires a thorough immersion in, and understanding of, the nature of the corporation's business, its people, its culture, and its competitive environment. The breadth of the responsibilities and substantive content of the job can be both stimulating and rewarding. Being general counsel is "a continuous learning experience, which is one of the reasons people like it and find it interesting."[9]

Moreover, the general counsel must have the people skills and relationships to navigate the corporate culture well. Job satisfaction—and success—can hinge on whether the CLO *likes* the business and the people. The business should involve taking prudent risks, while promoting the highest corporate integrity and "tone at the top," as well as "tone in the middle." Ben Heineman has expounded well the thesis of the CLO's crucial role as guardian of corporate integrity, while serving importantly as a business partner, and the inherent tensions in the general counsel's dual, partner-guardian roles.[10]

2. The "Multifaceted" Aspect

The general counsel of a major public company in North America is expected to be a bit of a "renaissance person"—the problem-solving "'Swiss Army

9. Interview with Kristin Campbell, Senior Vice President and General Counsel, Staples, Inc. (Oct. 28, 2009).
10. HEINEMAN, *supra* note 7; *see also* Heineman, *Lawyer-Statesman*, *supra* Introduction, note 1.

Knife' of the legal profession."[11] As we discuss in chapter 3, and as we catalogued in a 2006 article in *The Business Lawyer*,[12] the chief legal officer of a major public company has a very large portfolio of roles ranging from corporate officer to ethicist.

As business, legal, and ethical advisor, the chief legal officer is a key part of the senior management team that develops business strategy for consideration by the board of directors. As a persuasive counselor to that team, the chief legal officer should have the business acumen, independence, inquisitiveness, leadership skills, and courage to help shape and lead senior management's business decisions. And the CLO should be a pivotal part of the senior management team in presenting issues to the board so that the directors will *understand* the issues as thoroughly as possible. There may be times, as well, when the chief legal officer needs to say to the CEO and senior management, when appropriate, and before the matter reaches the board, that a particular proposed course of action is "legal but stupid,"[13] and to use her talents as the persuasive counselor to lead the decision in a better direction.

Corporate scandals and economic events of the past decade have led regulators, academic observers, and others to view some in-house counsel as enablers of corporate misfeasance. This, in turn, has led to cries that general counsel should act as gatekeepers, with a duty to protect the public interest rather than pursuing their clients' interests. But being merely an enabler or merely a gatekeeper does not get the job done for the CLO as a persuasive counselor. Nor does being a passive bystander. What does get the job done are well-earned respect and leadership. The quintessential persuasive counselor must be the embodiment of the classic leader—one who has and uses her vision, clarity, common sense, judgment, integrity, and ability to motivate a group of people toward a common goal of steering the company on the right course.

One usually thinks of the CEO as being the primary corporate leader, and the person in the company who most likely (and importantly) possesses these leadership attributes. The CEO is and must be. But the CLO in her

---

11. Omari Scott Simmons & James D. Dinnage, *Innkeepers: A Unifying Theory of the In-House Counsel Role*, 41 SETON HALL L. REV. 77, 88, 112 (2011).

12. E. Norman Veasey & Christine T. Di Guglielmo, *The Tensions, Stresses, and Professional Responsibilities of the Lawyer for the Corporation*, 62 BUS. LAW. 1 (2006).

13. *See, e.g.*, Interview with Susan Hackett, Senior Vice President and General Counsel, Association of Corporate Counsel (Sept. 2, 2009) (discussing the necessity of counseling with respect to an idea that is "legal but stupid"). The chief legal officer must also consider how her involvement in business decisions implicates important issues of attorney-client or work product privilege. *E. g.*, Veasey & Di Guglielmo, *supra* note 8, at 26–27.

special role as persuasive counselor needs to possess, nurture, and employ those qualities as well. Consider how the following perspectives on leadership might well apply to the CLO as well as to the CEO:

> "Management is doing things right: leadership is doing the right things."—Peter Drucker
>
> "The very essence of leadership is that you have to have a vision. You can't blow an uncertain trumpet."—Father Theodore Hesburgh
>
> "The essence of being a lawyer-statesman is to move beyond the first question—'is it legal?'—to the ultimate question—'is it right?' Such a role involves leadership, or shared responsibility, not just for the corporation's legal matters but for its positions on ethics, reputation, public policy, communications, corporate citizenship, country and geopolitical trends."—Ben Heineman

3. The "Lonely" Aspect

By "lonely" we do not mean to suggest that the general counsel is cloistered alone in a corner without any company or friends. Quite to the contrary, the life of the general counsel involves daily interactions with many people. But her decisions in carrying out the responsibilities as persuasive counselor are her own—although the decision-making process may be shared with staff, other senior officers, key directors, or her other advisors. Ultimately, though, the general counsel must be the final decision maker with respect to many difficult matters—a role in which she cannot often follow an "easy" path.

The "lonely" aspect of the job arises partially from the fact that the legal department generally, and the general counsel in particular, is frequently viewed as a naysayer or an obstacle to getting a deal done. As Adam Ciongoli, General Counsel of Willis Group Holdings, Ltd., explained:

> It can be a very lonely job, being general counsel. There are times when you feel like the rest of the management of the company strongly does not like what you are telling them they have to do. They sometimes view you as the "Business Frustration Department." Sometimes, all of the good work you have done over the course of the years goes out the window. It is all about this current issue. Under those circumstances, talking with someone else who has been through it as a GC is good for [gaining] perspective.[14]

14. Interview with Adam Ciongoli, General Counsel, Willis Group Holdings, Ltd. (Sept. 4, 2009).

Making connections with other general counsel, or other trusted advisors or mentors, can be very important to alleviate the type of "loneliness" that arises in the general counsel position by identifying resources and sounding boards to cross-check ideas and judgment calls. In our interviews, we asked the interviewees to whom they might turn when they need to have a wise head to help them navigate a "sticky wicket." The answers were varied and interesting. The interviewees noted that their "council of elders"[15] includes respected outside counsel, lawyer-friends, the CFO, former colleagues, spouses, and others. Many of the interviewees mentioned friends, mentors, and confidants among groups and networks of general counsel as particularly valuable resources.

The interviewees often premised their comments about being caught in the middle with the basic truism that the CLO's client is the corporate entity, not the CEO, the CFO, the board as a whole, or any director individually, though each of those groups sometimes exerts "ownership" over the CLO. Also, they mentioned that the CLO advises the CEO (who hires her but does not "own" her). The CLO advises the board (who should have been consulted by, and should have concurred with, the CEO on hiring, firing, and compensating the general counsel). The general counsel educates both the board and the CEO.

The CLO may be a bridge, a leader, or a mediator when tensions arise. She must deal not only with the management and the board, but also with the outside world, including third parties, outside counsel, government officials, politicians, media, adverse lawyers, and stockholders. The CLO must resolve inner conflicts in juggling responsibilities. For example, there may be pressure on her at times to compromise her professional judgment and moral standards to fit into, or "go along with," a problematic business decision. This, of course, is a tension that may well be baked into the job, and she must have the courage and leadership skills to resist the pressure. As persuasive counselor she must lead in helping to steer the corporate ship into the right channel.

4. The "Perilous" Aspect

The CLO is increasingly exposed to outside scrutiny. That is one source of potential peril in the form of risk of liability, reputational harm, or embarrassment. Another source of peril—real or perceived—is the risk of losing

---

15. Interview with Charles J. Kalil, Executive Vice President, Law and Government Affairs, General Counsel, and Corporate Secretary, The Dow Chemical Company (Nov. 10, 2009).

her job as a result of promoting her client's interests in the face of disagreement with her boss. She must balance her need for self-preservation with her need to serve her client—the corporation—with skill, integrity, and zeal. In her multifaceted and lonely world, her exposure and that of her staff lawyers to personal worries has become exacerbated in recent years. We need only to consider the reincarnation in the new reality of Judge Stanley Sporkin's famous rhetorical question following the savings and loan scandal of the late 1980s and early 1990s:

> Where were these [accountants and lawyers], a number of whom are now asserting their rights under the Fifth Amendment, when these clearly improper transactions were being consummated?
>
> Why didn't any of them speak up or disassociate themselves from the transactions?
>
> . . . .
>
> What is difficult to understand is that with all the professional talent involved (both accounting and legal), why at least one professional would not have blown the whistle to stop the overreaching that took place in this case.[16]

Little over a decade later, Enron, Worldcom, and other corporate scandals emerged. Following those scandals, Congress enacted the Sarbanes-Oxley Act, and particularly Section 307, which directed the SEC to develop minimum professional standards for lawyers.[17] On the Senate floor during the Sarbanes-Oxley debate in the 2002 election year, one of the Senators targeted corporate counsel with the following remarks:

> The truth is that executives and accountants do not work alone. Anybody who works in corporate America knows that wherever you see corporate executives and accountants working, lawyers are virtually always there looking over their shoulder. If executives and/or accountants are breaking the law, you can be sure that part of the problem is that the lawyers who are there and involved are not doing their jobs.[18]

The SEC implemented Section 307 by promulgating Rule 205, which includes elaborate provisions concerning when and how lawyers *must* report "evidence of a material violation" up the corporate ladder and *may*

---

16. Lincoln Sav. & Loan Ass'n v. Wall, 743 F. Supp. 901, 920 (D. D.C. 1990).
17. 15 U.S.C. § 7245.
18. 148 Cong. Rec. S 6524–02, S 6551 (daily ed. July 10, 2002) (statement of Sen. Edwards).

report outside to the SEC.[19] These rules contain significant responsibilities and potential perils for both supervising and subordinate lawyers.

Aside from adherence to the SEC rules implementing Sarbanes-Oxley, some general counsel have been swept up in criminal investigations, civil suits, and SEC professional responsibility proceedings. Indeed, some general counsel have gone to jail.[20]

Now, in the aftermath of the 2008–2010 economic meltdown from the subprime mortgage crisis and other debacles, there probably will be renewed scrutiny of general counsel and other in-house lawyers. It remains to be seen what the impact of the Dodd-Frank Wall Street Reform and Consumer Protection Act[21] will be. But it is clear that the fallout from the economic meltdown that began in 2008 has intensified regulatory, legal, and corporate governance challenges and, correspondingly, the responsibilities of the chief legal officer.[22]

But, as noted above, it is not only concern about the external perils like prosecution or ethical sanctions that may keep the general counsel awake at night. There is also the very real, potential internal peril of losing her job as a result of internal conflict with the other representatives of the client.[23] In-house counsel may be tempted to refrain from challenging courses of action sought by management for fear of placing their livelihoods at risk.[24]

---

19. Standards of Professional Conduct for Attorneys Appearing and Practicing Before the Commission in the Representation of an Issuer, 17 CFR pt. 205 (implementing Section 307 of the Sarbanes-Oxley Act).

20. *See, e.g.,* 2 *Years in Prison for Ex-Software Executive,* N.Y. TIMES, Jan. 17, 2007, at C13 (reporting two-year sentence for former general counsel of Computer Associates in connection with "scheme to increase the company's quarterly revenue artificially through backdated sales contracts"); *Comverse General Counsel Headed to Prison,* ETHISPHERE (May 20, 2007), *at* http://ethisphere.com/comverse-general-counsel-headed-to-prison/(reporting on sentencing of former general counsel of Comverse Technology in connection with securities backdating).

21. Pub. L. No. 111–203, 124 Stat. 1376 (2010) (codified in scattered sections of 7, 12, 15, 18, 31 U.S.C.).

22. *See infra* chapter VII (discussing these real, external perils).

23. *See* Veasey & Di Guglielmo, *supra* note 8, at 11–13.

24. *See* Deborah A. DeMott, *The Discrete Roles of General Counsel,* 74 FORDHAM L. REV. 955–56 (2005) ("[A] general counsel's dependence on a single client may call into question counsel's capacity to bring an appropriate degree of professional detachment to bear."); *id.* at 967–68 ("Conventional skepticism about the capacity of in-house corporate lawyers to exercise independent professional judgment focuses on the exclusivity of their relationship with a single client (their employer), which calls into question the feasibility of withdrawing from representation if professional norms so require."); *see also* Mary C. Daly, *The Cultural, Ethical, and Legal Challenges in Lawyering for a Global Organization: The Role of the General Counsel,* 46 EMORY L.J. 1057, 1099–1100 (1997) ("Whether in-house counsel can exercise the required degree of [professional independent judgment] is a question that has universally troubled the legal profession.

As we discuss in more detail later,[25] as compared with outside counsel, in-house counsel face a unique peril of losing their livelihood because they have only one client. The general counsel's financial dependence on a single client—the corporate employer—may raise questions concerning counsel's ability to courageously use her independent judgment when providing legal advice to the corporation or when examining corporate compliance practices. Whether or not this dependence raises an issue of compromised objectivity and the potential for conflict of interest is a concern.[26] But regardless whether objectivity is compromised or conflicts of interest are heightened, reliance on a single client poses a potential peril for the general counsel.

The corporation should design a compensation plan for in-house counsel that rewards exceptional and professionally independent legal work, as distinct from pure financial performance.[27] We recognize and applaud the common practices of well compensating in-house counsel. Including stock options as a portion of a general counsel's compensation package may or

Critics insist that a lawyer who is dependent on a single client, i.e., the corporate employer, for his or her livelihood cannot provide independent advice and judgment of the same caliber as outside counsel whose financial ties to a single client are presumably much weaker." (footnotes omitted)); *cf. also* Sally R. Weaver, *Ethical Dilemmas of Corporate Counsel: A Structural and Contextual Analysis*, 46 EMORY L.J. 1023, 1027 (1997) ("The first, and perhaps most critical, difference between [in-house] counsel and their colleagues in private practice is the economic dependence of [in-house] counsel on a single client.").

25. *Infra* chapter III.B. 3; *see also* Veasey & Di Guglielmo, *supra* note 8, at 11–13 ("In-house counsel may be tempted to refrain from challenging courses of action sought by management for fear of placing his or her livelihood at risk.").

26. Rule 1.7(a)(2) of the Model Rules of Professional Conduct provides that a lawyer shall not represent a client if that representation may be materially limited by the lawyer's own interests. MODEL RULES OF PROF'L CONDUCT R. 1.7(a)(2) (2006). *See also, e.g.*, Jill Barclift, *Corporate Responsibilities: Ensuring Independent Judgment of the General Counsel—A Look at Stock Options*, 81 N. DAK. L. REV. 1, 16 (2005) (noting that the commentary to Model Rule 1.7 "recommends that a lawyer withdraw from representing a client if the lawyer's financial interest in the client leads to the reasonable conclusion that the representation would be adversely affected," and suggesting that this may be the case for general counsel, particularly when they receive stock option compensation).

27. Jill Barclift has suggested that "[t]he general counsel should be rewarded for outstanding legal work, including compliance with ethical obligations of the SEC and the state bar. Salary and bonuses in recognition of outstanding performance are appropriate. Stock options are rewards for reaching financial performance goals. Millions of dollars in stock option wealth not only raises questions about where the general loyalties lie, but can compromise the general counsel's judgment in the same way other corporate executives are compromised by the lure of stock option wealth." Barclift, *supra* note 26, at 25.

may not raise issues in any particular corporation.[28] Those involved in designing and approving the package—and the general counsel who benefits from it—should consider what incentives and optics the various features of the package may create, and whether those mesh with the recognized and appropriate role of the general counsel in the corporation.

C. DEALING WITH THE NEW REALITY

1. New Laws and Prescriptive Regulatory Attitudes

We start with the premise that general counsel in the new reality must understand that there *is* a new reality. That is, the world clearly has changed. The general counsel must therefore gird herself and her colleagues to deal with it. If one merely opens the history books to the beginning of the twenty-first century, one immediately is faced with the Enron scandal. Fraud and accounting shenanigans were instrumental in driving that corporate enterprise into bankruptcy and some of the actors to prison. There were lessons from that debacle for many to learn—including future CLOs.

Congress stepped in with a big footprint and enacted SOX in midsummer of the election year 2002. SOX marked the beginnings of the new reality by effecting a paradigm shift aimed at enhancing the role, power, and responsibilities of the board of directors vis-à-vis management.[29] SOX not only imposed new laws relating to corporate governance in at least a partially federalized milieu, but it also ushered in new standards of professional responsibility for lawyers.[30]

---

28. *See* Interview with Scott Giordano, *The Evolving Role of General Counsel*, METRO. CORP. COUNSEL, June 2011, at 9 ("There is a conflict, for example, when the GC's compensation package is tied to company profitability and stock options. It raises questions of impartiality when there is a personal incentive to disregard playing the corporate cop and maximize payouts that might be a result of manipulated financial numbers. Similarly, when an M&A or joint venture may affect the GC's company shares, it raises the question of whether the GC will advise the board as a lawyer or as a business executive interested in passing an initiative.").

29. *See* Stephen M. Bainbridge & Christina J. Johnson, *Managerialism, Legal Ethics, and Sarbanes-Oxley Section 307*, 2004 MICH. ST. L. REV. 299 (summarizing the provisions of Sarbanes-Oxley that enhance board power vis-à-vis managerial power, and contending that section 307 of the Act, including the up-the-ladder reporting requirement, seeks to align lawyers with the board of directors and reduce informational asymmetry between management and the board).

30. Professor Bainbridge and Christina Johnson have argued that these rules further support SOX's goal of shifting the balance of power away from management and toward the board. *See id.* at 315 ("The nature of the market for legal services gives

The next high-water mark was the 2008–2010 global economic melt-down that galvanized Congress to pass the Dodd-Frank Act in midsummer of another election year, 2010. Dodd-Frank ushered in further federalized corporate governance mandates for most public corporations and tough new standards and regimens for financial institutions. Corporate lawyers, particularly general counsel, have had to master and manage the fallout from these laws and the follow-on regulations. That fallout includes height-ened scrutiny by regulators, increased investor activism, more litigation, and more media and congressional attention.

Our interviewees have focused us on this new reality. They have given us, and therefore our readers, their views of best practices. Given that the world has changed—indeed, there has been a "sea change"—since the dawn of this century, general counsel need not only to understand the depth of the new reality but also to help counsel and guide other corporate constitu-ents (principally senior management and the directors) in understanding and navigating the new landscape.

2. The Dodd-Frank Act of 2010 and Its Impact on Corporate Governance

The Dodd-Frank Wall Street Reform and Consumer Protection Act of 2010, signed into law on July 21, 2010, while perhaps the most recent factor, is only part of the new reality for U.S. business, in general, and general coun-sel, in particular. Much of the two thousand-plus-page act focuses on the financial services industry. We do not undertake in this book to analyze the myriad details of the Dodd-Frank financial-institution or corporate-gover-nance regulations. Instead, we refer the reader to two papers providing overviews of the provisions of the Act, some of which will affect virtually all U.S. public companies, regardless of industry.[31] Because of their significant

management a set of carrots by which to align the interests of corporate counsel with those of management. Sarbanes-Oxley did not attempt to change that set of incen-tives. Instead, Sarbanes-Oxley section 307 gave the SEC a set of sticks in hopes of enlisting corporate counsel in the prevention of fraud and related corporate scandals. In doing so, as we have seen, section 307 is part and parcel of the statute's goal of empowering boards of directors." (footnotes omitted)).

31. For a summary of Dodd-Frank provisions, including those applicable to financial institutions, see FINANCIAL REGULATORY REFORM: AN OVERVIEW OF THE DODD-FRANK WALL STREET REFORM AND CONSUMER PROTECTION ACT (2010), available at http://www.weil.com/files/upload/Weil%20Dodd-Frank%20Overview. pdf; Challenges of the Next Proxy Season: What to Expect from the Dodd-Frank Act and How to Begin to Prepare, WEIL BRIEFING (July 22, 2010), available at http://www.weil. com/files/Publication/a554708d-ac75–423c-84c2–76921424f294/Presentation/

impact on public companies, the Act's provisions and implementing regulations are bound to affect the role of the CLO.

Some key governance and disclosure provisions of the Dodd-Frank Act include the following:

- Express authority for the SEC to adopt proxy access rules
- Mandates for stockholder advisory votes on executive compensation ("say-on-pay" and "say-when-on-pay")
- Provisions relating to "golden parachutes"
- Further limits on discretionary voting by brokers
- New "pay vs. performance" and "pay equity" disclosures
- Heightened independence requirements for compensation committees and their advisors
- Required clawback policies that reach beyond those established in the Sarbanes-Oxley Act
- Enhanced incentives and protections for corporate whistleblowers
- New disclosure requirements regarding corporate policies on hedging by directors and employees
- Authority for the SEC to adopt rules increasing the transparency of securities ownership

As a result of the global financial crisis of 2008–2010 and in a political environment highly distrustful of corporate boards and executives, various members of Congress began in 2009 and early 2010 to draft multiple bills proposing a wide variety of changes to corporate governance rules. Supporters of new federal intrusions into state corporate governance laws contended that federal mandates are necessary to hold boards of directors accountable to investors. Others argued that board governance was the wrong target for the reform effort. The outcome was mixed.[32]

Fortunately, some widely discussed potential mandates in these earlier bills (e.g., mandatory and inflexible majority voting for directors, limits on

PublicationAttachment/e1ccd99b-8c6c-4cf4-a545–7e0a8cbad69f/Weil_Briefing_SEC_CG_July_Sept%202010.pdf.

32. For articles analyzing the conclusions in the report of the Financial Crisis Inquiry Commission regarding the root causes of the economic meltdown, see Ben W. Heineman Jr., *Financial Crisis Inquiry Commission: The Private Sector Failed*, Harv. Law School Forum on Corporate Governance and Financial Regulation (Jan. 31, 2011), http://blogs.law.harvard.edu/corpgov/2011/01/31/financial-crisis-inquiry-commission-the-private-sector-failed/; Holman W. Jenkins, Jr., *What Caused the Bubble?*, WALL ST. J., Jan. 29, 2011, at A17; Frank Partnoy, *Washington's Financial Disaster*, N.Y. TIMES, Jan. 30, 2011, at week in review 9.

executive compensation, mandatory board risk committees for non-financial companies, and mandatory separation of the CEO and board chair) did not make their way into the final legislation. Nevertheless, the Dodd-Frank Act makes important changes that will likely have the effect of empowering investors to assert a greater voice in corporate governance. Yet, these new congressional mandates and impending rules of federal agencies (notably the SEC), while not necessary or desirable, are manageable—sometimes with difficulty—by corporate boards and senior management, with significant general counsel leadership.

Corporate governance and other matters relating to the internal corporate affairs of U.S. companies have historically been governed by the law of the state of incorporation, principally Delaware law, given the large number of companies incorporated in that state. Federal law in the Sarbanes-Oxley Act intruded on state law to some extent.[33] Similar to what the Sarbanes-Oxley Act did with respect to audit committees, the Dodd-Frank Act mandates a number of governance structures and practices that traditionally have been regulated only by state law. These include proxy access, "say-on-pay,"[34] and "golden parachute" advisory votes; compensation committee and committee adviser independence; incentive compensation "clawback" policies; whistleblower provisions; and special governance requirements for financial companies. Disclosure provisions have long been properly situated in the federal-regulatory column.

The Dodd-Frank Act will have a significant regulatory effect on financial institutions, and will have some effect on corporate governance of these institutions and others. Although that latter effect, in itself, is not as intrusive as it might have been, it is a federal intrusion that is undesirable as a matter of principle and may serve to distract a board from their primary goal of advancing corporate strategy.

It does not, however, constitute a wholesale federal preemption of corporate law and corporate governance. Importantly—and the general counsel should impart this to senior management and the board—the Act does not alter or eliminate the protections traditionally provided to directors by

---

33. E. Norman Veasey, *What Would Madison Think? The Irony of the Twists and Turns of Federalism*, 34 DEL. J. CORP. L. 35 (2009); E. Norman Veasey et al., *Federalism vs. Federalization: Preserving the Division of Responsibility in Corporation Law*, in 2 THE PRACTITIONER'S GUIDE TO THE SARBANES-OXLEY ACT V-5–1 (John J. Huber et al. eds., 2006).

34. *See* Holly J. Gregory, *Proxy Advisors and Say on Pay: Greater Influence May Bring Closer Scrutiny*, PRACTICAL LAW, June 2011, at 20 (discussing some potential impacts of say-on-pay, including the impact on the perceived influence of proxy advisors).

the business judgment rule.[35] Beyond that, this federal law does not eclipse other state-based corporation law principles, including principles of fiduciary duty, mergers and acquisitions, and the like. Some opponents countered that federal mandates nevertheless represent an ill-advised departure from the flexible state-law-based system that has successfully eschewed a one-size-fits-all approach in favor of private ordering.[36]

The Dodd-Frank governance provisions and the SEC implementation of the authority conferred on it in the legislation will make life more challenging for directors and senior officers, including the general counsel, not only because regulators will be more active but also because the provisions strengthen the hand of activist investors.[37] There may or may not be merit to some of the financial-regulatory provisions in the Act. But there is a compelling view that the corporate governance provisions in the Act are unnecessary and of dubious relevance to the global financial crisis.[38] The extent to which the financial meltdown of 2008–2010 was the result of a pervasive failure of good governance practices of the boards of the thousands of U.S. public companies has been a controversial subject of political dialogue. Regardless of whether Dodd-Frank's provisions properly correlate with the problems they are supposed to address, the Act is here to stay and must be dealt with.

Many advances in corporate governance have been put in place in recent years, including majority voting (now the norm[39] for most public companies)[40] and proxy access under private ordering provisions of

35. *See infra* chapter V.A.4 (discussing the business judgment rule).

36. For articles discussing the historic and recurring federalism debate, see E. Norman Veasey, *The Challenges for Directors in Piloting Through State and Federal Standards in the Maelstrom of Risk Management*, 34 SEATTLE UNIV. L. REV. 1 (2010) [hereinafter Veasey, *Maelstrom*]; Veasey, *supra* note 33; Veasey et al., *supra* note 33, at V-5–1.

37. For example, the SEC has promulgated proxy access rules (rules allowing investors to nominate directors on the company's proxy, under certain circumstances) under Rule 14a-8 and Rule 14a-11. 17 C.F.R. § 240.14a-8; 17 C.F.R. § 240.14a-11; Facilitating Shareholder Director Nominations, SEC Release Nos. 33–9136, 34–62764 (Aug. 25, 2010), *available at* http://www.sec.gov/rules/final/2010/33-9136.pdf. The implementation of these rules has been stayed, however, pending the outcome of a suit by the U.S. Chamber of Commerce and the Business Roundtable challenging the validity of the adoption of the SEC rules. *See* Notice of Stay of Effective and Compliance Dates, 75 Fed. Reg. 64,641 (Oct. 20, 2010) (implementing stay of rules including Rules 14a-8 and 14a-11 pending resolution of Business Roundtable v. SEC, No. 10–1305 (D.C. Cir., filed Sept. 29, 2010)).

38. *See* BAINBRIDGE, *supra* note 2; Stephen M. Bainbridge, *Dodd-Frank: Quack Federal Corporate Governance Round II*, 95 MINN. L. REV. 1779 (2011).

39. CLAUDIA H. ALLEN, NEAL, GERBER & EISENBERG LLP, STUDY OF MAJORITY VOTING IN DIRECTOR ELECTIONS, at ii (2007), http://www.ngelaw.com/files/upload/majoritystudy111207.pdf.

40. Delaware law was amended in 2006 to provide that a corporation may depart from the statutory default of plurality voting in uncontested elections to require that

Delaware law.[41] Indeed, it is the freedom of corporate private ordering, subject to fiduciary duty enforcement, that is the "genius of American corporate law."[42]

The anger of the American public about the financial meltdown and the response in the media and in Congress in 2009–2010 created a "drum beat" of rhetoric urging the federal government to "do something!" That drum beat has focused, in large part, on perceived "excessive risk-taking" (mostly in financial institutions) as a major culprit in the global financial crisis. This rhetoric has resulted in calls for the scalps of some CEOs, CFOs, CLOs, directors, and other players in American business, with a wide swath of blame as well for the corporate structures in which these players function. Unfortunately, corporate governance was swept up in the frenzy.[43]

As a result of the Dodd-Frank Act, boards of directors' exercise of their fiduciary oversight duties of care and loyalty[44] will include ensuring management's compliance with the panoply of new Dodd-Frank regulations, thus adding to what is already a very full plate of oversight responsibilities. Boards also will need to be aware of changes mandated by the Act that directly affect their own composition and processes.

---

directors be elected by a majority of the votes cast, and that a pre-tendered resignation by a director who would not receive such a majority could be made irrevocable. 8 DEL. CODE ANN. tit. 8, §§ 141(b), 216(b). Under the majority voting protocol of many companies, the remainder of the board may elect to reject the tendered resignation. *See, e.g.,* City of Westland Police & Fire Ret. Sys. v. Axcelis Techs., Inc., 1 A. 3d 281 (Del. 2010) ("[T]he Axcelis Board unilaterally conferred upon the shareholders the right to elect directors by majority vote. But, the Board also conditioned that right upon the board's discretionary power to accept (or reject) the resignations of those directors who were elected by a plurality, but not a majority, shareholder vote."). The Delaware Supreme Court has, by way of dictum, suggested that such a vote by the remaining directors to retain a director not receiving a majority should be for bona fide reasons. *See City of Westland,* 1 A. 3d 281 ("The less-than-majority shareholder vote may be viewed as a judgment by the holders of a voting majority that those director-candidates were no longer suitable to serve (or continue to serve) as directors. Correspondingly, the Board's decision not to accept those resignations may be viewed as a contrary, overriding judgment by the Board. At stake, therefore, is the integrity of the Board decision overriding the determination by a shareholder majority. Stated differently, the question arises whether the directors, as fiduciaries, made a disinterested, informed business judgment that the best interests of the corporation require the continued service of these directors, or whether the Board had some different, ulterior motivation.").

41. Note that Delaware has acted to enable proxy access by private ordering. DEL. CODE ANN. tit. 8, §§ 112–13 (2009). Stockholders have always had the right, in Delaware at least, to have bylaw amendments proposed and voted on by the stockholders, including most recently proxy access and expense reimbursement.

42. ROBERTA ROMANO, THE GENIUS OF AMERICAN CORPORATE LAW (1993).

43. *See* Veasey, *Maelstrom, supra* note 36.

44. *See* Stone v. Ritter, 911 A.2d 362 (Del. 2006); *In re* Caremark Int'l Inc. Deriv. Litig., 698 A.2d 959 (Del. Ch. 1996).

The chief legal officer must be the point person in helping senior management and directors navigate these new duties. The CLO must be ahead of the curve in advising management and the board of the requirements of Dodd-Frank, not only to provide advice to directors for action they need to take but also to encourage them to be attuned to their oversight responsibilities inherent in the Act.

The Dodd-Frank Act includes several provisions that may profoundly affect the approach that management and the board will take when interacting with stockholders. In short, the provisions of the Act, in combination, will give investors—as a practical, if not a legal, matter—a greater voice in board composition, governance, and executive compensation.

3. Whistleblower Incentives and Protection[45]

The Act expands the rewards available to whistleblowers by authorizing financial awards to individuals who voluntarily provide "original information" to the SEC that leads to an enforcement action under the federal securities laws that results in monetary sanctions exceeding $1 million.[46] The whistleblower provisions also strengthen the prohibition against retaliation, creating a new cause of action for employees against whom an employer retaliates for providing information to or assisting the SEC. On May 25, 2011, the SEC adopted, by a 3–2 vote,[47] rules implementing the Dodd-Frank whistleblower provisions.

a. Incentives

The Act vastly expands the SEC's whistleblower rewards program. The SEC's existing rewards program is limited to insider trading cases, caps rewards

---

45. Dodd-Frank Wall Street Reform and Consumer Protection Act, Pub. L. No. 111–203, §§ 922–24, 124 Stat. 1376, 1841–50 (2010).

46. Pub. L. No. 111–203, § 922(a)(1), (b). For an overview of the whistleblower regulations approved by the SEC, see *Weil Alert: SEC Disclosure and Corporate Governance, Dodd-Frank Update: SEC Adopts Whistleblower Rules, Changing the Landscape for Corporate Compliance Programs and Enforcement* (June 3, 2011), *available at* http://www.weil.com/news/pubdetail.aspx?pub=10347.

47. Implementation of the Whistleblower Provisions of Section 21F of the Securities Exchange Act of 1934, 17 C.F.R. pts. 240, 249 (2011); SEC Adopts Rules to Establish Whistleblower Program, Press Release 2011–116 (May 25, 2011) [hereinafter SEC Whistleblower Press Release]; Edward Wyatt, *Overcoming Dissenters, S.E.C. Adopts Revised Whistle-Blower Rules*, N.Y. TIMES, May 26, 2011, at B3.

at ten percent of the funds collected as sanctions, and, according to a recent report from the SEC's Office of Inspector General, has enjoyed only "minimal" success.[48] Under the new, expanded program, an individual (or group of individuals acting jointly) who provides "original information" to the SEC that leads to a successful enforcement action resulting in monetary sanctions exceeding $1 million will be eligible for a reward of between ten percent and thirty percent of the amount of the sanctions collected.[49] The SEC has discretion to determine the amount of any award made to a whistleblower, taking into consideration (1) the significance of the information provided by the whistleblower to the success of the action; (2) the degree of assistance provided by the whistleblower and any legal representative of the whistleblower; (3) the SEC's programmatic interest in deterring securities law violations by making whistleblower awards; and (4) such additional relevant factors as the SEC may establish by rule or regulation.[50] These awards are available for a successful action brought by the SEC under any of the federal securities laws, including, for example, actions involving violations of the Foreign Corrupt Practices Act (FCPA).[51]

b. Protection from Retaliation

The Dodd-Frank whistleblower provisions prohibit employers from taking adverse employment action against whistleblowers and create a cause of action that allows whistleblowers to bring adverse-action claims directly in federal district court.[52] The protection provisions apply even if a whistleblower's tip does not lead to a successful enforcement action or the whistleblower otherwise fails to qualify for an incentive award.[53] The whistleblower protection provisions provide for employment reinstatement if the whistleblower has been discharged and recovery of two times back pay otherwise

---

48. SEC Office of Inspector General, *Assessment of the SEC's Bounty Program* (Mar. 29, 2010), *available at* http://www.sec-oig.gov/Reports/AuditsInspections/2010/474. pdf; *see also* Wyatt, *supra* note 47, at B3 ("Previously, the S.E.C. had authority to reward tipsters only in insider trading cases and was limited to paying 10 percent of the penalties collected.").

49. Pub. L. No. 111–203, § 922(a), (b).

50. *Id.* § 922(c)(1). The SEC may not, however, take into account the balance of funds left in the SEC's Investor Protection Fund from which such awards are to be paid. *Id.*

51. Steve Tyrrell, *SEC Whistleblowers: Boon or Bust*, BLOOMBERG LAW REPORTS— RISK & COMPLIANCE (2011).

52. Pub. L. No. 111–203, § 922(h). In contrast, the whistleblower provisions of the Sarbanes-Oxley Act required whistleblowers to file claims initially with the Department of Labor.

53. Tyrrell, *supra* note 51.

owed to the individual, as well as reimbursement for attorneys' fees and other litigation costs.[54] Similar, but not identical, whistleblower provisions exist for matters within the jurisdiction of the Commodity Futures Trading Commission (CFTC) and the new Bureau of Consumer Financial Protection, created under the Dodd-Frank Act.

c. Expansions of the Sarbanes-Oxley Act

The Dodd-Frank Act amends the Sarbanes-Oxley Act to clarify that its whistleblower protections apply not only to employees of a public company, but also to employees of a public company's subsidiaries and other affiliates whose financial information is included in a public company's consolidated financial statements. It also amends the Sarbanes-Oxley Act (1) to extend the statute of limitations for filing claims with the Department of Labor from 90 days to 180 days and by running the statute of limitations not only from the date of the discrimination, but also from the date on which the employee "became aware of the violation;" (2) to provide for jury trials; and (3) to make pre-dispute agreements to arbitrate Sarbanes-Oxley Act whistleblower claims unenforceable.

d. Implications of the Whistleblower Provisions

Observers have identified a number of concerns relating to the whistleblower provisions of the Dodd-Frank Act. A large influx of complaints, particularly those that may be low quality, may strain or overwhelm limited enforcement resources.[55] Critically, the expanded whistleblower incentives may undermine the effectiveness of companies' internal compliance programs.[56] Conditioning the incentive awards on the provision to the SEC of

---

54. Pub. L. No. 111–203, § 922(h)(1)(C).

55. *See* Ronald D. Orol, *SEC: Bigger Potential Payouts for Whistleblowers*, MARKET WATCH, May 25, 2011, *at* http://www.marketwatch.com/story/sec-bigger-potential-payouts-for-whistleblowers-2011-05-25?link=MW_latest_news ("Troy Paredes, [an SEC] commissioner, said that the volume of complaints will increase and that the agency may have a difficult time handling them. And if many tip[s] are deemed to be low-quality, it will make it harder to identify real problems, he said.").

56. *See* Jessica Holzer & Ashby Jones, *Bounty Plan Approved*, WALL ST. J., May 26, 2011, at C3 ("Business groups and others had argued that to earn such 'bounties,' employees should first have to report their findings through company channels before going to the SEC. 'Not informing the company of a potential fraud and waiting for the SEC to act is the equivalent of not calling the firefighters down the street to put out a

"original information" may provide an incentive for employees to circumvent internal compliance programs and go directly to the government with information about possible securities violations, even if the concerns are not well-founded.[57] The robust compliance programs currently in place in many multinational companies have greatly advanced—and added substantial private resources to the public resources allocated to—the fight against corruption, and their continued success should be encouraged and supported, not undermined.[58]

Relatedly, the juxtaposition of the whistleblower incentives with the federal sentencing guidelines, which give corporate defendants sentencing credit for self-reporting violations, may cause companies, under pressure from a belief that an employee may make a report, to themselves prematurely report to the SEC, before a thorough investigation can be completed.[59] During the rule-making process, the SEC stated that in determining incentive award amounts, it would consider whether and the extent to which a whistleblower reported a potential violation through the company's internal compliance processes before making a report to the SEC.[60]

The final rule does include some modest provisions aimed at encouraging employees to use the company's internal compliance system, including (1) maintaining eligibility for awards if a whistleblower reports internally and the company informs the SEC about the violations; (2) treating an employee as a whistleblower as of the date that the employee makes an internal report if the employee provides the same information to the SEC within 120 days; (3) considering a whistleblower's voluntary participation in an internal compliance program as a factor that can increase the amount of an award and a whistleblower's interference with internal compliance

---

raging fire,' David Hirschmann, president and chief executive of the U.S. Chamber of Commerce's Center for Capital Markets Competitiveness, said in a statement after the vote on Wednesday.").

57. Adele Nicholas, *Whistleblower Provisions of the Dodd-Frank Act Pressure Employers to Improve Compliance*, INSIDE COUNSEL, Oct. 2010. *But cf.* SEC Whistleblower Press Release, *supra* note 47 ("'While the SEC has a history of receiving a high volume of tips and complaints, the quality of the tips we have received has been better since Dodd-Frank became law.'" (quoting SEC Chairman Mary L. Schapiro)); Wyatt, *supra* note 47, at B3 ("Robert Khuzami, the S.E.C.'s director of enforcement, said the S.E.C. had seen 'an uptick' in the number of complaints since the Dodd-Frank Act went into effect last July, but there had not been a flood. The quality of the tips has improved as well, he said, and they are often accompanied with detailed corroboration.").

58. Tyrrell, *supra* note 51.

59. Nicholas, *supra* note 57.

60. Tyrrell, *supra* note 51.

and reporting as a factor that can decrease the amount of an award.[61] Nevertheless, the lure of incentive payments may result in a sharp rise in non-meritorious allegations, burdening enforcement resources and erroneously stigmatizing corporations while non-meritorious charges are pending.[62]

Companies can take steps to mitigate these risks by evaluating and reinforcing their compliance programs, and by ensuring that employees feel that their concerns are heard and addressed internally.[63] Similarly, companies can reduce the likelihood of reports by making sure that senior executives are aware that they are excluded from the ability to recover whistleblower incentives,[64] and that legal, compliance, audit, supervisory, and governance personnel likewise are familiar with the limits on their eligibility for awards based on information that they receive in the course of performing their respective duties.[65]

4. New Challenges Beyond the Horizon

The new reality is not a static state of play. Rather, it is dynamic. Federal legislative activity is often triggered by something like a major scandal (e.g., the Enron era) or a downward spiral (e.g., the 2008–2010 financial meltdown). Cynics might say that after the "battle," Congress takes to the field to shoot the wounded. Realists might say that we should not indulge in such cynicism because such indulgence is not productive.

The realists are looking beyond the present-day new reality to see what is beyond the horizon. Unless one is exceptionally prescient, one cannot

---

61. SEC Whistleblower Press Release, *supra* note 47; *see also* Wyatt, *supra* note 47 ("One of the changes [to the final rules from the rules first proposed in 2010] included a potential bonus if corporate employees first report suspected wrongdoing through their company's internal compliance system.").

62. Tyrrell, *supra* note 51.

63. *See* Nicholas, *supra* note 57 ("'Employees don't usually become whistleblowers unless they feel they've been ignored internally,' says Betsy Lewis, a partner at Cooley.").

64. *Id.*

65. *See* SEC Whistleblower Press Release, *supra* note 47 (outlining that under the final implementing rules the following individuals, among others, are generally ineligible for whistleblower awards (and noting the exceptions): attorneys, including in-house counsel, who attempt to use information obtained from client engagements to make whistleblower claims; compliance and internal audit personnel; and public accountants working on SEC engagements, if the information relates to violations by the client). For a discussion of a best practices approach to whistle blowers, see STEPHEN M. BAINBRIDGE, THE COMPLETE GUIDE TO SARBANES-OXLEY 105–08 (2007).

forecast the next scandal or catastrophe. Nor could one reasonably be expected to foresee how those who embrace a strong federalization agenda will react. Even now a movement is afoot to federalize mandatory disclosure of beneficial ownership of certain entities—all in the name of ferreting out terrorism.[66] Where that effort will go or what else might be beyond the horizon cannot now be anticipated with specificity. But the general counsel needs to avoid being complacent about the status of the "here and now."

D. KEY TAKEAWAYS FOR THE GENERAL COUNSEL'S CHALLENGES IN THE NEW REALITY

The modern landscape into which the general counsel has been thrust is exciting, wide-ranging, and scary, at times. The general counsel confronts rapidly changing and sweeping new laws and fierce regulatory and litigation obstacles. Concurrently, investor activism and media attention have ratcheted upward.

It is no coincidence that these new challenges for general counsel have come in an era following the Enron and other scandals of the early years of the twenty-first century. Not only did these scandals trigger an uprising in the media and among stockholders, but they also kick-started aggressive legislative and regulatory reactions, exemplified by the Sarbanes-Oxley Act.

Those events were bad enough. But they were compounded late in the first decade of the twenty-first century by a huge market meltdown followed by another round of legislative and regulatory reactions, exemplified by the Dodd-Frank Act and its implementing rules. Not only did the federal government step in with a big footprint in the area of financial regulation, but it also has stepped into the corporate governance arena.

The chief legal officer of public companies sails in the vortex of this tempest. The general counsel is a business partner and a guardian of the corporate integrity. As such, she must be a courageous renaissance person in playing the challenging hand she is dealt each day.

---

66. Stop Tax Haven Abuse Act, S. 1346, 112th Cong. (2011); Incorporation Transparency and Law Enforcement Assistance Act, S. 569, 111th Cong. (2009); *see also* Kelly Carr & Brian Grow, *A Little House of Secrets on the Great Plains*, REUTERS (June 28, 2011), *at* http://www.reuters.com/article/2011/06/28/us-usa-shell-companies-idUS TRE75R20Z20110628 (discussing Senator Levin's repeated introduction of a bill that would require "states to obtain and update information about the real owners of companies, and impose civil and criminal sanctions for filing false information" in order to combat "'financial fraud, drug trafficking, even terrorist financing'" (quoting Senator Levin)).

The chief legal officer lives and operates in the present tense. We will turn in the next chapter to the replay of the changes that the role has undergone over time. But even as the general counsel must live and operate in the present, she is aware that there is a future that will likely impact her world.

Understanding that there is a new reality. The general counsel of today knows that there has been a "sea change" in the environment in which she operates today. That environment brings new and aggressive actors that may challenge her every move. Those actors include the regulators, federal lawmakers, courts, and litigants.

Appreciating the job characteristics. The general counsel job is interesting, multifaceted, lonely, and perilous. The general counsel of today appreciates those characteristics of her job in both senses of the verb "appreciate": She embraces and enjoys the good characteristics (interesting and multifaceted) and she is prepared to recognize and navigate the more challenging characteristics (lonely and perilous).

Dealing with the New Reality. We have not seen the end of new laws. SOX, Dodd-Frank, and new regulations from the SEC and other agencies may be "throttled back" if the political landscape undergoes significant change and no new scandals arise. But expecting that state of affairs in the foreseeable future would be folly. Even now new challenges (e.g., federally mandated beneficial ownership disclosure) lie just over the horizon. So, when it comes to the present-day life of the general counsel, there may be no rest for the weary.

CHAPTER 2
Evolution of the Role of General Counsel

*Every generation thinks its generation is revolutionary. But what's happening in the role of the general counsel and the role of lawyers today is not even about change. It's about transformation. It **is** revolutionary.*

The drivers of that change and that transformation are everything from an increase in complexity to an incredible change in the scope of what it means to be a GC or an in-house lawyer. That scope is now covering not just the legal, but also the policy, the people, and the business issues.

There is an expectation by the stakeholders, by the shareholders, by the regulators that the GC and legal department are not only dealing with what you would call the traditional legal issues. But they are seeing the intersection and impact of regulation from every shape and form, whether it be local, state, federal, regulatory, E.U., et cetera, which have dramatically impacted the complexity, the multidimensional nature, and the intersection of issues.

I think the power-center of the change is the types of things that in-house lawyers and general counsels deal with today. The former view was that really the sexy stuff was going on only in law firms and that the in-house movie was rather dull and boring in the ordinary course. That has dramatically changed at most companies. Most legal departments these days and most general counsels are involved in the strategic work for the company. We are keeping the strategic work within the company and more selectively using outside counsel for much more targeted assignments.

The role has expanded. The expectation of the role has expanded. The complexity of the role has expanded. And I don't see it going back into the four-cornered box that was the more traditional GC role.

—Kim K.W. Rucker[1]

---

1. Interview with Kim K.W. Rucker, Senior Vice President and General Counsel, Avon Products, Inc. (Jan. 7, 2010).

A. HISTORICAL PERSPECTIVE

In the late nineteenth century, as the corporate form became dominant in American business, the position of general counsel in a major corporation grew in prestige and drew candidates from among the best and brightest members of the bar.[2] In-house counsel positions continued to be perceived as prestigious and powerful in the early twentieth century, an era that has been dubbed the "golden age of corporate counsel."[3] During that time, the general high regard for lawyers within the corporation was evident in the ranks of senior management itself, where many of the most senior executive positions were held by lawyers, whose "professional and business advice was considered critical."[4]

As the twentieth century progressed, however, senior management positions shifted to business school graduates. Correspondingly, in-house lawyer compensation lagged and advancement opportunities decreased, and corporate legal work shifted from in-house to outside counsel. In addition, "in-house counsel were stereotyped as inferior legal service providers" and were "unfairly viewed as lawyers 'who had not quite made the grade as partner' at their corporation's principal outside law firm."[5] Consequently, in-house counsel positions became less desirable.[6] Moreover, many business people saw the general counsel and other in-house counsel as "Mr. or Ms. No," as "the bad guys who were going to quash the deals."[7] Thus, business people frequently kept in-house counsel out of the loop, further marginalizing them and decreasing their effectiveness.[8]

As legislative, regulatory, and business complexity burgeoned in the 1970s and 1980s, and litigation by and against corporations proliferated,

---

2. Sarah Helene Duggin, *The Pivotal Role of the General Counsel in Promoting Corporate Integrity and Professional Responsibility*, 51 St. Louis U.L.J. 989, 995 (2007).

3. Carl D. Liggio, *A Look at the Role of Corporate Counsel: Back to the Future—or Is It the Past?*, 44 Ariz. L. Rev. 621, 621 (2002) [hereinafter Liggio, *Back to the Future*]; Carl D. Liggio, *The Changing Role of Corporate Counsel*, 46 Emory L.J. 1201, 1201 (1997) [hereinafter Liggio, *Changing Role*]; Duggin, *supra* note 2, at 995.

4. Duggin, *supra* note 2, at 995; Liggio, *Changing Role*, *supra* note 3, at 1201; Liggio, *Back to the Future*, *supra* note 3, at 621.

5. Simmons & Dinnage, *supra* chapter I, note 11, at 79 (quoting Abram Chayes & Antonia H. Chayes, *Corporate Counsel and the Elite Law Firm*, 37 Stan. L. Rev. 277, 277 (1985)).

6. Duggin, *supra* note 2, at 995–96; Liggio, *Changing Role*, *supra* note 3, at 1202; Liggio, *Back to the Future*, *supra* note 3, at 622.

7. Interview with Louis J. Briskman, Executive Vice President and General Counsel, CBS Corporation (Aug. 26, 2009).

8. *Id.*

the general counsel again rose to prominence within the corporation.[9] In-house legal departments began to focus on "[a]cquiring in-house special- ists" that gave companies the capacity to complete more specialized work in-house, as well as "the capacity to evaluate and find the best outside spe- cialists" for a particular issue.[10] Moreover, many senior managers began to recognize the value of having lawyers who were already well-versed in the corporation's operations, culture, and legal environment.[11] This recognition of the value of lawyers led, in turn, to the involvement of in-house lawyers early on in business activities, for strategic and preventive purposes.[12]

Thus, the inside-outside counsel balance began to shift again, with in- house counsel again taking on a more prominent role, and "the role of out- side counsel [becoming] one of an episodic provider of legal services."[13] Susan Hackett, former Senior Vice President and General Counsel, Association of Corporate Counsel, describes the shift this way:

> From an internal management perspective, the general counsel's role over the last twenty years has really moved from being one of a lawyer who is a counselor on legal issues toward one that is far more focused on a more holistic involve- ment in the corporation's strategic, financial, and legal risk. In short, enterprise risk management. The general counsel is no longer just the guy who answers the legal questions.
>
> What you see now is much more of a differentiation between what an in- house lawyer does and what an outside counsel does. They both practice law, but they do it in very different ways. In-house lawyers have much more focus on preventive practice internally. That is not to say outside counsel are not inter- ested [in prevention], but outside counsel get called when the milk is spilt.

---

9. Duggin, *supra* note 2, at 996–97; Liggio, *Changing Role*, *supra* note 3, at 1203–04.

10. Heineman, *supra* Introduction, note 2, at 95.

11. *See* Simmons & Dinnage, *supra* chapter I, note 11, at 84 (noting the "unique value that stems from in-house counsel linkages, networks, and integration with other firm activities").

12. Duggin, *supra* note 2, at 997–98; *see also* Simmons & Dinnage, *supra* chapter I, note 11, at 79 ("Today, however, in-house counsel, when compared to other legal providers, have a greater potential impact on corporate affairs, particularly by curbing corporate opportunism and creating value.").

13. Liggio, *Changing Role*, *supra* note 3, at 1201; *see also* David B. Wilkins, *Team of Rivals? Toward a New Model of the Corporate Attorney-Client Relationship*, 78 FORDHAM L. REV. 2067, 2070 (2010) (describing a trend through the 1980s and 1990s among corporations to "acquir[e] in-house expertise" and "mov[e] toward a spot-contracting model for procuring legal services"); Yuri Mikulka, *Be Careful out There*, CORP. COUNSEL, Mar. 2008, at 74 ("Unlike their counterparts 20 years ago, GCs these days are . . . pro- gressively more involved in business decisions and senior management meetings.").

In-house counsel are increasingly focused on how to keep the milk in the glass.[14]

Cost pressures have further catalyzed corporate internalization of legal services.[15]

B. MODERN REALITY

The complexity of the CLO's role has expanded to reflect the shift toward the general counsel's broader involvement in corporate affairs. For example, "the general counsel's role is increasingly consumed by regulation and government. For the general counsel of a publicly traded company, it is in the forefront. Disclosure, compliance, regulations, internal investigations—these are all increasingly a huge part of what every general counsel is working on."[16] The complexity of the general counsel role has also intensified as companies have expanded their global reach. "The global dimension of what general counsel do is vastly different for most companies than it was 20 years ago. Twenty years ago, you did not worry too much about Europe and antitrust; you did not worry too much about China. Now you could make a long list of those global challenges."[17] Moreover, as regulation of the U.S. securities markets has shaped the governance of some foreign companies,[18]

14. Interview with Susan Hackett, Senior Vice President and General Counsel, Association of Corporate Counsel (Sept. 2, 2009).

15. *See* Simmons & Dinnage, *supra* chapter I, note 11, at 80 ("A growing number of corporations, facing increasing costs due to business and legal complexities, are deciding to internalize a greater proportion of their legal needs in lieu of procuring legal services from the wide array of outside law firms available in the marketplace."); *see also infra* chapter VI.D.1 (discussing the shift toward keeping legal work in-house in an effort to curb legal costs).

16. Interview with Adam Ciongoli, General Counsel, Willis Group Holdings, Ltd. (Sept. 4, 2009); *see also The Evolving Role of General Counsel, supra* chapter I, note 28, at 9 ("Today's GC needs to oversee corporate governance and compliance areas as well as play a key role in shaping governance, risk and compliance (GRC) management policies. The role has expanded to include proactive legal risk management and preventative law, becoming a critical pillar in an organization's risk management strategy."); Mary Swanton, *Mid-Term Report: A Look at Obama Administration Moves That Impact In-House Counsel*, INSIDE COUNSEL, Nov. 2010, at 51 (discussing legislative and regulatory initiatives creating complexity for businesses).

17. Interview with Brackett B. Denniston III, Senior Vice President and General Counsel, General Electric Company (Dec. 16, 2009).

18. Interview with Simon A. Fish, Executive Vice-President & General Counsel, BMO Financial Group (Dec. 2, 2009) ("Sarbanes-Oxley has had a significant impact on Canada. Many Canadian public companies either are listed on the New York Stock Exchange or are SEC registrants. In one way or another, the governance of Canadian

the role of general counsel in those companies may have shifted toward the U.S. model as well.[19]

As the role of in-house counsel—and particularly the general counsel—has expanded, so too has the influence of the general counsel in the corporate organization.[20] Expanded roles and influence again have increased the desirability of in-house counsel positions for bright, well-educated lawyers seeking interesting, influential work.[21] Louis Briskman, Executive Vice President and General Counsel of CBS Corporation, has explained how the shift toward a broader involvement by the general counsel in the myriad corporate activities keeps the job interesting:

> The CEO and the CFO want to have a team, and they want to have the General Counsel as one of the members of the team. When I first became General Counsel our CEO told me what he wanted was not a lawyer; he wanted a counselor. He wanted someone who would give him not just good legal advice, but also good business advice, good moral advice, and good reputational advice. He wanted someone to counsel him and not just to "lawyer up." To me that was very, very important, very significant. It was a great learning experience for me.[22]

As the roles and influence of the legal department and in-house counsel in the corporation have expanded, the general counsel herself has become a pivotal figure in the organization.[23] In this "platinum" age of general counsel, the general counsel's roles "call for a broader set of skills that . . . extend far beyond the law." Indeed, they extend further than ever before.[24] Accordingly, the general counsel's influence in the corporation matches

companies has tended to follow the U.S. model. We monitor very closely developments in U.S. regulation—U.S. securities in particular.").

19. *Id.* ("Having served as general counsel of three Canadian public corporations, I have certainly seen a change in recent years in the role of the general counsel and in the relationship between the general counsel and the CEO. Certainly, the role and the relationship are more similar to the U.S. model than perhaps a decade or even half a decade ago. . . . Heightened cross-border compliance may be one of the reasons for the change in the role of the Canadian general counsel in recent years.").

20. *See* Michael W. Peregrine, *Front and Center: Nine Tips on Enhancing the Profile of the Nonprofit General Counsel*, CORP. COUNSEL, Aug. 2008, at 63 (explaining "the importance of enhancing the organizational profile of the nonprofit general counsel" in order to increase the general counsel's influence in the organization and avoid governance problems).

21. Duggin, *supra* note 2, at 999; Liggio, *Back to the Future, supra* note 3, at 628.

22. Interview with Louis J. Briskman, Executive Vice President and General Counsel, CBS Corporation (Aug. 26, 2009).

23. Liggio, *Back to the Future, supra* note 3, at 629.

24. *Id.* at 634–35; *see also* Simmons & Dinnage, *supra* chapter I, note 11, at 112 ("The mixture of legal and business roles requires a broader set of skills particularly among

those broad roles and skills. With that prominence come heightened expectations, increased scrutiny, and attendant risks of liability.[25]

One factor in the evolution of the role of general counsel has been the dawn of the "new reality." While the evolution of the role of general counsel is partly a function of the increasing challenges of the new reality (such as the intense regulatory environment, stockholder activism, and growing litigiousness), it is also partly a function of other factors. Those other factors include those noted above in this chapter, such as the extensive upgrade in respect and quality of work, along with the benefit to the company that comes from the general counsel's understanding of and involvement in the company's business.

We pause here to probe further the CLO's functions as "business partner." It is clear that the CLO must be fully immersed in the company's business and competitive environment. Such immersion enables the CLO to evaluate and guide the company with respect to trends and anticipated changes in the legal, regulatory, and business environments that may impact the company. Further, the general counsel should not hesitate to express her views about the wisdom of a proposed business venture, even if the legality of the deal is beyond serious doubt. If the general counsel feels "in her gut" that the venture is "legal but stupid," she should not hesitate to say so (though delicate and diplomatic framing of the issue may be prudent, if still effective).[26]

It is clear that "as the amount of government attention and pressure on companies has increased, the difficulties of being a general counsel have also increased because the government expects general counsels to exercise some independence within the company."[27] The rewards of the job apparently continue to outweigh the challenges, however. Indeed, "the modern chief legal officer thrives on 'the challenge of operating effectively in an evolving global business environment, while at the same time implementing a company culture that combines high ethical standards with

general counsel, who must not only manage legal departments, but often navigate and influence corporate culture to limit legal risk and costs.").

25. *See* Mikulka, *supra* note 13, at 74 (quoting William Lytton, retired general counsel of Tyco International Ltd., as stating that "heightened scrutiny 'is the logical result of the increasing visibility and importance of GCs'"); *see also id.* ("[A]ll GCs are now expected to have a deeper knowledge of corporate decisions and applicable regulatory requirements . . . .").

26. We discuss this issue *infra* chapter III.B.4.b, including the tension between the CLO's participation in strategic decision-making as a business partner with the other senior management and preservation of the attorney-client privilege.

27. Interview with Adam Ciongoli, General Counsel, Willis Group Holdings, Ltd. (Sept. 4, 2009).

world-class performance.' In other words, the job is tougher than ever, yet it remains well worth the trouble."[28]

C. KEY TAKEAWAYS ON THE EVOLUTION OF THE ROLE OF GENERAL COUNSEL

This is not the "good old days." But reflection on the historical roles of the general counsel over the past century or so helps us gain some understanding of how the role has dynamically evolved to meet the challenges presented by the modern corporate context.

Our senior partner Ira Millstein recently articulated to us his view of the changes that have occurred in the general counsel role since he began practicing law with large corporate clients, some fifty or sixty years ago. He put it this way:

> When I started practice with larger clients in the late '50s–'60s, in-house counsel were not very significant in the corporate scheme of things. Generally, they were compliance-oriented note-keepers. They had very little role in strategy, risk, and worldly matters. Also, they generally came from the larger law firms and were planted in clients for safekeeping of the client relationship. Outside counsel then were the primary source of "important" legal advice. And rarely did in-house counsel have a major role in picking outside counsel. That was the job of the CEO or other top management.
>
> Over the years as corporate responsibilities kept growing—by law, best practices, and public expectations—general counsel inexorably took on more important, responsible roles in the corporation. This in turn led to a vast change in the quality of general counsel. Men, and then later women, were outstanding lawyers with career options who were recruited to the client, often leading to responsible management roles directly and indirectly, sometimes graduating to the board, heaven help them, in certain cases.
>
> Today, it has become a most sensitive position. The GC is in a tough position, reporting to the board, working for management, and technically having the "corporation" as a client.

So, with the "past as prologue," even one who has been an outside observer of the corporate scene over the years can see that the role has

---

28. Mikulka, *supra* note 13, at 74 (quoting Smith McKeithen, general counsel of Cadence Systems, Inc.).

undergone a transformative change—an evolution—over the past fifty-plus years, with that evolution picking up some speed in the past twenty years or so. But in the past decade, the evolution of the role has morphed into a revolution in responsibilities and expectations. Chief legal officers, their peers, and some of their colleagues know that intuitively. Our job in this book is to shine a light on that reality for all constituents and observers to see.

The CLO of today as partner/guardian is normally positioned within the highest ranks of senior management, while also serving as a legal advisor to the board of directors. The quintessential general counsel of today is the archetypical persuasive counselor—part gatekeeper, part enabler, part advocate, and (perhaps most of all) wise advisor.

How to live up to the expectations for the chief legal officer of today is "job one" for the incumbent in that position. And it is all about expectations.

The CEO may wish for and expect primarily an enabler. The CLO of today is part enabler. Otherwise, she would not last long in the position. The question is, what kind of enabler? The expectation should be that her skills at enabling will be leavened by a balanced mix of legal skills, responsibility, business knowledge, a dash of gatekeeping, and a heaping helping of integrity, independence, and common sense.

The board may wish for and expect primarily a legal and ethical guardian. This expectation is self-evident. With the shift from outside counsel to the CLO as the font of legal wisdom in the boardroom, the expectation is very high. The in-house general counsel must be able persuasively to communicate to the directors the confidence and security that she and her staff either (a) know the legal answer as applied to a business strategy or brewing trouble or (b) have the depth of knowledge of the outside practicing bar to obtain the best advice for the board.

The challenges arise in striking the right balance between the role of partner and of guardian, between the CEO's expectations and the board's expectations, in order to pursue the best interests of the corporate entity-client. We explore these challenges further in the following chapter.

CHAPTER 3

The General Counsel on the Balance Beam

The best training for being a general counsel were my years as a high school gymnast. The balancing act, the difficult positions, and sometimes pain, but handling it all with grace and calm, and making it look effortless are the general counsel's parallels to the life of the gymnast. Think of the challenges of being the business partner, but also the gatekeeper, the counselor to the CEO, but not being too close to the CEO, the counselor to the board and leader of a team, just to name a few. The number of different hats that the general counsel is asked to wear today is what makes the job very exciting and fulfilling at one end. But it also makes the job incredibly challenging and thoughtful at the other end, because you do have to wear a lot of different hats for a lot of different stakeholders but never lose focus on what is right for the company and its shareholders.

—Kim K.W. Rucker[1]

General counsel have to be prepared for and even enjoy a somewhat bumpy ride. That also means exercising very good judgment—and calm and cool judgment—in the face of things that are quite serious.

—Louise M. Parent[2]

The lawyer for the corporation—whether she is the general counsel, subordinate in-house counsel, or outside counsel—faces tensions, stresses, and professional responsibilities that often differ from those of lawyers who represent individuals. Of course, the primary reality that must be faced is that the corporate lawyer's client is—and should be—only the

---

1. Interview with Kim K.W. Rucker, Senior Vice President and General Counsel, Avon Products, Inc. (Jan. 7, 2010).
2. Interview with Louise M. Parent, Executive Vice President and General Counsel, American Express Company (Nov. 2, 2009).

corporate entity. The CEO, CFO, and the directors are "constituents" of the corporation, but they are not clients of the general counsel or of her subordinates.[3]

This chapter is an attempt to highlight some of the issues that corporate counsel, directors, executives, and other corporate stakeholders should seek to recognize and understand.[4] The various challenges faced by both in-house and outside lawyers representing corporations include the courageous maintenance of professional independence, dealing with "up-the-ladder" reporting obligations, seeking to serve the client's best interests through persuasive counseling, the separation of legal and business advice, and dealing with internal investigations, to name just a few.

As mentioned previously, the CLO's successful fulfillment of her dual roles as business partner and guardian of the corporate integrity turns on her ability to manage the tensions inherent in that partner-guardian role. That is, the CLO is a partner of the management when it comes to business decisions and she is the guardian of the corporate integrity when it comes to infusing ethics, morals, policy, compliance, and a range of other issues in her persuasive counseling of senior management and the board of directors.

There is a threshold question to be addressed at this point. That is, to whom does the CLO "report?" In some companies, the CLO reports to the CFO. To be sure, most CLOs would say that they have a strong, collegial relationship with the CFO. But that does not mean that the CLO should report to the CFO. The preferred—and perhaps the most prevalent—model is one in which the CLO reports to the CEO.[5] This reporting relationship is a natural one on an operational basis.

---

3. *See, e.g.,* MODEL RULES OF PROF'L CONDUCT R. 1.13 (2010).

4. A substantial portion of this chapter is based on E. Norman Veasey & Christine T. Di Guglielmo, *The Tensions, Stresses, and Professional Responsibilities of the Lawyer for the Corporation,* 62 BUS. LAW. 1 (2006).

5. *See* DeMott, *supra* chapter I, note 24, at 967 ("Although general counsel would, as a corporate officer, be appointed to office by the board of directors, in a large corporation the general counsel generally reports to the CEO and the CEO has a substantial if not exclusive role in choosing the general counsel." (footnote omitted)); Duggin, *supra* chapter II, note 2, at 1040 ("[G]eneral counsel should always have a reporting relationship to the board, as well as to the CEO, and open lines of communication with independent directors."); *Report of the New York City Bar Association Task Force on the Lawyer's Role in Corporate Governance,* as excerpted in 62 BUS. LAW. 427, 434 (2006) [hereinafter, *Lawyer's Role in Corporate Governance*] ("The General Counsel must have sufficient direct access to senior management and to the Board so that problems can be elevated and dealt with at the appropriate level. The General Counsel should report to one of the highest ranked company executives, typically the CEO. He or she should

Indeed, the verb "to report" is normal and well understood in corporate parlance. But the CLO's reporting responsibilities and relationships are not limited to the CEO.[6] She is also the principal and trusted legal advisor to the board of directors, normally implicating the expectation that she will attend all board meetings and many key board committee meetings. Although she usually is not a member of the board, she should be regularly called on for advice and should be free to speak up at board or committee meetings and even in executive sessions of independent directors, when invited to attend.

Special tensions arise for the general counsel because, as the chief legal officer with the corporate entity as her only client, she answers both to the CEO and to the board of directors. She is the principal advisor to both. She is invested in important business matters hatched in the C-Suite, with which she or her team should have been involved from the beginning. And she must advise the board as their independent legal advisor. This is particularly troublesome if the management's or board's expectations and understanding of the roles of the CLO may be unclear or in conflict. In fact, it is far worse when the CEO and the board have potential differences or conflicts on strategy or other matters. Sometimes these tensions may be palpable and difficult for the CLO to manage consistent with her ethical duties, advancement of corporate interests, and job security.

Most general counsel we know are up to the task and do not take for granted their challenges or the importance of managing those challenges effectively and collegially. The management of these challenges presents issues of how to establish and fulfill counsel's obligation to be independent, when to advise the corporate actors to seek outside counsel or a second business opinion, when to go up the ladder, and how to summon up the courage to do the right thing.

Following the spate of Enron-era corporate scandals, lawyers, directors, and academic observers have taken an increased interest in the professional responsibility challenges faced by corporate counsel. In this chapter we discuss some of the types of challenges and tensions general counsel must confront and resolve in order to serve their clients ethically and well. Since the CLO does not represent individually the chief executive officer, the board as a whole, or the individual directors and officers with whom she

have ready access, as well, to any other executives or directors responsible for compliance, governance or ethics issues, and to any company ombudsman.").

6. Whether the reporting relationships to the CEO and the board are thought of as a solid line and a dotted line, respectively, is of little consequence. Both reporting relationships are real, constant, and significant.

interacts, this dynamic exemplifies the issues that confront the general counsel and outside counsel.[7]

This chapter does not attempt to deal completely with all of the professional responsibility challenges that corporate counsel face. Instead, we raise here some issues in order to highlight a few of these challenges and tensions. Further discussion and debate concerning these issues are ongoing and will continue to evolve in C-suites, boardrooms, law offices, articles, case law, studies, and reports.[8]

In the preceding chapter we addressed the general counsel position in historical context, providing an overview of the multiple roles that the modern general counsel fills and noting the concept of tension among the general counsel's various roles as well as the advisory and reporting relationships of the position. Underlying these responsibilities and tensions is the importance of professional independence and courage for both in-house and outside corporate counsel, but especially for the chief legal officer. Independence and courage are the crucial attributes for a general counsel because she must provide unvarnished advice and endeavor to avoid circumstances in which it is hard to resist the temptation to "go along to get along."

The general counsel is often the bridge between management and the board. She must have sufficient courage to be candid with both. Her need to be independent is not only an ethical obligation,[9] but it is also a practical necessity to keep the corporate ship afloat and sailing the proper channel.

---

7. Of course, the issues may arise with different degrees of complexity or frequency for general counsel and outside counsel. In addition, subordinate in-house counsel face many of the same challenges, also to different degrees. *See, e.g.,* Lisa H. Nicholson, *Sarbox 307's Impact on Subordinate In-House Counsel: Between a Rock and a Hard Place,* 2004 MICH. ST. L. REV. 559 (discussing some of the special challenges faced by subordinate in-house counsel); *see also* Responsibilities of Supervisory Attorneys, 17 C.F.R. § 205.4 (2006) (codifying the SEC's rule describing and regulating the professional responsibilities of supervising lawyers); Responsibilities of a Subordinate Attorney, 17 C.F.R. § 205.5 (2006) (codifying the SEC's rule describing and regulating the professional responsibilities of subordinate lawyers); MODEL RULES OF PROF'L CONDUCT R. 5.1 (addressing the responsibility of partners, managers, and supervising lawyers); MODEL RULES OF PROF'L CONDUCT R. 5.2 (addressing the responsibilities of the subordinate lawyer).

8. *E. g., Lawyer's Role in Corporate Governance, supra* note 5. One excellent resource for directors with respect to some of these issues is the *Corporate Director's Guidebook,* now in its sixth edition. CORPORATE LAWS COMMITTEE, AMERICAN BAR ASSOCIATION, CORPORATE DIRECTOR'S GUIDEBOOK (6th ed. 2011) [hereinafter CORPORATE DIRECTOR'S GUIDEBOOK].

9. *See infra* chapter IV, notes 39–40 and accompanying text for discussion of MODEL RULES OF PROF'L CONDUCT R. 2.1.

A. THE MANY HATS WORN BY THE MODERN GENERAL COUNSEL

A major factor contributing to the variety and complexity inherent in the general counsel position is the multiplicity of roles inherent in the office.[10] In a broad view, the general counsel's roles within the corporation may be divided into four general categories:

- legal advisor
- corporate officer and member of the senior executive team
- administrator of the in-house legal department; and
- corporate agent in dealings with third parties, including outside counsel.[11]

Each of these categories encompasses numerous important functions. The general counsel's roles are not limited to purely legal functions— companies frequently assign functions other than legal to the CLO and the legal department. As Bruce Sewell, Senior Vice President and General Counsel, Apple Inc., explained:

> The general counsel's role has really expanded to encompass a portfolio that is not just legal, but includes matters such as government affairs, corporate social responsibility, reputational matters, and compliance. These all play into the reputational value of the corporate brand. More and more companies are organizing so that these functions are under the general counsel. For example, at Intel, the general counsel's role had four pillars: law, public policy, government relations, and corporate social responsibility. At Apple, the legal department includes law, government affairs, global security, and all of the compliance functions. I think companies are increasingly recognizing the relationship, the synergies, between a law function and the government affairs and compliance functions.[12]

Whatever the organizational structure of the legal department within the overall corporate organization may be, the wide range of more specific

---

10. For descriptions of the general counsel's many roles in the corporation, see, for example, DeMott, *supra* chapter I, note 24, at 955; Barclift, *supra* chapter I, note 26, at 5–7; Susanna M. Kim, *Dual Identities and Dueling Obligations: Preserving Independence in Corporate Representation*, 68 TENN. L. REV. 179, 201–04 (2001); Weaver, *supra* chapter I, note 24, at 1039–40.

11. *See* DeMott, *supra* chapter I, note 24, at 957–58; *see also* Daly, *supra* chapter I, note 24, at 1061–62 (categorizing the functions as management and review of outside legal services, performance of routine legal services and sometimes complex transactions or litigation, counseling clients and constituents on regulatory requirements, and creating compliance programs).

12. Interview with Bruce Sewell, Senior Vice President and General Counsel, Apple Inc. (Nov. 3, 2009).

functions that the general counsel often fulfills reflects the breadth and depth of the general counsel's roles.[13] Indeed, the broad scope of the job may even be key to enabling the general counsel "to address the myriad business-in-society issues facing modern corporations,"[14] as well as enhancing the general counsel's job satisfaction and personal fulfillment. As Daniel Desjardins, Senior Vice President, General Counsel and Assistant Secretary of Bombardier, described:

> It is important for the fulfillment of the role of the general counsel to go outside of the strong legal responsibility and take on more functions such as corporate social responsibility, because doing so enhances the scope of the daily life of the general counsel and serves them well in their personal fulfillment.[15]

The general counsel's functions often include:

- *Business as well as legal advisor.* The general counsel's position in the top levels of the corporation's management structure gives the general counsel a broad impact on strategic business planning.[16] This may often affect the style of lawyering that a *general* counsel brings to the table.[17] Indeed, top-notch general counsel are true generalists—even renaissance persons. The issues and concerns raised by the general counsel's role as a business advisor are the subject of detailed discussion later in this chapter.
- *Manager.* The general counsel must devote substantial time to managing or directing the management of the work and employees of the corporation's legal department, as well as the corporation's procurement and

---

13. Duggin, *supra* chapter II, note 2.

14. Ben W. Heineman, Jr., *Caught in the Middle*, CORP. COUNSEL, Apr. 2007.

15. Interview with Daniel Desjardins, Senior Vice President, General Counsel and Assistant Secretary, Bombardier Inc. (May 20, 2011).

16. *See* Liggio, *Changing Role, supra* chapter II, note 3, at 1209–10 ("No strategic plan can be developed which does not include the legal ramifications of the proposed conduct. To be effective, the earlier and the more involved that counsel is in this process, the more likely it is that counsel will be able to provide meaningful advice and help avoid problems."); Simmons & Dinnage, *supra* chapter I, note 11, at 84–85 ("When completed by competent professionals with well-honed ethical sensibilities, the strategic tasks that in-house counsel undertake add value because they are fundamentally different from the largely tactical outside law firm role.").

17. *See* Daly, *supra* chapter I, note 24, at 1068 ("The proactive model of lawyering springs from personal and professional traits seemingly unique to U.S. lawyers. It is characterized by a 'can do' attitude that focuses on problem-solving and mixes business and legal counseling with little concern for the boundaries between them.").

monitoring of outside legal services.[18] How the legal department is organized and how legal and related services are delivered can strongly influence the corporation's culture of integrity.

- *Promoter of values and ethics.* The CLO has a pivotal role in framing,
  implementing, and overseeing the company's values and ethical standards.[19] This role can include developing explicit policies instructing
  employees to seek guidance from counsel regarding the resolution of
  business and legal ethical issues.[20] In addition, as the top supervising
  lawyer in the legal department, the CLO must ensure the highest levels
  of ethics and professionalism of all lawyers and support personnel in the
  legal department.[21] The ethical tone set in the legal department can

18. *See* Liggio, *Changing Role, supra* chapter II, note 3, at 1219 (observing that corporate counsel must be skilled managers and administrators); Simmons & Dinnage, *supra*
chapter I, note 11, at 114 ("General counsel normally have absolute control over the
selection and management of outside counsel. This even applies to specialist areas such
as tax or intellectual property where there may be internal specialists who are quite
capable of working directly with outside legal providers."); *cf. also* Michele D. Beardslee,
*If Multidisciplinary Partnerships Are Introduced into the United States, What Could or
Should Be the Role of General Counsel?*, 9 FORDHAM J. CORP. & FIN. L. 1, 21 (2003) (quoting an interview with a general counsel, who described the general counsel position as
"a management job as opposed to a practice job").

19. Heineman, *supra* note 14 ("The GC, either as a lead or supporting actor, should
be involved in . . . establishing global values and standards beyond what financial and
legal rules require . . . ."). This role may expand because the Sarbanes-Oxley Act and
the SEC's implementing rules as well as recent amendments to the self-regulatory
organizations' listing standards require that corporations subject to their regulation
enact a code of business ethics. *See, e.g.*, Sarbanes-Oxley Act § 406(a), 15 U.S.C. § 7264
(directing the SEC to adopt rules requiring issuers to disclose "whether or not, and
if not, the reason therefor, such issuer has adopted a code of ethics for senior financial officers, applicable to its principal financial officer and comptroller or principal
accounting officer, or persons performing similar functions"); Code of Ethics, 17 C.F.R.
§ 229.406 (2006) (codifying the SEC's final rule implementing § 406 of the Sarbanes-
Oxley Act); Disclosure Required by Sections 406 and 407 of the Sarbanes-Oxley Act of
2002, Exchange Act Release No. 33–8177, http://www.sec.gov/rules/final/33–8177.
htm (releasing and discussing the final rule); N.Y. STOCK EXCH., LISTED COMPANY
MANUAL § 303A. 10 (2010), http://nysemanual.nyse.com/LCMTools/PlatformViewer.
asp?searched=1&selectednode=chp_1_4_3_1&CiRestriction=303A&manual=%2Flcm
%2Fsections%2Flcm-sections%2F ("Listed companies must adopt and disclose a code
of business conduct and ethics for directors, officers and employees, and promptly disclose any waivers of the code for directors or executive officers.").

20. *See* Daly, *supra* chapter I, note 24, at 1084 n. 116 (citing IBM's instruction to its
employees to consult IBM's in-house counsel when faced with a business decision that
raises ethical concerns).

21. *See, e.g.*, 17 C.F.R. pt. 205; MODEL RULES OF PROF'L CONDUCT R. 5.1. *See gener-
ally* Andrew M. Perlman, *Unethical Obedience by Subordinate Attorneys: Lessons From
Social Psychology*, 36 HOFSTRA L. REV. 451 (2007); Mark A. Sargent, *Lawyers in the
Perfect Storm*, 43 WASHBURN L.J. 1 (2003); Christopher J. Whelan, *Some Realism About
Professionalism: Core Values, Legality, and Corporate law Practice*, 54 BUFF. L. REV. 1067

reverberate throughout the organization, as the lawyers interact with all groups, connecting the dots between various service lines or business units. The general counsel also frequently participates in shaping the corporation's corporate social responsibility policies and other aspects of the company's "role as a corporate citizen" and how it balances its "private interests with the public interests affected" by its actions.[22]

- *Problem solver.* As a trusted member of senior management, with specialized skills and a strong dose of independence, the general counsel is often a problem solver on a wide range of issues. She fulfills this role both proactively and as a key go-to person for people throughout the organization who have concerns about legal issues, compliance, ethics, corporate integrity, or other issues.

- *Mediator among corporate constituencies.* The general counsel often acts as a middleman, ferrying between two groups, such as the board and senior management, in an effort to reach a solution to a problematic issue.[23] The general counsel may also participate in communications with large stockholders, institutional investors, or stockholder advisory firms. Some corporations also call upon the general counsel or in-house counsel in a more formal way to help resolve disputes or issues among individuals or groups within the corporation.[24]

- *Compliance program designer and implementer.* As the complexity of corporate compliance programs has increased, so too has the general counsel's

(2007); Donald C. Langevoort, *Someplace Between Philosophy and Economics: Legitimacy and Good Corporate Lawyering*, 75 FORDHAM L. REV. 1615 (2006).

22. Heineman, *supra* note 14.

23. Interview with Louis J. Briskman, Executive Vice President and General Counsel, CBS Corporation (Aug. 26, 2009); *see also* Duggin, *supra* chapter II, note 2, at 1020 ("Yet another informal role that general counsel often play is that of arbitrator among corporate factions. While many different people may serve in this capacity within an organization, lawyers often have a skill set uniquely suited to identifying the issues at the core of internecine disputes and negotiating workable resolutions. As chief legal officers, general counsel are ideally situated to appreciate the impact of factionalization and the damage that it can do, particularly when disgruntled employees fairly or unfairly believe that their rights have been violated or that another group within the entity has engaged in inappropriate behavior. As lawyers trained in the art of negotiation, general counsel also have skills that often prove invaluable in resolving intra-corporate disputes among business units or administrative departments." (footnote omitted)); Simmons & Dinnage, *supra* chapter I, note 11, at 134 ("In-house counsel are perhaps well-suited for this [mediation] function because they develop a broad panoramic view of corporate problems that extends well beyond provincial department concerns and legal expertise.").

24. *See* Beardslee, *supra* note 18, at 24 (describing one general counsel's role as the corporation's internal mediator).

involvement in the planning or management of those programs.[25] Practice varies as to the management of the compliance function. In some corporations, the general counsel is also the chief compliance officer, in others, there is a chief compliance officer (CCO) who may report to the CLO, the audit committee of the board of directors, or another senior officer.[26] Moreover, the whistleblower rules adopted by the SEC, pursuant to the Dodd-Frank Act, present a new layer of challenges to the management of the corporation's compliance program, and, thus, to the general counsel's role in the program.[27]

- *Manager of legal and reputational risk* and *educator*. General counsel perform the increasingly important function of assessing legal risks and translating those risks into business terms in order to facilitate decision-making concerning those risks.[28] The CLO's role in risk assessment

25. *See* Richard S. Gruner, *General Counsel in an Era of Compliance Programs and Corporate Self-Policing*, 46 EMORY L.J. 1113, 1113 (1997) (discussing "the changing roles of corporate general counsel and inhouse attorneys as architects of and participants in the management of corporate law compliance"); *see also Compliance Readiness—General Counsel's Expanded Role*, METRO. CORP. COUNSEL, Sept. 2006, at 1. *See generally* Sarbanes-Oxley Act § 404, 15 U.S.C. 7262 (directing the SEC to prescribe rules requiring corporations to report annually regarding management's assessment of internal controls).

26. For discussion of the relationships and responsibilities of the general counsel and the chief compliance officer, see *General Counsel as Persuasive Counselors: The Role and Responsibility of Today's General Counsel*, METRO. CORP. COUNSEL, Aug. 2007 (interview with Robert H. Mundheim, former Senior Executive Vice President and General Counsel, Salomon Smith Barney Holdings Inc.), http://www.metrocorpcounsel.com/current.php?artType=view&artMonth=August&artYear=2007&EntryNo=7013; Duggin, *supra* chapter II, note 2, at 1011–12; Ben Heineman, *Don't Divorce the GC and Compliance Officer*, CORP. COUNSEL, Dec. 2010, op. ed. (discussing various reporting relationships and responsibilities of chief compliance officer and general counsel), http://belfercenter.ksg.harvard.edu/publication/20612/dont_divorce_the_gc_and_compliance_officer.html; José A. Tabuena, *The Chief Compliance Officer vs. the General Counsel: Friend or Foe?*, COMPLIANCE & ETHICS MAGAZINE, Dec. 2006, at 4.

27. *See supra* chapter I.C.3.

28. *See* Howard B. Miller, *Law Risk Management and the General Counsel*, 46 EMORY L.J. 1223, 1223 (1997) ("General counsel are managers of law risk. Law risk is a kind of commercial risk, similar to credit risk, interest rate risk, currency risk, or market risk faced by modern businesses. What distinguishes and obscures law risk is the extent to which it is composed of transactional and dispute resolution inefficiencies. . . . The general counsel, comfortable in the worlds of business management and law, can translate and mediate between the concepts of business risk and the vocabulary of the law."); *see also* Beardslee, *supra* note 18, at 32 ("'The level of risk the company is assuming is often undertaken without a conscious decision having been made. . . . While the managers involved in each project may have made a careful judgment about what they believe to be the legal risk involved, in fact the scope of that risk, its wider consequences for the company, the relationship between that risk and others, and the aggregate risk being assumed by the company often are matters that only the General Counsel is in a position to assess in their entirety.'") (quoting STEPHEN J. FRIEDMAN & C. EVAN STEWART,

and risk management may be akin to her role in respect to compliance issues.[29] In their role in risk management, general counsel are well positioned to counsel decision-makers regarding the potential, nuanced implications of a course of action, in addition to the strictly financial implications of the course of action.[30] Educating employees about compliance is a critical component of managing legal risk.[31]

• *Public Policy Advisor*. The general counsel may also be in charge of or have a major role in government affairs for the company.[32] Public policy is an area of varied functions, including broad public policy activity as well as more targeted lobbying or other government affairs.

THE CORPORATE EXECUTIVE'S GUIDE TO THE ROLE OF THE GENERAL COUNSEL 1) (alteration in original)).

29. *Cf.* Stephen M. Bainbridge, *Caremark and Enterprise Risk Management*, 34 IOWA J. CORP. L. 967 (2009) (outlining doctrinal similarities between cases in which corporate losses arise from compliance issues and cases in which they arise from lax risk management); Veasey, *Maelstrom*, *supra* chapter I, note 36, at 8 ("Although risk management is the job of senior management, the board of directors is responsible for ensuring that the corporation has established appropriate risk-management systems, much as they must establish compliance systems.").

30. *See* Beardslee, *supra* note 18, at 32 ("It is the General Counsel's job to appraise [*sic*] the other Senior Managers of the [company's overall legal risk position] and as one General Counsel pointed out to 'encourage [them] to think of risk in terms other than money.'" (quoting interview with anonymous general counsel)); *see also* Timothy P. Terrell, *Professionalism as Trust: The Unique Internal Legal Role of the Corporate General Counsel*, 46 EMORY L.J. 1005, 1009 (1997) ("What every corporation needs is this sophisticated lawyer who respects not only the strong foundations of the law but the nature and significance of its constraints as well.").

31. *See* Duggin, *supra* chapter II, note 2, at 1005–06 ("Another critical task of general counsel is to educate corporate constituents. General counsel serve as educators at the highest levels of their organizations and set in motion the programs designed to alert employees at all levels to their legal obligations. Education of client constituents is a core element of proactive lawyering in American corporations that 'animates entire legal departments.' As the principal in-house legal advisor for the client, a general counsel has the responsibility to find ways to inform business managers and constituents throughout the company about what they can and cannot lawfully do as they pursue business objectives. This function is particularly important when major new legal obligations. [such as SOX and Dodd-Frank] come into existence." (footnotes omitted)); James F. Kelley, *The Role of the General Counsel*, 46 EMORY L.J. 1197, 1198 (1997) ("[T]he general counsel's role in th[e area of shaping corporate operations to avoid liability] is mostly educational . . . . Compliance programs are just frameworks for the actual process of educating corporate employees about the need for compliance and managing the implementation of that process."); *see also Compliance Readiness—General Counsel's Expanded Role*, *supra* note 25, at 24 (stressing the importance of providing within a compliance program education regarding regulatory developments).

32. *See, e.g., Corporate Counsel: Taking Stock*, 40 AZ. ATTORNEY 12 (Nov. 2003) (reporting the governmental affairs duties of the general counsel of the Dial Corporation); Michael A. Lampert, *In-House Counsel and the Attorney-Client Privilege*, at http://library.findlaw.com/2000/Oct/1/128767.html.

- *Corporate advocate, gatekeeper to the securities markets*, or *persuasive counselor*. General counsel's role with respect to the corporation's access to the securities markets has been the subject of significant recent debate. In chapter VII.A, we discuss counsel's potential gatekeeping and enabling roles and the issues raised with respect to lawyers' ability to counsel their clients and advocate clients' interests. We then suggest our preferred model under which corporate counsel, as persuasive counselors, can serve to protect the firm by guiding its constituents to the right course, without compromising their ability to provide to the corporation excellent and independent legal advice, service, and advocacy.[33] Moreover, the general counsel often sets the standards and tone for the professional services to be rendered to the corporation by outside counsel.[34]
- *Corporate secretary*. Although the duties of general counsel and corporate secretary are discrete and these positions are often held by different persons, the general counsel sometimes acts as or supervises the corporate secretary in carrying out that increasingly complex and important role.[35] Indeed, one of the key functions of the CLO and/or the corporate secretary relates to documenting board decision-making and oversight in minutes and other corporate records.[36] The corporate secretary is also an important bridge between management and the board, assisting in effective governance of the organization.

In short, general counsel "function in a strategic capacity . . . at the intersection of most corporate activity," which affords them "(i) access to information and institutional knowledge, (ii) the power to promote internal action, (iii) responsibility for outside counsel, and (iv) the capacity to engage in preventive law."[37]

---

33. *See* Veasey & Di Guglielmo, *supra* chapter I, note 8, at 28–30 (discussing the vision of the general counsel as persuasive counselor).

34. Contrast this model with the views expressed in a 2011 *New York Times* op-ed piece by Mark Emerson. Mark W. Emerson, *Lawyers and Accountants Once Put Integrity First*, N.Y. TIMES, June 19, 2011, Week in Review at 8.

35. *See* Weaver, *supra* chapter I, note 24, at 1035 (suggesting that the most common additional officer designation of general counsel is that of corporate secretary). Even where the offices of corporate secretary and general counsel are separate, as they often are, the officers serving in those positions must coordinate their activities. For discussion of a particular context in which such coordination is usually necessary—recording minutes for meetings of the board and its committees—see *infra* chapter III.B.5.c.

36. For discussion of this role with respect to minutes and record keeping, see *infra* chapter III.B.5.c.

37. Simmons & Dinnage, *supra* chapter I, note 11, at 113.

As discussed below, the general counsel's deep and daily understanding of, and involvement in, the corporation's business brings different value to the organization than is brought by outside counsel, who does not have the same familiarity with the business.[38] General counsel's business involvement can also work, paradoxically, to increase both her professional fulfillment and the tensions she experiences. Greater knowledge and familiarity often leads to greater recognition of problems (for example, the ability to ascertain the accuracy or inaccuracy of corporate disclosures), which in turn can lead to increased exposure to ethical dilemmas.[39]

The many and varied roles and functions of the general counsel are impacted from company to company by such widely divergent matters as corporate culture and risk tolerance, individual personalities of executives and directors, the business and regulatory environment of a particular company and its industry, the general counsel's personal and professional experiences, and many others. Thus, there can be no "one-size-fits-all" approach to handling the multifaceted responsibilities and expectations of the lawyer for the corporation.

B. THE LONELY MIDDLE: RELATIONSHIPS WITH SENIOR MANAGEMENT AND THE BOARD

1. Independence and Courage

The trick and one of the real challenges of being a general counsel is maintaining independence without the erosion of trust.
—Alan Braverman[40]

If you're either asleep or afraid, you don't belong in the position.
—Michele Mayes[41]

38. *Infra* notes 124–25, 127–29 and accompanying text; *see also* Simmons & Dinnage, *supra* chapter I, note 11, at 84 ("In-house counsel value is not simply a function of individual value-producing activities; it also encompasses the networked and embedded nature of the role, which contributes to the enhancement of corporate value and competitive advantage in unique ways that outside counsel cannot easily replicate.").

39. *See* Gruner, *supra* note 25, at 1185 ("Since general counsel and other inside attorneys will often have greater knowledge about past corporate operations and misconduct than their outside attorney counterparts, the likelihood that they will recognize the incompleteness or inaccuracy of proposed disclosures is correspondingly greater. Hence, the chances that inside counsel will face significant ethical dilemmas while overseeing disclosures about corporate misconduct are unusually high.").

40. Interview with Alan Braverman, Senior Executive Vice President, General Counsel and Secretary, The Walt Disney Company (Nov. 12, 2009).

41. Interview with Michele Coleman Mayes, Senior Vice President, General Counsel, and Chief Legal Officer, The Allstate Corporation (Aug. 25, 2009).

As general counsel, you've got to understand you're not running for a popularity contest. You're not going to be unnecessarily contentious, but at the same time, you have to be firm. That comes down to building trust and respect.
—Kim K.W. Rucker[42]

For many general counsel, certain tensions arise out of their relationships with other corporate actors, including the directors and senior executives. Additional issues for the general counsel may arise out of tensions among the various members of the senior management group. Before considering how those relationships affect the general counsel's professional responsibilities, we must first recognize the importance of independence and courage as professional qualities for lawyers generally and the CLO in particular.[43] Independence has several aspects[44] and must be evaluated in light of the particular circumstances of any proposed or ongoing representation.

As a general matter, independence requires that corporate counsel "must exercise professional judgment in the interests of the corporate client, independent of the personal interests of the corporation's officers and employees"[45] or the lawyer's own personal interests.[46] The CLO must continually wrestle with her need to support management and the board as persuasive counselor on the one hand and her need to exercise courage and independence in providing unvarnished advice and to "apply the brakes"

---

42. Interview with Kim K.W. Rucker, Senior Vice President and General Counsel, Avon Products, Inc. (Jan. 7, 2010).

43. *See, e.g.,* GEOFFREY C. HAZARD, JR. & W. WILLIAM HODES, 2 THE LAW OF LAWYERING § 17.7 (2d ed. Supp. 2004) (noting the importance of a corporate lawyer's exercising "independent professional judgment to determine what is truly in the client's best interest—setting aside, if need be, the views of other highly placed agents"); Lawrence J. Fox, *MDPs Done Gone: The Silver Lining in the Very Black Enron Cloud,* 44 ARIZ. L. REV. 547, 553 (2002) (describing independence as one of the "core values" of the legal profession); E. Norman Veasey, Chief Justice of the Delaware Supreme Court, Response for the Court at the Delaware Bar Admission Ceremony (Dec. 15, 2003) (on file with authors) (reflecting on the importance of independence among lawyers); E. Norman Veasey, The Lawyer's Higher Calling, Remarks at the Wake Forest School of Law Hooding Ceremony (May 14, 2006) (on file with authors) (discussing the importance of independence and courage among lawyers in the pursuit of doing the right thing).

44. *See* Fox, *supra* note 43, at 553–54 (examining some of the many facets of lawyer independence, including "independence from influences that would compromise our ardor for our clients" and "independence from the client" so that the lawyer can "be free of client influence [in order] to do the right thing").

45. ABA Task Force on Corporate Responsibility, *Report of the American Bar Association Task Force on Corporate Responsibility,* 59 BUS. LAW. 145, 157 (2003) [hereinafter Cheek Report]; *see also* MODEL RULES OF PROF'L CONDUCT R. 2.1 (discussed *infra* chapter IV, notes 39–40 and accompanying text).

46. *See* Cheek Report, *supra* note 45, at 157 ("There are times, moreover, when the corporate lawyer must recognize that his or her own independence may be compromised by relationships with senior executive officers . . . .").

when needed, on the other hand. Thus, the general counsel must be "more than a technician. The CEO and the board need to respect and trust the general counsel's judgment, not just her technical legal ability. That's very important. The general counsel has to be able to say 'no' to the board or say 'no' to the CEO, but has to be able to do that in a way that is reasonable and with respect."[47] In other words, the general counsel must navigate the tension between "go[ing] native as a yes-person for the business side" and "be[ing] an inveterate naysayer excluded from core corporate activity."[48]

Perhaps, in some contexts, a word that may be better than "independence" is "objectivity," because it better captures the nature of in-house counsel's relationship with management as a partnership.[49] In fact, in many circumstances, the in-house counsel brings to the table a greater built-in objectivity than another executive working on a particular issue, because the other business person may be too close to a problem to think critically about it.[50] The point is that a general counsel advising senior management or the board needs to think critically and not hesitate to express an unbiased and unvarnished view. In order to function effectively, the general counsel must demonstrate her support for management as well as the courage to go against the grain when necessary. "The general counsel wants to support management, but at the same time management needs to know, and the general counsel has to demonstrate, that when it comes to doing the right thing for the corporation, the general counsel will do that even if that is antagonistic toward management's own particular departmental goals or their own personal goals. Fortunately, there is usually a lot of

47. Interview with Larry D. Thompson, Senior Vice President, Government Affairs, General Counsel and Secretary, PepsiCo (Dec. 9, 2009).

48. Heineman, *supra* note 14.

49. *See* Interview with David G. Leitch, General Counsel and Group Vice President, Ford Motor Company (Feb. 1, 2010) ("I shy away a little bit from the word 'independence' because it almost implies a crusade. I want my lawyers to be partners with their business units. Maybe 'objectivity' is a better word. We are all part of the overall organization, so I do not want the lawyers feeling like they are somehow separate or above or independent of the overall entity. But they do need to give objective legal advice. Sometimes that takes support from headquarters and courage on their part."); *cf. also* Simmons & Dinnage, *supra* chapter I, note 11, at 90–92 (warning against "a myopic focus on independence" and promoting a vision of the in-house counsel role that "consider[s] how the input of in-house counsel could positively impact business enterprises and the design of corporate reform," particularly in light of in-house counsel's greater ability to monitor the corporation as compared with outsiders).

50. Simmons & Dinnage, *supra* chapter I, note 11, at 142. A tendency toward bias or a lack of objectivity are not issues that face only internal corporate actors. *See id.* ("Just as internal corporate actors may be too close to problems to think critically about them and thereby prone to provincialism, lawmakers and other outside observers may rely on crude, readily available heuristics, such as share price, that do not provide adequate insight into the health of a corporate organization.").

middle ground here, but in the end the general counsel is responsible for making the sometimes unpopular call."[51] Thus, balancing the trust the general counsel must build in order to do her job well with the independence necessary to the exercise of professional judgment is one of the key challenges of the job:

> In the relationship between management and the board, the general counsel has to balance the needs for maintaining loyalty, trust, and independence at the same time. You cannot be effective with management unless you are trusted, but you cannot do your job as general counsel unless you are independent. And I think the trick and one of the real challenges in being a general counsel is maintaining independence without the erosion of trust because [no matter how effective you are], you can find yourself in situations where [trust and independence] are really conflicting, so that the assertion of independence could be viewed as a betrayal of trust.[52]

Some general counsel choose to establish that trust by explicitly communicating with senior management—before the need arises—about the lawyer's independent role, coupled with her desire to solve problems and facilitate business objectives rather than to create problems and impede business. Doug Hagerman, Senior Vice President, General Counsel, and Secretary of Rockwell Automation, Inc., takes this approach. As he describes it:

> Before a matter arises where I as CLO will be asked to give advice to the CEO or other management person, I have found it best to make them feel at ease with me by saying something like: "When you come to me for advice about whether a certain action should be taken, I will probably give you one of the following four answers, when I have formulated an answer:
> (1) Yes;
> (2) Yes, if . . .;
> (3) No, but . . .; or
> (4) No!
> My first choice is #1 and my least-preferred choice is #4. Choices # 2 and # 3 are my second and third choices, respectively.[53]

51. Interview with Louis J. Briskman, Executive Vice President and General Counsel, CBS Corporation (Aug. 26, 2009).

52. Interview with Alan Braverman, Senior Executive Vice President, General Counsel and Secretary, The Walt Disney Company (Nov. 12, 2009).

53. Douglas M. Hagerman, Senior Vice President, General Counsel, and Secretary, Rockwell Automation, Inc. (Sept. 16, 2010).

So, general counsel and other in-house counsel can explicitly establish their independent role at the outset of the attorney-client relationship. But they, like outside counsel, must also remain vigilant about evaluating their independence not only at the outset of the attorney-client relationship but also with respect to working on a particular matter for the client. For example, if management seeks to engage regular outside counsel in conducting an investigation of questionable conduct, that counsel should consider whether the investigation might implicate counsel's earlier work for the corporation and thus present a conflict of interest, or whether limitations imposed by management on the investigation might impede proper and competent representation of the entity's interests in the investigation.[54] In the latter case, the Enron debacle teaches that referring the matter to independent outside counsel is the better course of action.[55]

A general counsel should apply careful judgment when determining when to flex her independence muscles, however. Maintaining and exercising independence does not mean that the general counsel should be constantly at odds with other members of management and the board. "One of the keys in being a successful general counsel is to know when you have to speak up. If you speak up every time that someone says something, then you start to lose credibility."[56] Instead, the general counsel must "pick her battles." The frequency and vigor with which the general counsel must actively exercise her independence thus may become a way of judging both the courage with which she fulfills her role and how well the company is functioning in terms of integrity and compliance. Kenneth Fredeen, General Counsel of Deloitte & Touche LLP (Canada), advises the lawyers in his group as follows:

> As you stand on the mountain and look out over the valley, you will see many, many other mountains and hills, and you know you cannot fight on every one of those hilltops. You have got to find out the ones that really matter and be chal-

---

54. *Cf., e.g.*, Robert W. Gordon, *A New Role for Lawyers?: The Corporate Counselor After Enron*, 35 CONN. L. REV. 1185, 1187–88 (2003) (describing the potential conflict issues arising in the internal investigation conducted at Enron by its regular outside counsel, and the ethical implications of the limitations imposed by senior management on the scope of the investigation); Susan P. Koniak, *Corporate Fraud: See, Lawyers*, 26 HARV. J.L. & PUB. POL'Y 195, 209 (2003) (arguing that Enron's regular outside counsel should not have accepted the task of investigating Sherron Watkins's allegations).

55. *See* Milton C. Regan, Jr., *Teaching Enron*, 74 FORDHAM L. REV. 1139, 1167 (2005) (observing some issues that may arise when existing counsel undertake investigation of their client).

56. Interview with Adam Ciongoli, General Counsel, Willis Group Holdings, Ltd. (Sept. 4, 2009).

lenging on those. The other ones, you should let go. There should be very few that you really have to take a stand on. If you are fighting on every hilltop, you (and the organization you work for) will be in trouble.[57]

The necessity of continual evaluation of one's professional independence applies equally to outside and in-house counsel. For example, a general counsel should objectively evaluate whether the board or a committee of the board should rely solely on her advice regarding a particular matter or consider using regular outside counsel or obtaining separate and independent counsel. The general counsel may decide that independence considerations demand special counsel in certain situations, such as a management buyout, a special litigation committee, or an internal investigation. In these types of situations,

> the facility for the board to seek independent legal advice is a safety valve for potential conflict situations. . . . But the corollary—that the CEO or [management] would seek independent counsel—would completely undercut the role of the general counsel. If the situation is such that the general counsel has to work on either the management side or the board side, then generally the general counsel should be more aligned with management and should be able and willing to seek independent counsel for the board. That is often the best way to balance competing interests. But in the vast majority of circumstances, there is a complete alignment of interest between management and the board. In that case, the general counsel absolutely operates as the trusted advisor for both management and the board.[58]

Thus, situations in which independent counsel for the board or the independent directors is necessary are generally limited. But the general counsel should be secure enough in her role to be comfortable suggesting that the board might want a second opinion in appropriate circumstances. Ultimately, the board or the independent directors must decide whether and when they need special outside counsel. In making this decision, they should be able to turn to the general counsel or regular outside counsel, who must have the professionalism, independence, courage, and integrity to provide the directors with unvarnished, objective advice. And, indeed, regular outside counsel may sometimes serve the corporate entity best if

---

57. Interview with Kenneth Fredeen, General Counsel, Deloitte & Touche LLP (Canada) (Dec. 7, 2009).

58. Interview with Bruce Sewell, Senior Vice President and General Counsel, Apple Inc. (Nov. 3, 2009).

he recommends that the board or the independent directors should consider and probably retain separate and independent outside counsel.[59]

Whether it is in-house or outside counsel, determining the independence of counsel requires a context-specific inquiry. When independent outside counsel is needed, that counsel need not necessarily be a stranger to the company. On the one hand, outside counsel's work may be more valuable if counsel has an established familiarity with the business and culture of the company. On the other hand, absence of significant prior legal work for the company may augur well when a court is scrutinizing counsel's independence.[60] But that counsel's independence with respect to the particular matter at hand must be evaluated. And the possible benefit of counsel's familiarity with the company's business must be weighed against the possible desirability and favorable optics of a completely "fresh face."

The tensions arising from a lawyer's relationships with other corporate actors may be particularly acute for a general counsel because of her

---

59. *See* E. Norman Veasey, *Separate and Continuing Counsel for Independent Directors: An Idea Whose Time Has Not Come as a General Practice*, 59 BUS. LAW. 1413, 1414 (2004) ("It is the general counsel, with a fully-staffed office, who must shape the quest for best practices by the board, and it is she who must make a professional decision about her counseling and reporting responsibilities in a variety of contexts, some of which may be very troubling. And, one would expect that a highly professional general counsel would have the intellectual honesty to counsel directors when they should consider separate representation."); *cf.* Cheek Report, *supra* note 45, at 157 & n. 54 (stating that a lawyer for a corporation must recognize when relationships with senior executives compromise her independence and must sometimes then ensure that "the corporate client retains other counsel who can exercise the requisite professional detachment"). *But cf.* Geoffrey C. Hazard, Jr. & Edward B. Rock, *A New Player in the Boardroom: The Emergence of the Independent Directors' Counsel*, 59 BUS. LAW. 1389, 1391, 1396 (2004) (suggesting that independent directors may now prefer to have regular, "genuinely independent counsel" rather than being represented by the in-house general counsel or the company's main outside counsel).

60. *Compare* S. Muoio & Co. v. Hallmark Entertainment Investment Co., 2011 Del. Ch. LEXIS 43, at *47–48 (Del. Ch. Mar. 9, 2011) ("Finally, I do not recognize any legitimate issue that can be raised concerning the Special Committee's independence or the integrity of its process in its selection of one of the attorneys, Mark Gentile of RLF. . . . Based on Lund's recommendation, and the firm's reputation, the Special Committee retained RLF as its counsel. . . . Finally, no evidence exists that Gentile had any ties to Hallmark or had any reason to favor Hallmark's interests over those of the Special Committee and Crown's minority stockholders. Based on this record, I find that the Special Committee (including its members, formation, and selection of counsel) is independent of Hallmark."), *with In re* Tele-commc'ns, Inc. S'holders Litig., 2005 Del. Ch. LEXIS 206, at *41 (Del. Ch. Dec. 21, 2005) ("The effectiveness of a Special Committee often lies in the quality of the advice its members receive from their legal and financial advisors. Rather than retain separate legal and financial advisors, the Special Committee chose to use the legal and financial advisors already advising TCI. This alone raises questions regarding the quality and independence of the counsel and advice received." (footnotes omitted)).

position within the corporation's organizational structure. The general counsel simultaneously is a part of the client-corporation and a lawyer—an advisor and advocate—for that client, while also maintaining a close working relationship with the client's managers and the board.[61] These structural features of the general counsel's job may sometimes place the general counsel in an anomalous position of "rendering legal advice to himself or herself."[62] Ben Heineman cogently refers to the CLO's complex role as "partner-guardian."[63] As "partner," the general counsel may have developed, vetted, and approved a business plan with other members of management. Then, as "guardian," she gives legal advice to senior management and the board and satisfies herself, management, and the board of the integrity and merit of the plan and the process necessary to effectuate it. But we do not suggest that this is a bad phenomenon.

The general counsel usually is subject to a dual reporting structure. The CEO often controls the selection, hiring, firing, and compensation of the general counsel, and the general counsel generally reports to the CEO within the management hierarchy.[64] In our view, it is important that the board have a role in the hiring, firing, and compensation of the CLO. The general counsel also has a duty to report to and advise the board of directors—either in the normal course under the corporation's policies, or when special situations arise requiring reporting "up-the-ladder" to the board as the highest authority in the corporation.[65] The tensions created by this dual reporting structure may be particularly pronounced for general counsel because of (1) the close collegial relationships that develop between general counsel and the other members of senior management, (2) the general counsel's financial dependence on a single client, and (3) the need to give independent, courageous, and unvarnished advice to both senior management and the board.

In the face of such challenges to independence that all corporate counsel (particularly the general counsel) experience, they must courageously assert their views in the best interests of their corporate client, whether the constituent wants to hear it or not. Courage is a necessary complement to lawyer independence. It is the critical quality for the lawyer to express

---

61. See Beardslee, *supra* note 18, at 22 (discussing the general counsel's position as the client's lawyer and as "part of the client"); Kim, *supra* note 10, at 196 (describing the "[t]riangular relationship between the lawyer, the client, and the client's agents").

62. Terrell, *supra* note 30, at 1006–07.

63. *E. g.*, Heineman, *Lawyer-Statesman*, *supra* Introduction, note 1.

64. DeMott, *supra* chapter I, note 24, at 967.

65. For discussion of these duties, see MODEL RULES OF PROF'L CONDUCT R. 1.13 (2010); 17 C.F.R. pt. 205, discussed *infra* chapter IV.B.

and advocate her independent views in order to make a difference and add value for her client.[66] It is also the quality that enables the general counsel to "advocate aggressively on behalf of the company without crossing a line that is going to get the company or the general counsel in trouble," in the face of legal questions that are answered in shades of gray and business interests that may warrant "taking an aggressive but defensible view of the law."[67] As Judy Lambeth, former executive vice president and general counsel of Reynolds American Inc., has pithily put it: "The general counsel must gauge the risk appetite of her executives, never catering to their dark side."[68]

2. Hiring, Firing, and Reporting Lines

The normal hiring and firing mode in U.S. companies is for the CEO to do the screening (or have it done), to interview candidates, and to select the person he thinks should become the general counsel. But there are variations on that theme. In some cases, the CEO may be considering more than one candidate. Also, the preferred model for hiring the general counsel is for there to be a genuine buy-in by the board or a subset of the board concerning the selection of the general counsel. Consider these observations with respect to the board's role in hiring, firing, and compensating the general counsel:

> Public corporations should adopt practices in which . . . [t]he selection, retention, and compensation of the general counsel are approved by the board of directors.[69]
>
> * * * * *
>
> If the general counsel understands that he or she will be supported by the board, the general counsel becomes much stronger, much more effective, and much better in his or her job in giving legal advice and trusted as the persuasive counselor.

66. *See, e.g.,* E. Norman Veasey, Chief Justice of the Delaware Supreme Court, Response for the Court at the Delaware Bar Admission Ceremony (Dec. 15, 2003) (on file with authors) (observing the relationship between independence and courage); E. Norman Veasey, The Lawyer's Higher Calling, Remarks at the Wake Forest School of Law Hooding Ceremony (May 14, 2006) (on file with authors).

67. Interview with Adam Ciongoli, General Counsel, Willis Group Holdings, Ltd. (Sept. 4, 2009).

68. E. Julia Lambeth, Remarks to Real World Challenges and Pitfalls of the Lawyer for the Corporation class at Wake Forest University School of Law (Nov. 1, 2010).

69. Cheek Report, *supra* note 45, at 161.

The GC has to report to the CEO. The board should be engaged in the process, obviously, and the board will need to respect the general counsel, have confidence in his or her ability and independence. So, the board really has to be engaged in that selection process. It is very important for the general counsel as she takes on a role that she knows that she has the support of the board. That only happens if the board is involved in the process of hiring.[70]

* * * * *

As general counsel, I have always reported directly to the CEO and been a member of the senior executive group. My compensation is in-line with that of the other senior executive officers. I was recruited directly by the CEO. During the process, I met with both the Chair of the Board of Directors and the Chair of the Governance and Nominating Committee of the Board. It was very clear that my appointment was a dual appointment.[71]

When the hiring of a new general counsel is being considered, the question often arises whether a promotion from the in-house legal department or an outside hire is preferable. There are benefits and drawbacks to each approach, which must be evaluated when the hiring decision is made. Consider the following:

The advantage to coming in from the outside is that you have some honeymoon period where you're recognized as the authority and perceived as having these new experiences to bring to bear on issues, so other executives probably give you a little bit more latitude on issues than you would have if you had come up the ranks. Coming up the ranks has the great benefit of enabling you to really know the company inside and out and to have numerous relationships and informal networks. This enables you to spot risk and simply know how to get things done. And so it just really depends upon the company as to which is more valuable at any point in time.[72]

* * * * *

I think it's much easier for a general counsel to come from the inside because what makes a general counsel successful is being able to navigate within the culture. Most high performance companies have strong cultures. It's not a negative to have a strong culture. It's actually essential if you're a global company with people around the world to knit people together with a strong culture.

70. Interview with Kenneth Fredeen, General Counsel, Deloitte & Touche LLP (Canada) (Dec. 7, 2009).

71. Interview with Simon A. Fish, Executive Vice-President & General Counsel, BMO Financial Group (Dec. 2, 2009).

72. Interview with Deirdre Stanley, Executive Vice President and General Counsel, Thomson Reuters Corporation (Jan. 25, 2010).

For an inside person, being effective in a complex operating environment and working within a culture comes second nature to them. If you've been a lawyer on the inside, you've had the benefit of getting increasingly senior exposure to sophisticated problems, and you're just very comfortable and familiar with the culture. No matter how good a lawyer is coming from the outside, and no matter how great the relationship that person has with the CEO, they're going to spend a fair amount of time learning to be more broadly effective within that particular operating environment. Some people are good at that. But I do think that some lawyers probably overweight their professional qualifications and underweight the necessity of being effective within a corporate culture.[73]

As to the firing, resignation, or retirement of the incumbent general counsel, the board of directors should certainly be consulted, and preferably involved when a termination or hiring decision is to be made. In those cases, some issues may lurk beneath the surface, such as a conflict between the CEO and the CLO or between the CEO and the board. Such issues may involve the CLO's assertion of her independence, and the board should monitor and evaluate the situation to determine whether any such issues are implicated.

Finally, there is the matter of the day-to-day reporting relationship between the general counsel and others. In some models, the CLO may report to the CFO or another senior officer other than the CEO. But the consensus among general counsel whom we interviewed seemed to be that the preferred model is that the CLO reports to the CEO.

3. Financial Dependence on a Single Client

If the general counsel is not thoroughly objective and courageous, she may be tempted to refrain from challenging courses of action sought by management for fear of placing her livelihood at risk.[74] The inclination to

---

73. Interview with Louise M. Parent, Executive Vice President and General Counsel, American Express Company (Nov. 2, 2009).

74. *See* DeMott, *supra* chapter I, note 24, at 956 ("[A] general counsel's dependence on a single client may call into question counsel's capacity to bring an appropriate degree of professional detachment to bear."); *id.* at 967–68 ("Conventional skepticism about the capacity of in-house corporate lawyers to exercise independent professional judgment focuses on the exclusivity of their relationship with a single client (their employer), which calls into question the feasibility of withdrawing from representation if professional norms so require."); *see also* Daly, *supra* chapter I, note 24, at 1099–1100 ("Whether in-house counsel can exercise the required degree of [professional independent judgment] is a question that has universally troubled the legal profession.

"go along to get along" is sometimes difficult to resist for corporate counsel. It is clear that this temptation must be resisted, but it often is not easy
to do so.

In-house counsel's inability, as distinct from the ability of most outside
counsel, to spread employment risk over multiple clients may result in a
temptation at times to "go along with"—perhaps by rationalizing problematic business decisions—the courses of action sought by the managers who
hold the power to hire, promote, compensate, and fire them.[75] But the
employment relationship may also enhance an in-house lawyer's job security as compared with that of outside counsel, giving the in-house lawyer a
greater opportunity to have a positive influence on the company's legal
policies.[76]

In-house counsel's financial dependence on a single client—her corporate employer—may raise questions concerning her ability to be courageous and to exert independent judgment when providing legal advice to
the corporation or when examining and advising corporate constituents on
compliance practices or risk-taking decisions. Whether or not this dependence raises an issue of compromised objectivity and the potential for conflict of interest is a concern. It may raise a potential conflict of interest
question under Rule 1.7 of the Model Rules of Professional Conduct if the

Critics insist that a lawyer who is dependent on a single client, i.e., the corporate
employer, for his or her livelihood cannot provide independent advice and judgment of
the same caliber as outside counsel whose financial ties to a single client are presumably much weaker." (footnotes omitted)); *cf. also* Weaver, *supra* Chapter I, note 24, at
1027 ("The first, and perhaps most critical, difference between [in-house] counsel and
their colleagues in private practice is the economic dependence of [in-house] counsel
on a single client.").

75. *See, e.g.,* HAZARD & HODES, *supra* note 43, § 17.7 ("[B]ecause in-house counsel
has only a single client, and that client controls professional advancement and salary
increments, there may be more of a tendency to avoid confrontation [than is experienced by outside counsel]."); Cheek Report, *supra* note 45, at 152 (observing that
in-house counsel's "desire to advance within the corporate executive structure[ ] may
induce lawyers to seek to please the corporate officials with whom they deal rather
than to focus on the long-term interest of their client, the corporation"); Kim, *supra*
note 10, at 204 ("The outside lawyer who seriously offends or disagrees with managers
of the corporation ultimately risks losing a client, but the inside lawyer who does the
same thing risks losing a job and being professionally blacklisted. Therefore, inside lawyers face stronger pressures to conform to the wishes and objectives of managers who
have the authority to hire and fire them."(footnote omitted)); Weaver, *supra* chapter I,
note 24, at 1032 ("The inevitable divergence between the goals and objectives of the
individual constituents of the organization and the best interests of the organization
can, and do, create career threatening situations for corporate counsel.").

76. HAZARD & HODES, *supra* note 43, § 17.7.

effectiveness of her professional service is "materially limited" by her "own interests."[77]

Stock options need not create a conflict for the general counsel[78] or dilute her independence, but they do give the general counsel a direct financial interest in her corporate client as well as imposing pressures similar to those faced by other senior executives to see that the stock price remains high, perhaps even when actual performance does not support the price.[79] But equity-based compensation for the general counsel may not create such incentives in all circumstances. Thus, whether there should be concern must be evaluated in the context of a particular corporation.

The issue of the general counsel's financial dependence on a single client should be considered in certain contexts when the lawyer's independence is severely put to the test. Corporations can implement a number of policies to reduce the concerns that arise from the general counsel's employment relationship with her client.

First, as noted, the board of directors should at least have approval responsibility for selecting, retaining, and compensating the general counsel.[80] This "buy-in" by the board provides it with an investment in the tenure of the CLO, leverages the board as a buffer between the general counsel and

77. Rule 1.7(b) of the Model Rules of Professional Conduct provides that "[a] lawyer shall not represent a client if the representation of that client may be materially limited by the . . . lawyer's own interests." *See also, e.g.,* Barclift, *supra* chapter I, note 26, at 16 (suggesting that the commentary to Model Rule 1.7 "recommends that a lawyer withdraw from representing a client if the lawyer's financial interest in the client leads to the reasonable conclusion that the representation would be adversely affected," and that this may be the case for general counsel, particularly when they receive stock option compensation).

78. The stock option compensation issue is not necessarily limited to general counsel. Outside counsel is sometimes compensated with stock options as well. *See* Jason M. Klein, *No Fool for a Client: The Finance and Incentives Behind Stock-Based Compensation for Corporate Attorneys,* 1999 COLUM. BUS. L. REV. 330 (suggesting that stock compensation for outside lawyers may be appropriate because it would simply parallel a common form of compensating in-house lawyers).

79. *Cf.* Barclift, *supra* chapter I, note 26, at 17 ("[A] large personal equity interest might raise questions on the in-house lawyer's ability to represent a client if the legal advice might result in a significant financial loss of the lawyer's equity interest."); Emerson, *supra* note 34, Week in Review at 8 (arguing that "[outside lawyers] and accountants who were once the proud pillars of our financial system have become the happy architects of its circumvention" and that general counsel and other senior executives should be paid "handsome, multiyear fixed salaries . . . without equity participation," so as to "sharply limit the temptation to inflate shareholder value at the expense of business substance"). But see Klein, *supra* note 78, for discussion of some potential benefits of inside or outside counsel's compensation in stock or stock options.

80. *See* Cheek Report, *supra* note 45, at 161 ("Public corporations should adopt practices in which . . . [t]he selection, retention, and compensation of the corporation's general counsel are approved by the board of directors."); *cf. also* Veasey, *supra* note 59,

the CEO, and ensures the new general counsel that she has the support of the board as she begins her work. This may serve to reduce the pressure on the general counsel to accede to dubious management plans despite her important reservations.[81]

Second, the corporation, through the board and the CEO, should design a compensation plan for the general counsel and other in-house counsel that rewards exceptional and professionally independent legal work, as distinct from pure financial performance.[82] This may or may not include a bonus system as well as stock option compensation for the general counsel, depending upon the corporation's particular circumstances. Most general counsel adhere closely to their professional responsibilities and personal integrity, unswayed by the potential for stock option wealth. The common practices of well compensating in-house counsel is laudable. Thus, a board-level review of the corporation's compensation structure for the general counsel and senior in-house lawyers is appropriate, with sensitivity to the challenging independence issues previously discussed.

4. Partnering with the Management Team

a. The CLO's Relationships with Senior Management

As discussed above, corporate counsel must exercise independent judgment on behalf of the corporate client when advising directors, officers, and employees of the client. But general counsel's position as a member of the senior management team can place special pressure on that independence, beyond the tensions created by the employment relationship. This pressure arises naturally from the interactions and relationships that develop as individuals work together on the senior management team to

at 1414 ("[T]he board must have a voice in the selection and retention of the general counsel. . . .").

81. *See* DeMott, *supra* chapter I, note 24, at 980 ("Strengthening the board's relationship with general counsel may weaken the bonds between the CEO and general counsel, as would instituting a practice of regular meetings between general counsel and a committee or other group of independent directors.").

82. Jill Barclift has suggested that "[t]he general counsel should be rewarded for outstanding legal work, including compliance with ethical obligations of the SEC and the state bar. Salary and bonuses in recognition of outstanding performance are appropriate. Stock options are rewards for reaching financial performance goals. Millions of dollars in stock option wealth not only raises questions about where the general loyalties lie, but can compromise the general counsel's judgment in the same way other corporate executives are compromised by the lure of stock option wealth." Barclift, *supra* chapter I, note 26, at 25.

advance the firm's business prospects.[83] It does not necessarily require overt instructions or demands from other executives.[84]

For example, some commentators have suggested that a general counsel may develop a "loyalty to superiors" that can compromise her ability to view management plans with an independent, critical eye.[85] Others have observed that close working relationships create a sense of identification or association between the general counsel and other senior managers.[86] Professor DeMott has characterized this effect as "socialization" and has described some of the personal benefits that individual lawyers working in these positions may derive from such relationships:

> [T]o the extent general counsel is socialized as a member of the senior manage-
> ment team, general counsel may be reluctant to jeopardize ongoing membership
> in the team and inclusion in its informational loops, which underlie effective
> power within the corporation. The impact of such socialization on a general
> counsel may run stronger and deeper than the impact that socialization into a
> corporate employer may carry for subordinate members of the legal depart-
> ment. This is so both because the stakes associated with general counsel's posi-
> tion are higher and because the bonds of personal loyalty between general
> counsel and other members of the senior management team may bind more
> tightly than the more impersonal ties between a subordinate lawyer and a cor-
> porate employer.[87]

83. *Cf., e.g.*, Weaver, *supra* chapter I, note 24, at 1028 ("[T]he close working relationship between management and corporate counsel may create confusion and uncertainty about the role of corporate counsel in the representation of the organization."); *id.* at 1045 ("The problems related to independence, or lack thereof, are most likely to arise when the interests of the corporation diverge from the interests of any of its constituents, especially constituents with whom corporate counsel have a particularly close working relationship.").

84. *See, e.g.*, DeMott, *supra* chapter I, note 24, at 969 ("[A]s a member of the senior management team, counsel may tend to address legal questions in a manner that pays allegiance to the wisdom of executive-level commitments and perspectives, even in the absence of explicit instructions from other members of the team.").

85. *See, e.g.*, Barclift, *supra* chapter I, note 26, at 3 (suggesting that the independent judgment of general counsel may have been compromised by loyalty to superiors, contributing to recent corporate scandals); *id.* at 24 ("The integrity of public disclosures [is] dependent on the perception that the general counsel's loyalty to superiors will not influence his or her independent advice to executive management or the board of directors."); DeMott, *supra* chapter I, note 24, at 968 (noting "the bonds of personal loyalty between general counsel and other members of the senior management team").

86. *See* Kim, *supra* note 10, at 252–53 ("The close, day-to-day working relationships that inside lawyers develop with corporate constituents and the personal feelings associated with being a valued member of a corporate team produce a deeper and ongoing identification of the lawyer with the client.").

87. DeMott, *supra* chapter I, note 24, at 968 (footnote omitted).

Whether described in terms of identification, socialization, or loyalty, the social or psychological tendency not to abandon or violate these relationships may give rise to tensions that present special challenges. Thus, human nature, and not just financial dependence on a particular employment position, may also enhance the tensions experienced by general counsel when they seek to take the right course for their corporate clients.

Of course, many general counsel effectively manage these tensions and serve as strong, independent advisors to, and advocates for, their clients. The general counsel's position on the senior management team and her intimate knowledge of the corporation's affairs can also achieve a host of benefits for the corporation.[88] For example, in addition to enhancing her effectiveness as a persuasive counselor to the board and senior management, a strong familiarity and close working relationship with other senior managers may give the general counsel greater knowledge, credibility, and authority in dealing with other corporate agents. The general counsel will have more influence with managers if the general counsel's perceived relationship with the CEO and the directors conveys to managers the message that the general counsel is speaking for the CEO and the board. A direct reporting relationship between the CEO and the CLO ensures that no intermediary is "bottlenecking or spinning what is getting from the general counsel up to the CEO" regarding important issues.[89] Furthermore, general counsel's position as an employee of the corporation and a member of the corporate "team" increases incentives to ensure the long-term viability of the enterprise.[90]

b. The General Counsel as Business Partner

Some observers have noted that perhaps the most prominent distinction between the general counsel of several decades ago and contemporary

88. *See* Geoffrey C. Hazard, Jr., *Ethical Dilemmas of Corporate Counsel*, 46 EMORY L.J. 1011, 1018–19 (1997) (discussing in-house counsel's superior access to "water cooler" or "back-channel" information and the importance of such information); *see also* Beardslee, *supra* note 18, at 26 (observing that general counsel "specialize" in their clients' business, and suggesting that this strong familiarity with the business is an important asset to their clients that differentiates them from outside counsel).

89. Interview with Adam Ciongoli, General Counsel, Willis Group Holdings, Ltd. (Sept. 4, 2009).

90. *See* Kim, *supra* note 10, at 206–07 ("Inside lawyers tend to feel as though they are integral members of a team, and their goals are centered on furthering the long-term success of the corporate enterprise.").

general counsel is the modern general counsel's more sophisticated combination of business with legal advice.[91] As Simon Fish, Executive Vice-President and General Counsel of BMO Financial Group, articulated:

> I simplistically bundle all of the various activities in which I am involved into two parts: those activities related to revenue generation—basically, the sales side—and those activities that are related to oversight—the gatekeeper role and the compliance side.
>
> On the revenue generation side, the GC's role involves providing support or leadership on corporate or commercial transactions. This role is something that in-house lawyers have always done, but the role has become more sophisticated over time.[92]

For many general counsel, the business aspects of their jobs are interesting and professionally fulfilling. The business aspects of the job may even at times predominate in the daily work of the general counsel.[93] Indeed, the challenges and variety of work undertaken by those engaged in this type of lawyering often are what draw general counsel to their positions.[94]

In this dual role of lawyer and business advisor, the general counsel becomes a key player in assessing and understanding risk and matching strategies to risk tolerance. Gary Kennedy, Senior Vice President, General

91. *See* Daly, *supra* chapter I, note 24, at 1062 ("This new generation of in-house lawyers . . . frequently offers business as well as legal advice, and its members decidedly reject any notion that their role is limited to counseling clients on purely legal matters. A 'can do' attitude characterizes their lawyering."); *see also* HAZARD & HODES, *supra* note 43, § 17.7 (observing that in-house counsel are typically more integrated into the daily operations of the corporation than are outside counsel and that they are therefore "more likely to be called upon to participate in making business judgments as well as legal judgments on behalf of the company"); Beardslee, *supra* note 18, at 23 (describing general counsel's involvement with "non-legal aspects of all kinds of business projects, such as development of new products, marketing, hiring, internal restructuring"); Amy L. Weiss, Note, *In-House Counsel Beware: Wearing the Business Hat Could Mean Losing the Privilege*, 11 GEO. J. LEGAL ETHICS 393, 393 & n. 4 (1998) (discussing the many business-oriented roles that in-house counsel fill, including "as business advisors, negotiators, investigators, accountants, messengers, corporate directors, and corporate officers").

92. Interview with Simon A. Fish, Executive Vice-President and General Counsel, BMO Financial Group (Dec. 2, 2009).

93. *See* Beardslee, *supra* note 18, at 23–24 ("Not only do General Counsel have non-legal responsibilities, but they are often business people first and lawyers second.").

94. *See, e.g.*, Weaver, *supra* chapter I, note 24, at 1035 ("[C]orporate counsel often consider the opportunity to participate in business decisions to be one of the principal reasons that they prefer the in-house environment to private practice.").

Counsel, and Chief Compliance Officer, American Airlines, Inc., explains this role as follows:

> The GC plays a mixed role of true legal counselor versus businessperson. Lawyers help explain the risks, balance the risks, give an opinion whether or not those are acceptable risks from a legal perspective. And so, the GC, in my view, participates directly in those discussions. They have got to be an integral part of that whole set of developing the strategy, assessing it, agreeing with it, bringing it to the board and then, the board will often will turn its head and say, "Have we considered adequately the risk associated with it? Does counsel think that it is appropriate?"[95]

The general counsel's involvement in business strategy and offering business advice can create pressure, often asserted by corporate managers, on the lawyer to enable transactions rather than to act as a "bottleneck" to getting the deal done.[96] A corporate culture that emphasized getting the deal done quickly with too little regard for getting the deal done in an ethically and legally appropriate manner—and company lawyers' inability or unwillingness to apply the brakes—may have been a factor contributing to the corporate scandals around the turn of the twenty-first century. The pressure on general counsel and other in-house counsel to enable rather than "inhibit" deals may be strong in those companies where managers are particularly skeptical about the value of the legal department.[97]

The general counsel's ability to step beyond a strictly legal role also enhances her ability to counsel management that a proposal is "legal but stupid." This requires her to exercise her business—and common-sense personal—judgment, in addition to her legal judgment, and to earn credibility with management in those areas. "In order for the general counsel's business judgment to be taken seriously, good general counsel have to demonstrate that they understand the business, that they're interested in the

95. Interview with Gary Kennedy, Senior Vice President, General Counsel, and Chief Compliance Officer, American Airlines, Inc. (Nov. 10, 2009). For discussion of questions the board and management should be asking and the CLO's role in encouraging that process, see *infra* Chapter V.B.2.b.

96. Regan, *supra* note 55, at 1220 ("[C]orporate lawyers today want to be seen as creative business problem solvers and team players, not obstructionists who tell the client what it cannot do.").

97. *Cf.* Beardslee, *supra* note 18, at 51 ("'[I]n-house legal departments are frequently challenged to demonstrate the value, efficiency, and cost-effectiveness of their services—even to justify their very own existence . . . .'" (quoting Susan S. Samuelson, Book Review, *Sally Gunz's New Topics for Research in Legal Studies: The Role of Corporate Counsel. The New Corporate Counsel*, 30 Am. Bus. L.J. 335, 337 (1992)).

business, and that they understand the realities of business. . . . There are sometimes things that are perfectly legal that are not very nice."[98] Amy Schulman, Senior Vice President and General Counsel, Pfizer Inc., explains the partnership between general counsel and management as follows:

> My job is to help clients understand risks. Sure, if they're speeding, I'll stop them. But it's a far more interactive, iterative process where our lawyers are saying, "Well, let's map this journey out together. Let's figure out what kind of car we're in. Let's figure out who's driving and what we know about the driver. Let's figure out all of the nuances that go into helping us to determine how fast we can go on a particular stretch of road."
>
> If you look at your job that way and you're at a company that views the general counsel that way, then your role is unlikely to conflict because you're going to be an integral part of the conversation about the company's approach to risk and strategic planning.[99]

The tendency—at times—of general counsel to blend legal and business advice can have important implications for preserving the attorney-client privilege. It is well-settled that the attorney-client privilege applies when the client is a corporation.[100] It is also clear that the entity itself, and not the various agents who speak on the corporation's behalf, is the client for privilege purposes.[101] There are many facets to be explored when one is analyzing the attorney-client privilege and work product doctrine in the corporate context. There are the elements of the privilege, the communications involved, the waiver issues, the exceptions to the privilege, the applications in stockholders' suits, and the like. For an excellent, recent, and comprehensive analysis of issues that are applicable to both the attorney-client

98. Interview with Adam Ciongoli, General Counsel, Willis Group Holdings, Ltd. (Sept. 4, 2009).

99. Interview with Amy W. Schulman, Senior Vice President and General Counsel, Pfizer Inc. (Mar. 17, 2010).

100. *See* HAZARD & HODES, *supra* note 43, § 9.8 (discussing the application of the attorney-client privilege in the corporate context); *see also* Upjohn Co. v. United States, 449 U.S. 383 (1981).

101. *See* HAZARD & HODES, *supra* note 43, § 17.3 (stating that the client-lawyer relationship in the corporate context is understood under the "entity theory," and discussing the difficulty that lawyers may encounter in practice in "maintaining the distinction between an organization and its constituents"); *id.* § 17.7 ("The linchpin of the entity theory is that unless arrangements for multiple client representation have been made, a lawyer representing an organization represents *only* the organization, and that highly placed agents (or 'constituents') of the entity are not themselves clients.").

privilege and the work product doctrine, the reader is referred to an outstanding work prepared by Karen Valihura.[102]

For general counsel, of course, the understanding of these issues is crucial, whether it comes to establishing the privilege or the work product, protecting it from waiver, using it in negotiations with the government in the context of an investigation, or applying it in various litigation settings.[103] But there has been some recent split of authority and academic opinion concerning what types of communications qualify for the protection of the privilege, in particular when in-house counsel are involved. The concern is that the involvement of in-house lawyers in both legal and business affairs may "blur the line between legal and non-legal communications."[104] Thus, communications that might contain some legal advice (or convey information to the attorney for the purpose of obtaining such advice) could be found not to be covered by the privilege and therefore become subject to discovery.[105] Because of this, the general counsel's role in providing

102. KAREN L. VALIHURA, ATTORNEY-CLIENT PRIVILEGE AND WORK PRODUCT DOCTRINE: CORPORATE APPLICATIONS (2010).

103. *See In re* Teleglobe Corp. v. BCE, Inc., 493 F.3d 349 (3d Cir. 2007) (discussing elements of the privilege and analyzing its application when there are multiple parties in litigation).

104. Rossi v. Blue Cross & Blue Shield of Greater N.Y., 540 N.E.2d 703, 705 (N.Y. 1989); *see also* Weiss, *supra* note 91, at 398 (discussing various tests applied by courts in determining whether a communication is protected by the attorney-client privilege, including whether the contents are "primarily legal" or whether they are "for the express purpose of securing legal advice"); *cf.* Fox, *supra* note 43, at 552–53 (discussing the risks to client confidentiality and the attorney-client privilege that arise when lawyers practice in a multidisciplinary setting, and asserting that "the fact of lawyers providing services in a multi-service firm will make it too easy to argue that any particular consultation between lawyer and client was related to something other than legal advice," placing the "sanctity of the lawyer-client encounter" at risk).

105. *Cf. Rossi*, 540 N.E.2d at 705 (noting the need to apply the attorney-client privilege "cautiously and narrowly" in the corporate context in order to avoid sealing off disclosure through "mere participation of an attorney," because lawyers mix legal and business advice and "their advice may originate not in response to the client's consultation about a particular problem but with them, as part of an ongoing, permanent relationship with the organization"); *cf. also* Weiss, *supra* note 91, at 393 (stating that "[c]ourts are narrowing the scope of the attorney-client privilege in the corporate context," and suggesting that the protection offered by the privilege is eroding where the client is a corporation).

It is worth noting that whether a particular communication might be protected by the privilege becomes less important when governmental bodies use "strong-arm" tactics to induce extensive privilege waivers. *See* ABA Task Force on the Attorney-Client Privilege, *Report of the ABA's Task Force on the Attorney-Client Privilege*, 60 BUS. LAW. 1029 (2005) (observing that law enforcement and regulatory authorities have recently "employed practices and procedures that suggest that if corporations disclose documents and information that are protected by the corporate attorney-client privilege and work-product doctrine, they will receive credit for cooperation," leaving companies

business advice is not universally accepted. A distinguished and well-respected practitioner and academic friend of ours, Lawrence J. Fox, has stated that the general counsel should stick to legal advice and avoid stating her views on a proposed business transaction or strategy. The bases for his point of view appear to be the following: (a) the chief legal officer was hired for her legal acumen and she is not ordinarily an expert in business; (b) when she mixes legal and business advice, there is significant risk that the attorney-client privilege will be compromised; (c) this undermining of the corporate privilege has already manifested itself in the form of hostility to attorney-client privilege claims for communications with in-house counsel, following the draconian lead of the European Union;[106] and (d) in-house counsel's involvement in business decisions results in much higher risks of liability for the lawyers.[107]

Regardless of one's view of the extent to which the general counsel should be involved in business decisions, the corporation will be well-served by hiring or promoting candidates for general counsel who not only possess legal acumen, but who also are persons of high intelligence and common sense. As for the attorney-client privilege, it must be kept in mind that not all communications with counsel (whether in-house or outside counsel) are privileged: The privilege does not apply to communications between lawyer and client that do not satisfy the criteria for conferring privileged status.[108] So, when the general counsel expresses *solely* a business

---

with "no practical choice but to comply, since the agencies can employ their discretionary exercise of prosecutorial or enforcement authority under criminal law or civil regulation to impose a substantial cost on corporations that assert rather than waive the privilege"). For discussion of the evolution of the Department of Justice's policy with respect to seeking privilege waivers, including the current policy, embodied in the U.S. Attorney's Manual, that waivers of attorney-client privilege and work-product protection are not prerequisites for cooperation credit under the Department's prosecution guidelines, see *infra* chapter V.B.2.c.

106. Case C-550/07 P, Akzo Nobel Chemicals, Ltd. v. European Commission.

107. Larry expressed these views in an April 2011 panel discussion at the Georgetown Law Center, under the auspices of the American Inns of Court.

108. The court in *In re Teleglobe Commc'ns Corp. v. BCE Inc.* stated the elements necessary to a finding of attorney-client privilege, as follows:

> The attorney-client privilege protects communications between attorneys and clients from compelled disclosure. It applies to any communication that satisfies the following elements: it must be "(1) a communication (2) made between privileged persons (3) in confidence (4) for the purpose of obtaining or providing legal assistance for the client." RESTATEMENT (THIRD) OF THE LAW GOVERNING LAWYERS § 68 (2000). "Privileged persons" include the client, the attorney(s), and any of their agents that help facilitate attorney-client communications or the legal representation. *Id.* § 70.

493 F.3d 345, 359 (3d Cir. 2007).

opinion, it is of course not privileged. But other advice given by the general counsel, when *solely* legal advice is given, should be privileged.[109]

Because the distinction between legal and business advice may sometimes be blurred, it is difficult to anticipate which functions or communications will be considered legal in nature and which will be considered business-oriented when performed by a lawyer. For example, in *Georgia-Pacific Corp. v. GAF Roofing Manufacturing Corp.*,[110] an in-house lawyer at GAF had negotiated the terms of a contract with Georgia-Pacific. The contract became the subject of litigation between GAF and Georgia-Pacific, and Georgia-Pacific sought to compel deposition testimony relating to certain aspects of the attorney's role in the negotiations. Georgia-Pacific opposed the motion, claiming that the testimony was protected by the attorney-client privilege. The court rejected the privilege argument, finding that in negotiating on behalf of management, he was "acting in a business capacity."[111]

Courts have recognized that lawyers often do include consideration of non-legal issues when advising clients on the best course of action with respect to a legal matter—and doing so may be critical to providing good counsel. But when lawyers do mingle business advice with legal advice there arises a degree of uncertainty regarding whether a court would ultimately find the advice to be predominantly legal or non-legal in nature when determining whether it is protected by the attorney-client privilege. It is not clear, however, that in-house counsel offer business advice more frequently than do outside counsel,[112] suggesting that courts should not be more skeptical of the legal nature of a communication simply because it involved in-house counsel.

There is no single model or "right" answer to the legal/business conundrum. A good lawyer's skepticism about the business wisdom of a transaction may be very valuable, often as a "gut feeling" or an expression

109. *See* Veasey & Di Guglielmo, *supra* chapter I, note 8, at 26–27 (discussing implications for the attorney-client privilege raised by the general counsel's participation in business functions).

110. 91 Civ. 5125 (RPP), 1996 U.S. Dist. LEXIS 671 (S.D.N.Y. Jan. 25, 1996).

111. *Id.* at *12; *see also* E.I. duPont de Nemours & Co. v. Forma-Pack, Inc., 718 A.2d 1129 (Md. 1998) (rejecting claim of attorney-client privilege because transmission of documents was for the "purely business purpose of debt collection" rather than for a legal purpose).

112. *Cf.* Weiss, *supra* note 91, at 399 (discussing a study by Professor Vincent Alexander that found that "47.8% of outside counsel and 46.7% of in-house counsel said that they give business advice frequently," and therefore suggesting that "outside corporate counsel . . . give business advice just as frequently as in-house counsel do" (citing Vincent C. Alexander, *The Corporate Attorney-Client Privilege: A Study of the Participants*, 63 ST. JOHN'S L. REV. 191, 228–31 (1989))).

of common sense, practical wisdom. And we do not suggest that counsel should stand down and be mute when she senses an irrational folly in a business decision that may be able to be avoided even if legal. We merely suggest that counsel be aware of which "hat" she is wearing—and the potential risks to the privilege. Most general counsel are keenly aware of the distinction and will express views appropriately and carefully.

5. Bridging the Gap: The General Counsel and the Board

a. The CLO's Relationships with the Board and Board Committees

I think the role of the general counsel with the board is straightforward: We should be the fountain of truth and information and provide candid and timely counsel.
—Louis J. Briskman[113]

The expansion of the general counsel's roles in the corporation has been paralleled by a simultaneous trend toward greater independence of the board of directors, as well as a growing sense of accountability of the board of directors. As a result, "boards are more focused on being advised about their responsibilities as they relate to shareholders, and they really look to the general counsel to provide that advice. So, the general counsel is increasingly in the role of a counselor to the board as well as a counselor to management."[114] In most public companies, the general counsel is a fixture in the boardroom. "Corporate counsel is the front-line resource for keeping the board's leadership abreast of emerging trends in the legislative and regulatory arena. Effective GCs marshal company resources and support from internal auditors and compliance and ethics officers to ensure that the board is prepared and well informed."[115]

Serving as a "bridge"—a "diplomat," perhaps—between management and the board, the general counsel can play a unique role in facilitating the information flow between those groups.[116] If the general counsel is

---

113. Interview with Louis J. Briskman, Executive Vice President and General Counsel, CBS Corporation (Aug. 26, 2009).

114. Interview with Alan Braverman, Senior Executive Vice President, General Counsel and Secretary, The Walt Disney Company (Nov. 12, 2009).

115. Interview with Ira M. Millstein, *NACD: Creating Our Best Directors*, METRO. CORP. COUNSEL, June 2011, at 43.

116. *See* Interview with Adam Ciongoli, General Counsel, Willis Group Holdings, Ltd. (Sept. 4, 2009) ("Part of a good general counsel's job is diplomacy. The general counsel, I think, naturally, more than any other executive except maybe the CEO, deals directly with the board."); *see also* Simmons & Dinnage, *supra* chapter I, note 11, at 135

performing that role well, the independent directors should view the general counsel as a trusted independent advisor, seeking her advice not simply on legal issues, but also on whether the board has received the appropriate information and engaged the processes needed to make a particular decision, and memorialized those processes and the decision appropriately in the corporate records. Daniel Cooperman, former Senior Vice President, General Counsel, and Secretary, Apple Inc., has described how a close working relationship between the general counsel and the board is "essential":

> A very close relationship with members of the board is quite essential [for the general counsel, who can serve as] an intermediary. It is not that the CEO does not have access. Of course he does, and as frequently as he wishes. But on some issues, the board is much more comfortable raising them with the general counsel than with the CEO. Therefore the general counsel really can serve quite an effective purpose in frequent conversations with the directors and to try to channel that back to the management in a discreet way.[117]

When evaluating the adequacy of information flow to the board, the general counsel should consider both the quality and the timeliness of the information provided. Alan Braverman, Senior Executive Vice President, General Counsel and Secretary of The Walt Disney Company, describes the general counsel's role in this context as follows:

> The board will turn to the general counsel and want to know whether they should feel comfortable that they have received the right information, whether the information and whether their deliberative process about whatever decision needs to be made fulfills their fiduciary obligations.
>
> One of the things that's on my worry list always is, if we are asking the board to make a decision, are we, the management, providing to the board the quality of information and on a timely enough basis to enable the board not only to make an informed decision, but also to make an informed decision following a process that would stand scrutiny if they're ever challenged. Those two things should always happily marry up.[118]

("[The general counsel's and other in-house counsel's] intimate knowledge of the organization and legal acumen makes them an important part of the overall information flow within a corporation . . . .").

117. Interview with Daniel Cooperman, Senior Vice President, General Counsel and Secretary, Apple Inc. (Sept. 1, 2009).

118. Interview with Alan Braverman, Senior Executive Vice President, General Counsel and Secretary, The Walt Disney Company (Nov. 12, 2009).

Sometimes, even when the general counsel determines that the quality of the information and the deliberative process engaged in by the board are both good, the best advice from the general counsel still is "I know you're ready to make a decision, but I think you ought to sleep on it."[119] Or, stated differently but with equal and cogent force, is this view: "Sometimes buying time is the greatest solution to any problem. So rather than letting it come to a head and perhaps go the wrong way, just a quieting period, postponement, or a request for further information and discussion often leads to the right answer."[120]

When determining what information to provide to the board, the general counsel must not sugar-coat or shy away from delivering bad news when bad news needs to be communicated. Moreover, the general counsel should also try to avoid surprises by anticipating trouble spots and laying the groundwork with the board regarding issues that may not seem to be particularly serious or require close attention at the time but may bubble up in the future. Louis Briskman, Executive Vice President and General Counsel of CBS Corporation, suggests that this may be one of the most important factors in establishing a strong working relationship between the general counsel and the board:

> As long as [the general counsel provides truth and information to the board] and the board finds credibility in the way we communicate, there will be a good working relationship with the board. That sometimes entails telling the board bad news because there are bound to be operational or litigation surprises. It is very hard for a general counsel to stand up and face 12 to 14 people and report to them unpleasant news.
>
> But even doing your best, there are often surprises, and when something goes awry, you have to quickly, quickly communicate it. Hopefully, you have left a nice foundation in your prior discussions that you contemplated that this type of thing might happen, and you have given the board some type of fair warning. But every once in a while there is a surprise. So at the end of the day, the general counsel has to be there and provide both the facts and the information necessary for the board to fulfill its responsibility.
>
> I think the trick is that with your board, with your committees, you have to be as candid as you can be and they have to have complete trust in you; and if either fails, all fails.[121]

---

119. *Id.*
120. Interview with Louis J. Briskman, Executive Vice President and General Counsel, CBS Corporation (Aug. 26, 2009).
121. *Id.*

When the independent directors meet in executive session, as should be the norm these days,[122] the independent directors should consider making it a practice of inviting the general counsel to attend or be available to attend at least part of the sessions, absent some personal involvement of counsel in the issues to be considered by the independent directors.[123] This is an evolving issue and depends on the culture and the practices with which the independent directors are most comfortable in encouraging candor in the executive sessions. It must be emphasized that the decisions whether and when the general counsel should be invited to attend executive sessions will vary.

As noted above, the general counsel's position within the corporation provides added value that is rarely matched by outside counsel. In-house counsel, and the general counsel in particular, usually have a deeper and broader knowledge of the client's business than do outside counsel.[124] In addition, in-house counsel—and the general counsel—may be selected based on specialized skills that particularly complement the corporation's needs.[125]

But, in addition to increasing her value to the corporation, the general counsel's superior access to information may also increase the incidence of

122. See *infra* text accompanying chapter VII, notes 52–53 for discussion of current recommendations regarding the relationship between counsel and the board, including the independent directors.

123. *See, e.g.,* Cheek Report, *supra* note 45, at 161. In addition to personal involvement of the CLO in a particular issue, other sensitive issues, such as consideration of CEO performance or compensation, may counsel the CLO's not being included in an executive session.

124. *See, e.g.,* Daly, *supra* chapter I, note 24, at 1060–61 (noting that general counsel add value through specialized knowledge of their clients' business and the strategic goals of the corporation); Hazard, *supra* note 88, at 1018–19 (discussing in-house counsel's superior access to "back-channel" information and the importance of such information); Kim, *supra* note 10, at 199–200 (discussing the "added value" of in-house counsel's advice because it "is enhanced by in-house lawyers' direct knowledge of and involvement in the company's business affairs"); *see also* Beardslee, *supra* note 18, at 25 (noting the activities in which the general counsel engages in order to maintain strong knowledge of the business and industry); Terrell, *supra* note 30, at 1007 (describing "a perception among American lawyers—and perhaps business people as well—that general counsel bring to their corporate employment something more than just legal 'service.' They also bring (or should bring) to the business context a subtle but vital extra quality that is their own brand of legal 'professionalism.'").

125. *See* Kim, *supra* note 10, at 203 ("Because inside lawyers develop skills that are specialized to serve the corporation's needs, they perform many functional legal services efficiently without consulting outside counsel."); *cf. also* Beardslee, *supra* note 18, at 25 ("[T]he one thing General Counsel do 'specialize' in is their client's business.").

ethical dilemmas with which she must grapple. This is the "water cooler" phenomenon, which Professor Hazard has explained this way:

> Here lies the most significant difference between corporate counsel and lawyers in independent practice. The difference, simply stated, is in the factual conditions of their day-to-day work. To put the point bluntly, a lawyer in independent practice is sheltered from the informal, back-channel information that flows around the company water cooler. Instead, engagement of an independent law firm is necessarily predicated on a distillation of the facts about the matter in question. This is so even when the outside lawyer is given all of the documents and access to all of the company employees. Back-channel information simply cannot be recreated. And there are times, I have been told, when outside counsel may be retained on the basis of selected facts precisely to accommodate a response that provides a desired outside opinion.[126]

In-house counsel's enhanced knowledge of all aspects of their clients' business enables them to be "proactive as opposed to purely reactive because the lawyers' involvement could occur at an earlier phase of any given transaction."[127] This greatly enhances the lawyers' capacity to structure transactions in a manner that is appropriate for the company. The proactive model of in-house lawyering involves "performing legal risk analysis, [in which] an in-house lawyer blends both legal and business advice by drawing 'upon the corporation's conception of itself embedded in its cultures and policies.'"[128] This proactive model of lawyering means that lawyers are "innovative counselors" instead of mere "scribes" and "legal servants."[129]

---

126. Hazard, *supra* note 88, at 1019.

127. DeMott, *supra* chapter I, note 24, at 960–61; *see also* Kim, *supra* note 10, at 201 ("The in-house lawyer today is actively involved 'in shaping corporate events, in assessing corporate policies, and in establishing the tone and standard for corporate conduct.' In-house lawyers serve as legal advisors to management on all transactions and matters that have significant legal ramifications for the corporation. The lawyers are consulted before these transactions occur and not merely after the fact; in other words, in-house lawyers practice preventive law. Because outside lawyers have no way of insisting that corporations involve them early in matters, the role of outside counsel is usually reactive. Inside lawyers, however, play a much more proactive role because they are involved in earlier phases of transactions." (footnote omitted)); Simmons & Dinnage, *supra* chapter I, note 11, at 113 ("In-house counsel often acquire institutional knowledge concerning business operations and corporate culture that inevitably allow them to offer legal guidance in a more proactive *ex ante* manner.").

128. Daly, *supra* chapter I, note 24, at 1070.

129. *Id.* at 1078; *cf. also* Gruner, *supra* note 25, at 1116; Liggio, *Changing Role, supra* chapter II, note 3, at 1209–10. See *infra* chapter VII.A for discussion of a "persuasive counselor" model of corporate lawyering.

The corporation's lawyer, particularly the general counsel, must be continuously mindful of what is over the horizon. She must also be assertive about legal and ethical issues while matters are still "ripe"—that is, while decisions or changes may still be made. She needs to think ahead and anticipate what may be coming, and develop and prepare solutions or responses.[130] Corporate counsel should try to maintain a clear distinction between her legal and business roles.

In addition to enhancing general counsel's value to the corporation, the breadth of their responsibilities and familiarity with the business may make them implicitly (but not necessarily realistically) charged with knowing everything that is going on in a company.[131] It is, of course, unfair to impute knowledge to the general counsel of bad things that happen at the company "on her watch" simply because she is the quintessential generalist. But the corporation should attempt to limit structural and other barriers that may sometimes make it difficult for the general counsel to access all the information that she in fact needs to do her job.

The general counsel can take some steps in this regard through the way she structures and manages the legal department. For example, many corporate law departments operate in a compartmentalized or decentralized manner.[132] The general counsel often must manage these challenges by either modifying the structures (i.e., increasing centralization) or developing ways of increasing connections between decentralized parts of the legal department and law department headquarters. Daniel Desjardins, Senior Vice President, General Counsel and Assistant Secretary of the Canadian firm Bombardier Inc., described to us how he has adjusted over time the balance between centralization and decentralization of certain functions of the law department:

> It is important for the legal department always to be in charge of legal issues and to select external counsel whether in a centralized or decentralized model. This is ingrained as part of the culture [at Bombardier], and it is necessary for this to be clear.

130. *See generally infra* chapter V.B.2.b. (discussing the standard of conduct for directors relating to the best practices of having both management and directors ask probing questions, particularly in connection with risk analysis).

131. *See* Terrell, *supra* note 30, at 1007 ("Moreover, the general counsel, with overall legal responsibility for actions throughout the corporation, may perhaps be legitimately saddled with at least constructive knowledge of virtually everything occurring within the company.").

132. Nicholson, *supra* note 7, at 595–96 (discussing the problems and benefits associated with such structural organization of legal departments).

An important issue for general counsel is when to centralize and when to decentralize the function of the legal department. When I first came in as general counsel and as I was concentrating on the learning curve, I tended more toward the centralized model. As I grew in confidence it became appropriate to decentralize many of the functions in the business units, but to keep centralized at the corporate office legal department all of the financial and M&A issues and the like—in other words, all of the material transactions having a direct link to the capital structure and the balance sheet of the Corporation. At Bombardier, I have along with my team sometimes struggled with our decentralized model, but over the years we were able to fine tune our internal governance. Now, with more than 13 years under my belt, I have come to appreciate the flexibility and agility we have as a legal department in helping our company to execute projects in 80 countries around the world.

The challenge for the General Counsel is to keep communication open and keep a proper governance in place while not slowing down the delivery of the legal services even though the department is geographically widespread.

Although the lawyers in the field work with the business people in various units, it is the responsibility of the general counsel to meet with the business leaders and legal teams in offices and social gatherings. One must make certain that all aspects of the firm are strong because the chain is only as strong as the weakest link.[133]

An even greater—though perhaps less prevalent—obstacle may be intentional exclusion by other senior executives of the general counsel from the information loop.[134] The reasons for such exclusion are not clear, and are likely not valid. But one explanation might be fear that corporate lawyers are acting as "cops" and not as advisors and advocates.[135] Such distrust is generally unfounded,[136] but the mere perception of untrustworthiness is one

133. Interview with Daniel Desjardins, Senior Vice President, General Counsel and Assistant Secretary, Bombardier Inc. (May 20, 2011); *see also* DeMott, *supra* chapter I, note 24, at 970 (discussing challenges that may arise in a decentralized legal department).

134. *See* DeMott, *supra* chapter I, note 24, at 966 ("Although many reasons may keep general counsel out of informational loops that operate at the senior management level, one structural explanation is the ability of other members of senior management to exclude general counsel from any particular loop.").

135. *See* Nicholson, *supra* note 7, at 597 (observing that some general counsel see themselves as internal cops); *see also infra* chapter VII.A for discussion of the gatekeeping role that some observers have suggested that corporate counsel should fill.

136. *Cf.* Terrell, *supra* note 30, at 1007 ("Every constituency that comprises the dynamic business corporation, whether it perceives this fact or not, ultimately trusts the general counsel—as the chief (or only) lawyer in the organization—to provide, and in fact emphasize, an unusual sense of context for all corporate decision making.").

reason for lawmakers and corporate decision-makers to consider carefully any policy changes that may negatively impact the trust between the corporate lawyer and the client-corporation and its managers and directors.

These informational obstacles also highlight the need for corporations to develop and implement policies to ensure that the optimal quantity and quality of information flows to and from the general counsel. Professors Fisch and Rosen have suggested some key features of such systems and the benefits they might secure:

> One method of increasing information flow to corporate decision-makers is the development of information reporting systems relating to legal representation. Some corporations already provide structures through which the general counsel, the board or the CEO demands information from inside and outside counsel on a regular basis. Systems through which lawyers are regularly required to provide information on risks, liabilities and other potential problems relieve the lawyer of the responsibility for coming forward with information about potential misconduct. Structures in which lawyers regularly report directly to the board or a key corporate official allow lawyers to bypass managers without creating the risk of retaliation that might result from sporadic reporting up.[137]

Thus, policies requiring regular interaction and reporting between the general counsel and the board and the senior management team provide dual benefits. They enable the corporation's legal department to operate to the best advantage of the corporation and they relieve the tensions placed on corporate counsel by certain structural features of in-house lawyering as well as newly formalized rules such as up-the-ladder reporting.

In addition to serving as a bridge between the board and senior management, the general counsel regularly advises both the board as a whole, the key committees of the board (particularly the independent audit and nominating/governance committees), or the independent directors. There are many fact-specific dimensions and nuances to the fabric of this advice, and it is not practicable to attempt to catalog the issues that may be involved in the varying factual settings. As a general matter of counseling, however, it is productive for the general counsel to focus the members of the board on the crisp descriptions of their responsibilities as set forth in the new, sixth edition of the *Corporate Director's Guidebook*.[138]

---

137. Jill E. Fisch & Kenneth M. Rosen, *How Did Corporate and Securities Law Fail? Is There a Role for Lawyers in Preventing Future Enrons?*, 48 VILL. L. REV. 1097, 1135–36 (2003).

138. CORPORATE LAWS COMMITTEE, AMERICAN BAR ASSOCIATION, CORPORATE DIRECTOR'S GUIDEBOOK (6th ed. 2011). For the range of topics covered by the *Guidebook*, see appendix A, which reprints the table of contents of that text.

As the reader will see by perusing the table of contents and the excerpts from the *Guidebook*, that text covers representative slices of the life and responsibilities of the director. These slices of life and responsibilities include the director's legal obligations in which the general counsel is often directly involved, such as the duties of care and loyalty, as well as the director's role in sale transactions and financial distress situations; risk management; compliance and oversight; board structure, process, and operations; duties of board committees; and some duties under the federal law.

In chapter V, we outline in more detail some of the crucial legal issues relating to corporate law, corporate governance, and other laws on which in-house corporate legal departments and sometimes outside counsel must advise the directors.

b. Director Confidentiality and Candor

The *Corporate Director's Guidebook* contains many statements of "best practices" for directors. There is a corresponding link to some of the advisory responsibilities of corporate counsel. This is particularly the case with the general counsel who should often be present in the boardroom and committee meetings. Although we will not undertake to comment on all—or even a large number—of the best practices developed in the *Guidebook* in terms of how they relate to the general counsel's advice to the board,[139] we will mention in particular two: the director's obligation to be candid with his fellow directors and the duty of confidentiality. All that is necessary at this juncture is to quote two passages from the *Guidebook*. With respect to director candor, the *Guidebook* states:

> Candid discussion among directors and between directors and management is critical to effective board decision-making. Generally, directors must inform other directors and management about information material to corporate decisions of which they are aware. Directors occasionally also have legal or other duties of confidentiality owed to another corporation or entity. In such a situation,

---

139. Subsection D of Section 3 of the *Guidebook* lists issues surrounding some of the legal obligations of directors as follows: the duty of care (including issues relating to the time devoted to board duties and regularly attending meetings; the need to be informed and prepared; the right to rely on others; inquiry; and candor among directors), the duty of loyalty (including issues of good faith, conflicts of interest, and fairness to the corporation), the business judgment rule, the duty of disclosure, and director confidentiality. *Id.* at 19–29. These obligations often or continually involve the general counsel's advice.

a director should seek legal advice regarding the director's obligations, including reporting confidentiality obligations to the other directors and not participating in consideration of the matter.[140]

With respect to director confidentiality, the *Guidebook* states:

> A director must keep confidential all matters involving the corporation that have not been disclosed to the public. Directors must be aware of the corporation's confidentiality, insider trading, and disclosure policies and comply with them. Although a public company director may receive inquiries from major shareholders, media, analysts, or friends to comment on sensitive issues, individual directors should avoid responding to such inquiries, particularly when confidential or market-sensitive information is involved. Instead, they should refer requests for information to the CEO or other designated spokesperson.
>
> A director who improperly discloses non-public information to persons outside the corporation can, for example, harm the corporation's competitive position or damage investor relations and, if the information is material, incur personal liability as a tipper of inside information or cause the corporation to violate federal securities laws. Equally important, unauthorized director disclosure of non-public information can damage the bond of trust between and among directors and management, discourage candid discussions, and jeopardize boardroom effectiveness and director collaboration.[141]

One further word about candor and about confidentiality. As to candor, there are many times when a director needs to be candid with his fellow directors as to any relevant information he may have acquired in certain circumstances from other sources or any potential (even peripheral) personal interests he may have as to a matter under consideration by

---

140. *Id.* at 22–23.

141. *Id.* at 28–29. On the duty of confidentiality, consider Brophy v. Cities Service Co., 70 A.2d 5 (Del. Ch. 1949); Oracle Corp. Derivative Litig., 867 A.2d 904, 934 (Del. Ch. 2004); Hollinger Int'l v. Black, 844 A.2d 1022, 1061–62 (Del. Ch. 2004).

Somewhat related to the issue of director confidentiality, a current, live topic in corporate governance circles is the matter of permitting board members to interact with institutional investors. There are many points of view on this issue, but one point of agreement is that directors should be very cautious about not violating Regulation FD, which provides that when a securities issuer or a person acting on its behalf discloses material, nonpublic information to certain persons, the issuer must publicly disclose that information. Regulation FD, 17 C.F.R. §§ 243.100–.103; *see also* Selective Disclosure and Insider Trading, SEC Release Nos. 33-7881, 34-43154, IC-24599, File No. S7-31-99 (Aug. 15, 2000), http://www.sec.gov/rules/final/33-7881.htm (releasing final rule regarding Regulation FD, among others).

the board. As to confidentiality, recent events have highlighted some issues that can arise. For example, there was the infamous 2009 Hewlett-Packard "leak case" and ensuing difficulties arising from unfortunate internal efforts to probe the leak.[142] The scandal resulted in the forced resignation of several Hewlett-Packard executives, including the general counsel, and the filing of criminal charges against some of them (though not the general counsel).[143] And in 2011, the media chronicled an incident in which a director of Goldman Sachs, Rajat Gupta, was alleged to have provided confidential, inside information to a manager of hedge fund Galleon Group LLC, Raj Rajaratnam. Rajaratnam was convicted of insider trading, and Gupta was cited by the SEC in an administrative order concerning his alleged breach of confidentiality.[144]

c. Minutes, Records, and Notes

i. Board and Committee Minutes

Whether or not the general counsel is also the corporate secretary, she should be integrally involved in the process of keeping or closely supervising the keeping of the corporate minutes. Although opinions differ regarding the various methods of minute-taking, the issue's importance has been magnified by recent events. In particular, the proliferation in the past decade of stockholder demands for inspection of corporate books and records under laws such as section 220 of the Delaware General Corporation Law[145] "puts a premium on the preparation of [minutes] that can be produced in response to a Section 220 demand that show informed decision-making by disinterested and independent directors acting in good faith."[146]

---

142. *See* Damon Darlin, *Ex-Chairwoman Among 5 Charged in Hewlett Case*, N.Y. TIMES, Oct. 5, 2006, at A1 (reporting on the Hewlett-Packard pretexting scandal).

143. *Id.* The scandal also led to the passage of federal legislation banning the practice of pretexting. Telephone Records and Privacy Protection Act of 2006, 18 U.S.C. § 1039.

144. For news reports relating to these events, see John Helyar et al., *Rajat Gupta's Double Life*, WILMINGTON NEWS J., May 22, 2011, at D4; Peter Lattman, *Ex-Goldman Director Accused of Passing Illegal Tips*, N.Y. TIMES, Mar. 2, 2011, at B1; Michael Rothfeld et al., *Fund Titan Found Guilty—Rajaratnam Convicted of Insider Trading*, WALL ST. J., May 12, 2011, at A1.

145. *See, e.g.*, DEL. CODE ANN. tit. 8, § 220 (permitting stockholders to inspect books and records for a proper purpose).

146. Stephen A. Radin, *The New Stage of Corporate Governance Litigation: Section 220 Demands—Reprise*, 28 CARDOZO L. REV. 1287, 1412 (2006).

The general counsel and the corporate secretary can provide substantial support to the board, and the corporation generally, in minimizing litigation problems "by ensuring that corporate actions likely to be challenged by shareholders, such as mergers and acquisitions, transactions with controlling shareholders and executive compensation awards, are documented in carefully prepared minutes and board materials ready to be produced upon receipt of a Section 220 demand."[147]

The famous *Disney* case provides just one example of how problematic minutes can contribute to protracted litigation. *Disney* involved decisions by the board of The Walt Disney Company concerning the hiring and termination of Michael Ovitz as president of the company.[148] The court's comments on the minutes that were entered as evidence at trial highlight that what is *not* in the minutes can be as important as what *is* in the minutes. For example, with respect to the minutes of the compensation committee's meeting at which Ovitz's employment agreement (the OEA) was considered, the court observed: "It would have been extremely helpful to the Court if the minutes had indicated in any fashion that the discussion relating to the OEA was longer and more substantial than the discussion relating to the myriad of other issues brought before the compensation committee that morning."[149]

Interestingly, the Chancellor made this observation in the context of his comparison of the processes of the Disney board (and its compensation committee) with that of the TransUnion board in the famous *Smith v. Van Gorkom* case.[150] The Chancellor in *Disney* compared the facts he found there with those in *Van Gorkom*, noting that the "parallels . . . at first appear striking, [but] a more careful consideration will reveal several important distinctions between the two."[151] He noted that in *Van Gorkom*, "the TransUnion

---

147. *Id.* at 1413.
148. *In re* Walt Disney Co. Deriv. Litig., 906 A.2d 27 (Del. 2006), *aff'g* 907 A.2d 693 (Del. Ch. 2005).
149. *Disney*, 907 A.2d at 768 n. 539; *see also Disney Decision Refuses to Assess Director Liability and Provides Important Guidance for Directors*, WEIL BRIEFING: CORPORATE GOVERNANCE 3–4 (Aug. 12, 2005), *available at* http://www.weil.com/news/pubdetail.aspx?pub=3160 (discussing the importance of good minutes and noting that stockholders may use minutes to survive a motion to dismiss); *Delaware Supreme Court Affirms Chancellor's Judgment of No Liability for Directors in Ovitz Case*, WEIL BRIEFING: CORPORATE GOVERNANCE 2 (June 16, 2006), *available at* http://www.weil.com/wgm/cwgmhomep.nsf/Files/Briefing006_2006/$file/Briefing006_2006.pdf (reflecting on the importance of good documentation of board decision-making processes in avoiding lengthy and expensive litigation).
150. 488 A.2d 858 (Del. 1985) (holding directors liable in damages for violation of their duty of due care).
151. 907 A.2d at 767.

board met for about two hours to discuss and deliberate on this monumental transaction [sale of the company] in the life of TransUnion." Then he observed that "the length of the compensation committee meeting, and more specifically the length of the discussion of [Ovitz's contract] is difficult to establish." But by a painstaking process of hearing live testimony from several witnesses at trial and looking at what minutes there were, the Chancellor was able to conclude that the discussion took "about 25–30 minutes, significantly more time than the brief discussion in the minutes would seem to indicate."[152] Clearly then, the moral of this story is that the minute taker (usually the corporate secretary or the general counsel) does not want to subject the company and its directors to the painful and expensive ordeal of a trial (the *Disney* trial as a whole took thirty-seven days) to establish what well-crafted minutes would have shown.

The decision in *In re Netsmart Technologies, Inc. Shareholders Litigation*[153] provides another cautionary tale of the importance of well-prepared minutes. In *Netsmart*, the Court of Chancery preliminarily enjoined a going-private merger between Netsmart Technologies, Inc. and two private equity firms. The court concluded, in part, that the plaintiff had established that the board "likely did not have a reasonable basis for failing to undertake *any* exploration of interest by strategic buyers."[154] The court criticized on several fronts the minutes of the special committee formed to consider the transaction, citing the complete lack of minutes of certain board and special committee meetings,[155] a "tardy, omnibus" approval by the special committee at a single meeting of the minutes of ten meetings ranging over a two-month period,[156] as well as omissions from the minutes of

152. *Id.* at 768.
153. 924 A.2d 171 (Del. Ch. 2007).
154. *Id.* at 177.
155. *Id.* at 182; *see also id.* at 186 ("In any event, given the un-minuted nature of the May 19 meeting and the lack of good recollection by the defendants involved, it is difficult to determine what exactly motivated the board's decision [to forgo exploring strategic alternatives], or if decision is really even the right word."); *id.* at 187 ("[T]he Special Committee apparently decided on a very targeted approach to marketing the company . . . . I use the word 'apparently' because as with the meeting of May 19, no minutes exist for these Special Committee's deliberations that appear in the Proxy. As such, one cannot determine who was present for this meeting or what specifically was said or done. One might even reasonably speculate that no formal meeting took place as the Committee's chairman, Calcagno, testified that there were no Special Committee meetings at which minutes were not taken. In that case, Calcagno may well have signed off on the shopping list suggested by [the financial advisor] outside of the meeting room." (footnote omitted)).
156. *See id.* at 191 ("After this litigation commenced, the Special Committee met on December 21, 2006 and approved formal minutes for ten meetings ranging from August 10, 2006 through November 28, 2006. That tardy, omnibus consideration of

various meetings.[157] It also pointed to the minutes to ascertain the "directional force" of management's and the board's focus on a going-private, as opposed to a strategic, deal.[158]

The importance of board and board committee minutes has also come into sharper focus as courts, legislators, and regulators have given increased scrutiny to the processes of boards and board committees. For example, the comprehensive final rules of the SEC on "Executive Compensation and Related Person Disclosure,"[159] released by the Commission in the summer of 2006, and the Dodd-Frank Wall Street Reform and Consumer Protection Act,[160] enacted in 2010, have created significant challenges for directors and counsel, some of which are not yet entirely clear. It has been a best practice for board compensation committees to adhere to disciplined procedures that include recording minutes that accurately reflect the materials considered by the committee and the discussions at each session of the committee.[161]

In light of the new legislation and regulation, however, the required discipline has become even more exacting. In particular, the Executive Compensation and Related Person Disclosure rules mandate that detailed information be included in a "Compensation Discussion and Analysis" (CD&A) that must be *filed* with the Commission, thereby potentially implicating rules and penalties related to material misstatements.[162] The burden

meeting minutes is, to state the obvious, not confidence-inspiring, especially when considered along with the total absence of minutes for the May 19 board meeting and the lack of clarity whether the Special Committee ever met to approve the limited set of private equity firms to be canvassed." (footnote omitted)).

157. *See id.* at 184 ("The supposed important decision—not reflected in any minutes or resolution—to forsake approaching these [strategic] buyers appears to have only been justified by reference to the sporadic pitches to strategic players made [by Netsmart's CEO and financial advisor] over the prior decade.").

158. *Id.* at 182.

159. *See* Press Release 2006–123, U.S. Securities and Exchange Commission, SEC Votes to Adopt Changes to Disclosure Requirements Concerning Executive Compensation and Related Matters (July 26, 2006), http://www.sec.gov/news/press/2006/2006-123.htm (summarizing the new requirements). The text of the final rule itself fills hundreds of pages. Executive Compensation and Related Person Disclosure, Securities Act Release 8732A, Exchange Act Release No. 54,302A, Investment Company Act Release No. 37,444A, 71 Fed. Reg. 53,158 (Sept. 8, 2006).

160. Pub. L. No. 111–203, 124 Stat. 1376 (2010) (codified in scattered sections of 7, 12, 15, 18, 31 U.S.C.).

161. *See, e.g.,* REPORT OF THE NACD BLUE RIBBON COMMISSION ON EXECUTIVE COMPENSATION AND THE ROLE OF THE COMPENSATION COMMITTEE 17 (2003) (describing suggested procedures for the compensation committee).

162. 71 Fed. Reg. 53,167–68; *see also* Frank B. Manley, *A New Era for the Compensation Committee*, DIRECTORS MONTHLY, Aug. 2006, at 18, 19 ("The CD&A is a novella, not a short story. Be prepared to describe and defend every plan design feature, factors behind every plan change, and the rationale for every award decision.").

of compliance in this new reality rests with the directors, particularly the members of the compensation committee. But it is corporate counsel, whether in-house or outside counsel, who must master these rules to provide guidance to the committee to superintend the completeness and accuracy of the minutes as well as the content of the disclosure filings.

The legal issues lurking in the minute-taking process clearly are significant, and require substantial involvement of and vetting with the general counsel. Whatever process is ultimately implemented, those involved in preparing and reviewing the minutes must bear in mind that the minutes may be obtainable by court order as a corporate record.[163] Essentially, it behooves the minute taker to write the minutes as if for an audience of regulators, public stockholders (and their lawyers), and courts.

Given the critical importance of the minutes, the general counsel, another senior member of the in-house legal team, or the corporate secretary should draft or supervise the process of drafting the minutes so that they are professionally prepared and consistent from meeting to meeting. The drafter should memorialize each meeting of the board or a board committee, including regular and special meetings and executive sessions.

Each board or committee, with the advice of the general counsel, should decide what level of detail to include in the minutes. If the directors' actions or decisions later become the subject of litigation, a greater level of detail in the minutes may help the directors to demonstrate that they engaged in an appropriately deliberative process in reaching their decision. This is particularly true for a major transaction (such as a merger, sale, or acquisition) at the board level, and is essential also for a special board committee (such as one charged with a buyout transaction or a special litigation committee).

As a general rule, the minutes should set forth at least the following:

- the location, date, and time of the meeting;
- the chair and secretary of the meeting;
- the directors and other persons who attended the meeting (whether in person or by telephone), and the times that they entered and left the meeting;

---

163. DEL. CODE ANN. tit. 8, § 220; *cf.* Seinfeld v. Verizon Communications, Inc., 909 A.2d 117, 118 (Del. 2006) (concluding that plaintiff had not shown a "credible basis" from which the trial court could infer that there were possible issues of waste, mismanagement, or wrongdoing to support plaintiff's books and records request) (citing Stephen A. Radin, *The New Stage of Corporate Governance Litigation: Section 220 Demands*, 26 CARDOZO L. REV. 1595, 1647 (2005); E. Norman Veasey & Christine T. Di Guglielmo, *What Happened in Delaware Corporate Law and Governance from 1992–2004? A Retrospective on Some Key Developments*, 153 U. PA. L. REV. 1399, 1466–69 (2005)).

- any materials that the directors received before or during the meeting;
- a description of the topics discussed or considered, including a brief summary of the major terms and rationale discussed (without attributing particular words or points to particular directors) and who was present for those discussions;
- identification of anyone (e.g., lawyers, financial advisors) who provided information and advice at the meeting, and the subject matter of the advice (but not necessarily the advice itself);
- the outcome of any board vote on matters put to a vote (or a statement of decisions reached by consensus), indicating who was present for the vote and any director who dissented, abstained, or absented herself or himself from the vote;
- the material terms of any decision made by the board or committee;
- if discussions were held or information exchanged between or among some directors before the meeting relating to matters considered at the meeting, those facts should be reflected;
- the time that the meeting ended; and
- the identity of the person preparing the minutes.[164]

There should be some general relationship between the length of the minutes devoted to a particular issue and the time in the meeting devoted to the issue. But the minutes should not purport to constitute a verbatim record of the discussion. It is also a good practice to avoid adjectives or adverbs that suggest a quantitative or qualitative value judgment—such as "the board engaged in a *full* discussion." If such words or phrases are used, their omission in other sections of the minutes or in the minutes of other meetings might suggest that other discussions were not "full."

Among the commentaries on numerous aspects of the documentation problems in the *Disney* case are these observations and advice in a Weil Gotshal & Manges paper[165] following the Delaware Supreme Court decision:

> The Chancellor's 2003 decision denying motions to dismiss relied heavily on what did *not* appear in the company's Minutes and other documentation that

---

164. CORPORATE DIRECTOR'S GUIDEBOOK, *supra* note 8, at 52. The sixth edition of the *Corporate Director's Guidebook* includes a complete exposition of the issue of corporate minute-taking and serves as an excellent source of reference in this area.

165. *See Delaware Supreme Court Affirms Chancellor's Judgment of No Liability for Directors in Ovitz Case*, WEIL BRIEFING: CORPORATE GOVERNANCE 2 (June 16, 2006), *available at* http://www.weil.com/wgm/cwgmhomep.nsf/Files/Briefing006_2006/ $file/Briefing006_2006.pdf (advising that minutes should note when a subject has been discussed on a one-on-one or informal basis before a board meeting as well as the nature of discussions had and questions asked at a board meeting).

were produced in response to the plaintiff's demand for books and records under Section 220 of the Delaware General Corporation Law (DGCL), a pre-suit practice encouraged by Delaware Courts and increasingly used by plaintiffs' counsel before filing stockholder actions challenging board conduct.

To avoid the prospect of a long and expensive trial, directors and their counselors should be vigilant to the tension—highlighted by the facts in the *Disney* case—between informal consensus-building discussions outside formal board or committee meetings and the litigation imperative that matters requiring board or committee action must ultimately be discussed in full at well-documented meetings. One way to lessen the tension is to note in well-drafted minutes of formal meetings that there have been previous, informal one-on-one discussions on the subject. As we emphasized in our August 2005 Weil Briefing, the importance of keeping good minutes—showing what directors discussed and considered and whether questions were asked—cannot be overstated.[166]

The briefing then offers suggestions regarding the minutes, as follows:

> There is, of course, no "one-size-fits-all" checklist that will protect all directors in all cases. Adherence to the following suggestions . . . should, however, protect directors under almost all circumstances:
>
> . . . .
>
> • Review all board and committee materials and attend all meetings well-prepared to participate in discussion.
> • Review board and committee minutes carefully. Ensure that they reflect the board's deliberation by including the times that meetings begin and end and the times when persons present at the meeting enter and leave the meeting—particularly when people are leaving the meeting due to conflicts or potential conflicts. Seek to ensure that there is some relationship between the length of the minutes devoted to a particular issue and the time devoted to that issue. Ensure that the minutes accurately reflect the matters considered, and capture the general extent and nature of the board's questions, discussions, and decisions. Where information was provided to the board before the meeting or discussions among directors occurred before the meeting, reflect those facts in the minutes. (Minutes of executive sessions need not—and probably should not—be as detailed as other minutes, but should, at a minimum, indicate when the session began and ended, who attended, and what topics were discussed.)[167]

166. *Id.* at 2.
167. *Id.* at 4–5.

A draft of the minutes should be sent to each director or committee member promptly after the meeting, and the directors should promptly review and correct or comment on the draft. The final version of the minutes should then be considered and approved with any further changes at the next board meeting. Once the minutes have been finally approved, they become the official record of the meeting and should be retained as such by the corporation. Accordingly, to avoid confusion, preliminary drafts and notices relating to the minutes should not be retained.

Minutes can be crucial to the outcome of litigation. In *Netsmart*,[168] Vice Chancellor Strine (now Chancellor) was highly critical of the cavalier treatment of minutes, citing the appearance in the record of "minutes" when there had been no meetings, a lack of minutes when meetings had occurred, and the board's wholesale, blanket approval of past minutes submitted in a bunch.[169]

Also, in the epic opinion of former Chancellor Chandler in the *Airgas* litigation, the court noted that certain justifications for the board's perception of the threat to Airgas for the adoption of the poison pill were created by lawyers in litigation after the corporate events, and were not recorded in the minutes.[170] The court found the lack of evidence of the board's consideration of these justifications telling. But the court's decision favoring Airgas and supporting the directors' adherence to their fiduciary duties in resisting the hostile takeover attempt by Air Products ultimately did not turn on the absence of board discussions about certain justifications for the poison pill. Fortunately for Airgas, the absence of these discussions and absence of minutes referring to the threat in the formative stages of the resistance to the hostile takeover were not fatal to Airgas's defense. The lessons of the *Airgas* case in this connection are clear: (1) counsel need to anticipate what facts or positions are likely to be relevant to the directors and make certain they are considered or discussed during the formative corporate events; and (2) if these facts are true and if the board considers or discusses them, the minutes should reflect that consideration or discussion.

168. *In re* Netsmart Techs., Inc. S'holders Litig., 924 A.2d 171 (Del. Ch. 2007).

169. *Id.* at 182, 184, 187, 191; *see also* Caremark *and* Netsmart: *Ten Lessons for M&A Practitioners*, Weil Briefing (Mar. 22, 2007), *available at* http://www.weil.com/news/pubdetail.aspx?pub=7726 (discussing lessons learned from the *Netsmart* case).

170. Air Prods. & Chems., Inc. v. Airgas, Inc., 16 A.3d 48, 2011 Del. Ch. LEXIS 22, at *148–52 (Del. Ch. Feb. 15, 2011).

ii. Director Notes

The general counsel should evaluate and monitor the corporation's practices with respect to minutes and note-taking to minimize inconsistencies in format and approval that can arise from having multiple committees and note takers. Director note-taking raises issues that go beyond those implicated in the discussion of board and committee minutes. Because a director's individual notes are not subject to the careful process of drafting, review, and approval that applies to minutes, they may contain words or statements that could be misinterpreted or taken out of context in a litigation setting.

In particular, the general counsel should educate directors about the potential perils of taking and retaining individual notes, so that each director can make an informed decision about whether to take and retain notes. It may help if the general counsel would reassure directors that the official corporate records (including presentations to the board and minutes of the meetings) will contain information that will help demonstrate the board's informed business judgment and assist directors in recalling past events if they are deposed or called as a witness at trial. The text of the *Corporate Director's Guidebook* on director note-taking is a helpful guide. With respect to director note-taking, the *Guidebook* states:

> Directors are not obligated to take notes. Those who do take notes to help them participate should consider whether to retain them. Notes are not subject to a careful process of drafting, review, and approval, and may contain statements or notations that may be misinterpreted, taken out of context, or in fact, be incorrect, particularly if produced in litigation. For example, notes often capture only part of a discussion or fail to distinguish between words spoken and the note taker's thoughts. Similarly, notes and drafts of the secretary of the meeting should normally not be retained after approval of the official minutes.[171]

Thus, the general counsel can work with the board to develop a consistent policy for the retention of information provided to the board, such as board books and presentations, that, along with high-quality minutes, will create a reliable record of the board's deliberations and actions.

---

171. CORPORATE DIRECTOR'S GUIDEBOOK, *supra* note 8, at 53–54.

d. Crossing the Bridge: The General Counsel as Director

If the general counsel also serves as a member of the board of directors, that status itself may be a two-edged sword. On the one hand, being a director may play a substantial role in buttressing the general counsel's credibility and authority with the board as well as with the officers and other employees.[172] On the other hand, despite the increase in status that may be achieved when the general counsel serves as a director, it may not be advisable for the general counsel to be a director. It will doubtless add to the complexity of the general counsel's life, and it may be potentially conflicting for the general counsel, who already fulfills a dual role as part of senior management and independent legal advisor to the board. Thus, adding the directorship role as another "hat" to the general counsel's multifaceted position may be problematic.[173] The need for general counsel to be objective and independent may be put at risk in certain settings if she is a director as well as the chief legal officer.

The comment to Model Rule 1.7 advises that before accepting a position on the board of directors of a client, a lawyer should consider whether working in the dual role will compromise the lawyer's independent professional judgment. Specifically, the comment states:

> A lawyer for a corporation or other organization who is also a member of its board of directors should determine whether the responsibilities of the two roles may conflict. The lawyer may be called on to advise the corporation in matters involving actions of the directors. Consideration should be given to the frequency with which such situations may arise, the potential intensity of the conflict, the effect of the lawyer's resignation from the board and the possibility of the corporation's obtaining legal advice from another lawyer in such situations. If there is material risk that the dual role will compromise the lawyer's independence of professional judgment, the lawyer should not serve as a director. . . .[174]

---

172. *E. g.*, Geoffrey C. Hazard, Jr., *Three Afterthoughts*, 46 EMORY L.J. 1053, 1054 (1997); *cf.* Weaver, *supra* chapter I, note 24, at 1034 ("Corporate counsel often acknowledge the increased effectiveness that they enjoy when senior management believes that they are 'team players.' I do not dispute the accuracy of this perception; however, the close working relationship that often exists between corporate counsel and senior management offers many opportunities for confusion about the identity of the client that counsel represents.").

173. Similar and additional competing factors should also influence the determination of whether it is desirable for a corporation's outside counsel to serve on the corporation's board of directors. In our view, that situation should be avoided, particularly when outside counsel's fees are significant.

174. MODEL RULES OF PROF'L CONDUCT R. 1.7 cmt. [35]; *see also* MODEL RULES OF PROF'L CONDUCT R. 2.1.

This applies with force and reason where outside counsel is a director and his firm realizes substantial legal fees from the corporation. Such a practice was common years ago, but today it may compromise generally accepted understandings of director independence for many purposes and may complicate other issues, including preservation of the attorney-client privilege.[175] Today, it is generally considered a "no-no" for a lawyer whose firm is outside counsel to the company to serve on its board. There is usually no similar economic conflict with general counsel serving on her company's board, but the problems of independence and objectivity remain.

In order to render advice that is objective and will be perceived as objective, counsel, whether it is the general counsel or regular outside counsel, must determine how to remain close enough to the various corporate actors to achieve a depth of understanding and credibility, while also maintaining some degree of distance from the corporate client's representatives.[176] When the general counsel serves as a director of a corporate client, her advice may become—or at least may be perceived as being—less detached and more cautious because of extraneous concerns, including job security and personal liability.[177] In addition, the lawyer for the corporation— whether inside or outside counsel—will not be deemed to be independent for the purpose of considering many matters that come before the board of directors.[178]

175. *See* Marc I. Steinberg, *The Role of Inside Counsel in the 1990s: A View from Outside*, 49 SMU L. Rev. 483, 494 (1996) (stating that when in-house counsel serves as a director of the corporation, "application of the attorney-client privilege may be determined on an ad hoc basis depending on whether the attorney/director was acting as legal counsel or as a director. By assuming this dual function, therefore, the corporation's assertion of the attorney-client privilege may be subject to stricter scrutiny").

176. *See* Kim, *supra* note 10, at 187 ("Lawyer independence, however, is concerned primarily with the lawyer's relationship *with the client*. Lawyers must also keep a safe distance *from their own clients* because lawyers must maintain a separate identity if they are to render detached, objective advice.").

177. *See id.* at 233 ("Proponents of dual service argue that the corporation benefits by having its lawyer on the board because the lawyer knows he is at risk of personal liability as a director. That fact, however, may actually increase the threat to the lawyer's independence. Because the lawyer-director has placed himself in a position of being personally affected by the legal advice he renders, self-protection concerns may affect the lawyer-director's ability to render objective, detached advice. The result may be that the lawyer-director's opinion is far 'more cautious than it would otherwise be.' The corporate client suffers because it does not get the detached, objective, legal perspective it would normally receive from its counsel." (footnotes omitted)).

178. *See, e.g.*, N.Y. Stock Exch., Listed Company Manual § 303A. 02 (2004), *available at* http://www.nyse.com/RegulationFrameset.html?nyseref=&displayPage=/listed/1022221393251.html (establishing various tests for director independence for listed company boards); General Electric Governance Principles, *available at* http://www.ge.com/en/citizenship/governance/govprinc.htm (setting forth GE's principles

Some observers argue that it is not prudent for in-house or outside corporate counsel to serve on their clients' boards of directors under any circumstances.[179] Others take a different view. A view expressed by Professor Geoffrey Hazard in 1997 falls into the latter category:

> I once held that view [that it is never advisable for corporate counsel to serve as a director of a client], but no longer do. Rather, I hold to the more indeterminate view [that] [a]n in-house counsel should be very aware of the risks involved in that dual role. . . . My view of a lawyer's serving as both a director and general counsel changed as a result of a conversation with a very good lawyer who held that dual role. The lawyer served as general counsel to a major corporation and, prior and subsequent to that engagement, practiced with a leading law firm in a major city. My colleague's proposition was this: The risk of a dual role as general counsel and director can sometimes be offset by the advantage that members of the board of directors will regard legal advice much more seriously when it comes from a social equal in the corporate hierarchy than when it comes from someone who is in the hierarchy's second tier.[180]

In essence, Professor Hazard's argument is that a lawyer-director may be more effective at persuading other directors to follow her advice because the other directors know she is a peer and faces the same risk of personal liability as her fellow directors. Though this may make the advice more credible to other directors, it may not necessarily be in the corporation's best interest, as the desirability of credibility may be outweighed by the perceived independence problems.

This is a debatable issue that must be resolved within the context of the particular corporation and its culture. While there is no "one-size-fits-all"

---

of director independence); General Motors Corporate Governance Guidelines, *available at* http://www.gm.com/company/investor_information/corp_gov/guidelines_pg2.html#9 (setting forth GM's principles of director independence). Under Delaware law, independence is measured by considering the questions—independent from whom and for what purpose? Beam v. Stewart, 845 A.2d 1040, 1050 (Del. 2004).

179. *E. g.*, Weaver, *supra* chapter I, note 24, at 1039–40.

180. Hazard, *supra* note 172, at 1053–54; *see also* Kim, *supra* note 10, at 222 ("Proponents of dual service also argue that the corporation benefits by knowing that the corporate lawyer is on the hook as a board member. Corporate clients feel comforted when their lawyer serves on the board because the other directors know that the lawyer is subject to the same risk of personal liability that they bear as directors. Recognizing that they are at risk of personal liability as directors, lawyers presumably are likely to be more alert and diligent than they might otherwise be, and fellow board members are more likely to heed the lawyer's advice as a consequence. Outside directors in particular will find it easier to give weight to the legal opinions of someone who is taking the same risks that they are.").

solution, in most cases it is preferable for general counsel not to be a member of the board. But the general counsel should be present at board meetings and "in the loop" as the advisor to the board and its committees on almost all issues.

Ultimately, it is not easy to achieve or to determine ex ante the balance between effectiveness and the risks to professional independence. Corporate counsel should remember who is the client (only the entity) and carefully weigh the potential benefit of effectiveness against the potential cost to professional independence and objectivity when deciding whether to serve or to continue to serve on its board of directors.

We should add a word about the general counsel serving as a director on the board of another corporation. The concerns presented above concerning her service as a director on the board of her client, the corporation of which she is the chief legal officer, do not apply to her service on other boards. Indeed, the general counsel of corporation A might well make an outstanding director of corporation B (provided A and B are not in conflict or direct competition), and she may also become a very welcome and effective confidante of the general counsel of corporation B. Nevertheless, conflicts, laws, regulations, and time commitments must be carefully considered because her primary loyalty and full-time efforts are to serve corporation A. She should do nothing and should undertake no other professional commitments that could potentially interfere with that fiduciary and ethical responsibility.

C. OTHER RELATIONSHIPS

1. Relationships with Investors

Most public companies have investor relations departments. Those departments have on their staffs persons who are experts in reaching out to and responding to investors—including institutional investors, stockholders advisory services (e.g., RiskMetrics), and "retail investors."

The general counsel is not normally the first point of contact with these investors. But there may be times when legal issues may be implicated (e.g., a proxy contest or a merger or inside information implicating SEC Reg FD) when the advice and involvement of general counsel is called for. There is no "cookbook" on how general counsel should manage these contacts. But the general counsel often undertakes prospective, "clear day" advice to the investor relations staff on how to handle difficult scenarios.

A growing practice in many companies relates to entreaties by stockholders to meet with directors to engage in discussion about the business and affairs of the company. Of course, the CEO and the CFO often meet with institutional investors and analysts. But having directors—even lead directors or nonexecutive chairs—meet with investors is a practice that requires careful analysis and consideration. One must be careful not to reveal any material, nonpublic information for fear of violating SEC regulations, particularly Regulation FD.[181] There is no uniform practice in this area, and general counsel who have not had experience in director contact with stockholders (outside of annual meetings) should read some of the recent literature, consult with outside counsel, or reach out to other general counsel who have had some experience in this area. Again, there is no one-size-fits-all practice and there are many nuanced issues to consider.

2. Government Relations

Large, multinational corporations should develop a proactive, comprehensive government relations strategy and policy—one that extends beyond the short-term, reactive, and narrowly focused initiatives that comprise the bulk of some corporations' public policy or government relations efforts.[182] These proactive efforts—which Ben Heineman has termed "growth and government" initiatives[183]—are aimed at shaping major policies in global markets in ways that facilitate a company's growth, while also being consistent with good corporate citizenship.[184] The general counsel can play a pivotal role in such policy efforts.

The corporation's public policy initiative should ensure that the company has sufficient policy, political, and governmental process expertise in

---

181. Regulation FD, 17 C.F.R. §§ 243.100–.103; *see also* Selective Disclosure and Insider Trading, SEC Release Nos. 33-7881, 34-43154, IC-24599, File No. S7-31-99 (Aug. 15, 2000), http://www.sec.gov/rules/final/33–7881.htm (releasing final rule regarding Regulation FD, among others).

182. *See* Ben W. Heineman, Jr., *Hands Across the Water*, CORP. COUNSEL, Oct. 2006 ("Transnational companies need a coherent, forward-looking 'foreign policy,' but most don't have one. Although governmental decisions significantly affect global business success, many corporations and legal staffs are only involved in defensive, short-term, or narrowly self-interested 'government relations.'").

183. *Id.*

184. *See id.* (describing the types of growth and government initiatives that GE has undertaken, including, for example, "[s]timulating policy paradigm shifts" to "put[ ] more emphasis on early diagnosis and prevention in health care" or "[o]btaining government support for whole new markets, like wind or water, to advance important public goals").

place to address the myriad policy issues confronting the company, and that such expertise is built into planning processes.[185] "These experts need to help perform the difficult task of translating the desirable, from both a policy and business perspective, into something feasible."[186] The general counsel should have the overall responsibility for overseeing the integration of policy and politics with business strategy, because "[a]t the end of the day, policy, legislation, regulation, and (as necessary) test case litigation are about setting meaningful rules and achieving their intended impact in a variety of cultures"—goals that fit well with the general counsel's skills and resources.[187]

The general counsel's broad public policy role—as compared with lobbying with respect to more company- or industry-specific issues—may encompass a range of issues that may not be company- or industry-specific but that have significant impacts on the business. For example, general counsel of major corporations in Missouri have taken important action with respect to debate regarding judicial selection. Professor Roy A. Schotland has described these efforts as follows:

> Indeed, in Missouri, the general counsels of major corporations—and through them, the corporate community and its very effective lobbyists—have been a key group in converting attacks on the judiciary to support for it. One general counsel put it this way to legislative leaders in a private session: "We don't expect to win every case. But we do need judges who are well-qualified, free of improper political pressure, and able to decide cases promptly." That support has helped stop efforts to politicize Missouri's system of judicial selection.[188]

Chief legal officers frequently have trusted roles in a variety of important public policy efforts that may not directly impact their businesses.[189]

---

185. *See, e.g., id.* ("[T]he policy expert .... should be a key inside actor—an essential business team member .... [who] combine[s] expertise in the policy and politics of the field with an aptitude for business. This is the person who—through knowledge, experience, and networks—understands the trajectory of policy debates, and can spot and develop policy issues with the business teams. Ideally, this senior person has experience in government and so understands the interplay of policy, politics, and governmental process."); *see also id.* (articulating various types of policy issues that may confront a company operating in the global markets).

186. *Id.*

187. *Id.*

188. Roy A. Schotland, *New Challenges to States' Judicial Selection*, 95 Geo. L.J. 1077, 1100–01 (2007).

189. *See, e.g., How Can We Join Forces to Achieve a Moratorium?*, 4 N.Y. City L. Rev. 210, 221 (2002) ("The General Counsels of American companies have led on important

When hiring for the legal department, the general counsel should keep in mind the types of skills and personal characteristics—in addition to diversity considerations—that will enable corporate counsel to perform their legal functions within a broader policy and political paradigm.[190] Moreover, companies operating globally must face the challenges inherent in hiring policy experts who are foreign nationals and creating effective inside-outside partnerships with public policy experts.[191]

As part of the general counsel's public policy role, the chief legal officer frequently leads or plays an important role in the company's specific governmental relations or lobbying efforts. That is just one aspect of the general counsel's role in public policy, however, and should not cause the general counsel to lose sight of her broader role, as discussed above.

3. Media Relations

In today's "saturated media culture," public relations activities have become more important than ever before.[192] Corporate counsel are adapting to this new reality by finding ways to help their companies manage the public relations impacts of legal issues and controversies—in short, "legal public relations" has become "a legitimate and fundamental component of corporate legal services."[193] Public relations are critical to managing the value of a company's reputation, particularly because pre-trial settlement of most legal controversies has left "the court of public opinion [as] the most important battleground affecting not only good will and market share but [also] legal bargaining power, settlement negotiations, and future liability."[194]

public policy issues in the past, including some that certainly go beyond any direct impact on their businesses. These include the call for greater diversity in our profession, the support for *pro bono* and access to justice, and particularly the General Counsels' letter supporting increased funding for the Legal Services Corporation.").

190. Heineman, *supra* note 182.

191. *Id.*

192. Michele Destefano Beardslee, *Advocacy in the Court of Public Opinion, Installment One: Broadening the Role of Corporate Attorneys*, 22 GEO. J. LEGAL ETHICS 1259, 1259 (2009).

193. *Id. But cf. id.* at 1262–63 & n. 3 (citing sources demonstrating that "[m]any scholars, lawyers, and judges still believe that considering potential media spin or managing 'legal PR' is not or should not be part of legal services and that attempting to influence prosecutors, regulators, or trials in the media is inappropriate" (footnote omitted)).

194. *Id.* at 1262.

The relationship between public relations and legal issues is not a one-way street. Negative public perceptions of a company (whether accurate or not) can easily lead to litigation, not just the other way around.[195] Moreover, general counsel have reported that public relations considerations play a role before a legal strategy is even decided upon.[196]

Chief legal officers are actively managing legal public relations, albeit usually not as spokespeople.[197] They often work closely with their companies' public relations executives with respect to such issues as SEC filings, drafting press releases regarding legal issues or company disclosures, developing talking points regarding litigation or other legal issues, and addressing trademark protection issues.[198] A major challenge for general counsel in this context is balancing the "sound bite" sought by public relations executives with the accuracy and depth required for clear explanation of legal issues to the public.[199]

In this public relations role, the general counsel must also exhibit the personal characteristics that enable her to be the "right kind of public face" for the company. Kristin Campbell, Senior Vice President and General Counsel, Staples, Inc., articulated the necessary characteristics this way:

> The general counsel needs to be prepared to be the right kind of public face for the company. This involves complementing professionalism with a fair bit of humility, which is sometimes difficult for lawyers, for CEOs, and for other executives. For example, lawyers (and this applies to outside counsel as well as in-house counsel) can do a world of harm by going to a meeting with the government with an arrogant, obnoxious attitude that says, "we're going to win this and you can't stop us."[200]

The judgment and relationship skills that serve so well in other aspects of the general counsel role can serve fruitfully in the general counsel's role with respect to media relations (and other external relations) as well.

---

195. *See id.* at 1268 (quoting interview with general counsel of S&P 500 company, who stated that "If I'm painted as a bad company . . . and the stock price drops precipitously, I'm gonna be in a lawsuit" (alteration in original)); *see also id.* at 1269 (discussing the impacts of both accurate and inaccurate public perceptions).

196. *Id.* at 1270–72.

197. *Id.* at 1279.

198. *Id.* at 1280. In a significant number of companies, the legal department has direct oversight over the public relations department. *See id.* at 1287 (reporting that twelve percent of general counsel survey respondents reported direct legal department oversight of the public relations department).

199. *Id.* at 1280–81.

200. Interview with Kristin Campbell, Senior Vice President and General Counsel, Staples, Inc. (Oct. 28, 2009).

D. KEY TAKEAWAYS FOR THE GENERAL COUNSEL ON THE BALANCE BEAM

This is the longest chapter of the book, and rightly so. Kim Rucker's metaphor of the general counsel as a gymnast on the balance beam, with which we opened the chapter, is a particularly apt vision of the often competing forces with which the general counsel contends on a daily basis. In the preceding chapters we have touched on the CLO's challenging environment, as contrasted with the role's not-so-ancient history, and we began to develop the general understanding of the role of general counsel as persuasive counselor.

In this chapter, we have attempted, in part, to create a "bill of particulars" describing some of the many facets, opportunities, and perils inherent in the position. The chapter includes, for example, the broad-brush treatment of the need for independence, courage, and personal integrity while shepherding the corporation on a path of corporate integrity. Moreover, this chapter also includes more granular details, such as tips for keeping the corporate records, minutes, and the like.

Finally, the chapter highlights many corporate functions in which the general counsel is either the leader or a key player, ranging from counseling management and the board to shaping the company's interaction with the media. We have attempted to paint a picture of a modern renaissance person who is expected to perform a complex job for which different interested parties may have very different expectations. Thus, she teeters on a balance beam—while acting with strength, courage, and finesse—in an environment in which varied forces pull her in different directions.

Awareness of the need to juggle numerous responsibilities. The chief legal officer is aware of the many hats she wears, some of which are listed in this chapter. The multifaceted aspects of the position are simultaneously part of its attraction and part of its numerous challenges and tensions.

The reporting-line conundrum. If one is hired as general counsel solely by the CEO, without any board "buy-in," her tenure might be compromised. Problems arising from such a unilateral hiring are, of course, not inevitable. But a bilateral hiring process and reporting-line clarity is likely to be more salutary in the general counsel's life.

Financial dependence. We discuss in this chapter the CLO's singular economic dependence on the company as something that could tend to challenge her ability to be an independent, objective, and courageous actor. But this is an issue that she will have considered and resolved at the outset when agreeing to undertake the position.

Business-partnering should be fun, but beware of privilege issues. In the introduction to the book and in this chapter, we portray the business-partnering aspect of the position as one of its most stimulating aspects. And it is in that realm that the general counsel "earns her wings" as a knowledgeable, intuitive strategist who is prepared to advise the CEO and other actors in the C-suite of her studied or "gut" feeling about whether a proposed course of action is wise or folly, as well as whether it is legal. General counsel can and do participate with and advise the other corporate executives in business decisions, while remaining mindful of and managing the potential implications for attorney-client privilege and work product protection of her dual legal-business role.

Anticipating interaction with the board. When the general counsel is involved with members of the C-suite in analyzing a proposed business strategy, she is also thinking ahead to upcoming interaction with the board. She not only knows well the members of the board and their likely reactions, but she is also prepared to be a catalyst for them to probe prospective issues with questions and comments, while always avoiding surprises for the CEO. This mission of the CLO goes hand in glove with her legal analysis and communication as well as bringing out the best in board integrity and best practices by ensuring that matters such as candor and confidentiality are engrained in board behavior. Finally, the general counsel, whether or not she also holds the office of corporate secretary, has an important responsibility for the quality and value of minutes and other corporate records.

The general counsel and outreach. The CLO is a critically important corporate actor not only as a key internal player in the C-suite and the boardroom, but also as a crucial outside force—many times being the "face" of the company in dealing with investors, regulators, and media, as well as being a principal corporate negotiator and advocate.

CHAPTER 4

The General Counsel Leading
the Charge

The general counsel's job is to be a champion of integrity, compliance, and the rule of law. That is the way the organization looks upon the general counsel. That is a tremendously important role. It cannot be done effectively without buy-in from the CEO and the rest of the leadership. One of the things the general counsel can help do is ensure that the CEO understands what is being done and is supportive.

—Brackett Denniston[1]

[A] life of values is central to professional satisfaction and . . . one way to live such a life is to be the client, not just serve the client; to set the course as leaders and practical visionaries, not just provide advice and practical wisdom about what the course might be. . . . [S]uch leadership can be progressive and tough-minded, visionary and effective, humane and realistic. Deep personal engagement, the deep expression of one's self and one's values, can come from the ultimate responsibility and accountability for an institution or organization or school of thought that matters.[2]

—Ben Heineman

A. ESTABLISHING AND MAINTAINING A LEGAL AND ETHICAL CULTURE

If we had to roll the general counsel's indispensable responsibility into one term, it would be "guardian of the corporate integrity."[3] The general counsel

---

1. Interview with Brackett B. Denniston III, Senior Vice President and General Counsel, General Electric Company (Dec. 16, 2009).
2. Ben W. Heineman, Jr., The Robert H. Prieskel and Leon Silverman Lecture in the Program on the Practicing Lawyer and the Public Interest: Law and Leadership 8 (Nov. 27, 2006), *available at* http://www.law.yale.edu/documents/pdf/News_&_Events/HeinemanLecture.pdf.
3. *See supra* chapter I.A.

must be a key point person for monitoring and promoting ethical conduct throughout the corporate organization. Discourse about the general counsel's role sometimes limits the role to one of focusing on "compliance" or "legal affairs." The financial crisis and the various corporate scandals of the past decade—along with an associated uptick in prosecution of and enforcement actions against general counsel[4]—have resulted in a growing perception that chief legal officers and their subordinate in-house lawyers are expected to act as "cops on the beat." Just as the analogous, check-the-box, compliance-centric view is too limited to describe accurately the responsibility of the board of directors,[5] that view is especially cramped in describing the role expected of the general counsel. Rather, the general counsel is often looked to as having a key role in promoting a corporate culture and environment in which actors throughout the organization make decisions based on doing the right thing at every level. That means acting strategically, ethically, and with integrity. After all, "ethical behavior cannot be inspired or even directed through legal compliance mandates."[6] Instead, the general counsel must lead (though not alone) the corporate charge to build an ethical culture while working to help strengthen the corporation's business environment.

The increasing risk of liability that faces the general counsel and other in-house counsel may even have helped to drive the move of the chief legal officer toward the forefront of corporate efforts around ethics and integrity:

> The last 5 years have really brought an increased focus on accountability and transparency that has put a very difficult spin on the in-house lawyers' role. In-house counsel were in many ways the "consigliere" for the organization—not in a sense of being unethical, but in a sense of being the trusted private counsel who advised "from behind the curtain" about what should and should not take place. In-house lawyers would never have been seen as spokespersons. Lawyers would never have been seen as the folks you'd look at for liability. If something went wrong, lawyers were not at the front line. In the last few years, basically since Enron, I think what you've seen is a much greater focus on

---

4. *See infra* chapter VII.C (discussing the ways in which general counsel may be subject to liability).

5. Most jurisdictions describe the role of the board in language similar to that used in the Delaware General Corporation Law (DGCL): "The business affairs [of the corporation] shall be managed by or under the direction of a board of directors. . . ." DEL CODE ANN tit. 8 § 141(a).

6. Brian Martin, *Interactive Ethics*, INSIDE COUNSEL, Mar. 2011, at 10.

in-house counsel moving to the front of the stage within corporate management, acting as the conscience of the corporation, the ethical compass of the corporation. They are worried about their own liability, not only their professional liability, but also their fiduciary liability as a leader within the organization.

The professional rules were written in an environment that focused on whether lawyers could judge their own behavior and whether what you had done was appropriate. Now we are seeing an environment in which lawyers are responsible for the ethical behavior of others, not just their own ethical behavior, but for the client's ethical behavior. That's a sea change in how lawyers have traditionally looked at their role. Lawyers did not used to be responsible for what the client did with the advice.[7]

The perception of corporate counsel as "cops on the beat" views in-house lawyers as responsible for corporate compliance as well as the detection and deterrence of wrongdoing within the corporation.[8] Even strictly compliance-driven questions often come in shades of gray.[9] Thus, compliance-oriented decisions require the general counsel to exercise deep analysis and judgment. Moreover, the shades of gray with respect to compliance decisions operate to bring into play a variety of other considerations that are not strictly compliance issues. Such considerations may include a company's risk tolerance, operating and competitive environment, reputational considerations, and more.

Perhaps even more important than the judgment required to evaluate compliance issues is the general counsel's imperative role—in conjunction with the other senior executives—of establishing and maintaining a legal and ethical culture at all levels of the organization. In this role, the general counsel can guide others throughout the organization to develop the judgment that will allow them to apply ethical standards and company values in the "myriad scenarios" facing businesses operating in "the global business minefield" and to fill the gap between policy-based codes of conduct and

7. Interview with Susan Hackett, Senior Vice President and General Counsel, Association of Corporate Counsel (Sept. 2, 2009).

8. *E.g.*, Steven Andersen, *Greasy Palms*, INSIDE COUNSEL, Jan. 2009, at 34.

9. *See* Interview with Larry D. Thompson, Senior Vice President, Government Affairs, General Counsel and Secretary, PepsiCo (Dec. 9, 2009) ("I absolutely think that general counsel are currently more exposed to the threat of personal liability or ethical sanctions than in the recent past because so many [difficult] decisions come up to the general counsel. What bothers me is that most of this is in the gray area. I very seldom get a black or white issue. The general counsel could make the wrong decision. And I know people are then going to point fingers at the general counsel.").

real life.[10] Doing so may require the general counsel to understand and draw on disciplines beyond the law, such as organizational psychology, behavioral economics, and marketing.[11]

Creating a positive corporate culture is both the right thing to do and has major implications for the outcome of investigations and criminal prosecutions if something does go wrong.[12] A high "tone at the top" as well as a high "tone in the middle" are the key goals for proper corporate governance, with the general counsel at the heart of the effort to achieve and maintain this culture. "The most effective general counsel succeed in creating a culture in which awareness is high, messages are consistent, and close calls get reviewed. That requires a sincere commitment from the top of the company."[13] In effect, the CEO must make the business case, through words and conduct, for ethical conduct, sending the message that, "'If we stay out of trouble and don't embarrass ourselves and our clients, we will make more money,'"[14] and thus, the company "'would rather lose the sale than risk the company's reputation'" through unethical or illegal action.[15]

In addition to buy-in from the top, promoting an ethical culture throughout the organization also requires "deputizing" the subordinate lawyers in the legal department to carry out that mission. The entire legal team may thus form part of a collective "conscience" of the corporation. The general counsel, through both day-to-day example and in developing training programs for lawyers, can ensure that the entire legal team is on board by emphasizing the team's important role in this effort:

> I have used the phrase "conscience of the corporation" at work or when training the lawyers. I would say to them that they are the conscience of the company because I had 150 lawyers all over the world, in 21 countries. So they were the

10. Martin, *supra* note 6, at 10.

11. *See* Mary Swanton, *Combating Corruption*, INSIDE COUNSEL, Jan. 2011, at 39, 43 (discussing the approach of Marc Firestone, executive vice president of corporate and legal affairs at Kraft Foods, to establishing and maintaining ethical standards for the company).

12. *See, e.g.,* Andersen, *supra* note 8, at 35 ("There is no shortage of flagrant pay-offs to cite . . ., but the majority of corruption cases involve less blatant scenarios. Was a large donation to a politician's pet charity quid pro quo? Was a vacation package properly valued? Was paperwork misfiled by accident or design? As such, prosecutors look closely at corporate culture and patterns of behavior when deciding whether to indict.").

13. *Id.*

14. *See* Swanton, *supra* note 11, at 39, 44 (quoting Mark Ohringer, Global General Counsel of Jones Lang LaSalle).

15. *See id.* at 39, 44 (quoting CEO of Kraft Foods).

field marshals, if you will, of the code of conduct. I wanted them to feel that responsibility of being the conscience of the company because others would not take it as seriously as they would. I wanted them to be available to guide, to interpret the code for the employees located all over the world. And the general counsel is there to back up the lawyers with the full support of management and the board.[16]

Creating a consistent ethical culture requires ensuring that employees throughout the company are aware that any unethical or illegal conduct carries real, appropriate consequences. Daniel Desjardins, Senior Vice President, General Counsel and Assistant Secretary of the Canadian firm Bombardier Inc., put it well when he said:

Our philosophy is that integrity starts on the plant floor. We must have employees, no matter their status, who have high integrity. So it is not only the tone at the top but also it is necessary to have integrity throughout the organization because one has to trust all the employees.[17]

At the same time, creating that culture means avoiding an atmosphere of fear and defensiveness that chills productivity. One way to do this is to make clear the difference between unethical conduct—or dishonest mistakes—and honest mistakes that may be an outgrowth of prudent risk taking in business. Alan Braverman, Senior Executive Vice President, General Counsel and Secretary of The Walt Disney Company, explained how this works:

With regard to unethical practices we have zero tolerance. Our CEO likes to say: if you're in a creative business, not only do you tolerate mistakes, but also you expect them, because if you're not making mistakes you're not being creative. On the other hand, there is zero tolerance for any dishonest mistake. We have a very rigorous standard of business conduct that is administered not only through regular training but also a very robust hotline where complaints can be received anonymously.

I sit on a committee that "dispenses justice" after it investigates the complaints. There is no regard to rank, and it is pretty well known here that if you lie on an expense report, you're out, and it doesn't matter if you're a janitor or a

---

16. Interview with Daniel Cooperman, Senior Vice President, General Counsel and Secretary, Apple Inc. (Sept. 1, 2009).

17. Interview with Daniel Desjardins, Senior Vice President, General Counsel and Assistant Secretary, Bombardier Inc. (May 20, 2011).

senior vice president. You're out! And if you're in the accounting profession and you make a mistake that is viewed as deliberate, in order to succumb to the pressure of the quarter, you're out. And if you're the supervisor and you were aware of it or should have been aware of it, you're very likely out. That pervades the culture pretty quickly. This type of zero-tolerance approach is probably why there's no graffiti in Singapore.

The combination of reinforcing the ethical, zero-tolerance message with lawyers and a culture of ethical practices where there are real and visible consequences for transgressions very much means we walk the walk when it comes to tone at the top. It can't just be speeches. The institution has to have the courage of its convictions, and I've got to tell you it's really hard. We have fired people for a terrible lapse of judgment even over something that on a financial scale was pretty small. [In one situation,] it was maybe $1,000, but that person was let go. That decision reverberates throughout the organization more than any speech.[18]

Hewlett-Packard Company felt that reverberation in 2010, when the company ousted its chairman and CEO, Mark V. Hurd, "for the lowliest of corporate offenses—fudging his expenses."[19] According to public sources, H-P's general counsel, Michael Holston, courageously exercised his independence in ensuring corporate integrity as he, along with outside counsel, led an investigation of sexual harassment charges against Hurd.[20] Although the sexual harassment charges were found to be unsubstantiated, the investigation revealed that Hurd had violated H-P's Standards of Business Conduct[21] by submitting inaccurate expense reports to cover up dealings with a female marketing contractor with whom Hurd had developed a "close personal relationship."[22] Holston was quoted at the time as saying that Hurd's action "showed a profound lack of judgment that seriously

18. Interview with Alan Braverman, Senior Executive Vice President, General Counsel and Secretary, The Walt Disney Company (Nov. 12, 2009); see also Martin, supra note 6, at 10 ("[E]thics training should reflect the culture and reinforce it. If your company hires unethical employees or overlooks ethical lapses, your training program is not credible.").

19. Ashlee Vance, Hewlett-Packard Ousts Chief for Hiding Payments to Friend, N.Y. TIMES, Aug. 7, 2010, at A1.

20. Sue Reisinger, How HP General Counsel Michael Holston Handled CEO's Sex Harassment Nightmare, CORP. COUNSEL, Aug. 2010.

21. Id.

22. Vance, supra note 19, at A1.

undermined his credibility and damaged his effectiveness."[23] H-P's ouster of Hurd demonstrated that the company would not tolerate violations of its codes of conduct by employees at any level.

A consistent, strong message about the consequences of unethical conduct can be complemented by senior management's visible, assertive promotion of an ethical culture and the positive consequences of behaving ethically under difficult circumstances. In short, "[e]thics training is not an event; it is delivered through observable and consistent leadership."[24] David Leitch, General Counsel and Group Vice President, Ford Motor Company, has emphasized that a company's ethics training program must be backed up by a positive tone at the top, which can be created only by the senior executives' active, visible engagement in the process.[25]

Louise Parent, Executive Vice President and General Counsel of American Express Company, has explained how she achieves positive visibility in connection with the periodic promotion of her company's codes of conduct:

> We roll out our codes of conduct across the world every two years and I try to personally lead a few training sessions so I can talk about specific incidents that I have observed where people have made tough decisions that were consistent with the code of conduct. Being very visible in that way for the organization is extremely helpful.[26]

Daniel Desjardins, Senior Vice President, General Counsel and Assistant Secretary of Bombardier Inc., operates in a corporate culture where about two thousand white collar employees must affirm in writing each year their adherence to ethical codes of the company.[27] Such efforts appear to enhance awareness and observance of an ethical culture throughout the employee

---

23. Ben Worthen & Pui-Wing Tam, *H-P Chief Quits in Scandal*, WALL ST. J., Aug. 7–8, 2010, at A1.

24. *See* Martin, *supra* note 6, at 10.

25. *See* Swanton, *supra* note 11, at 42 ("Leitch emphasizes that establishing an ethical culture can't simply be done online. 'Sometimes you have to show up,' he says. 'You can't sit on the top floor [of Ford's headquarters] in Dearborn, Mich., and emit a tone. You have to get out and talk to people in the field about how they are doing business and what their concerns are.'" (alteration in original)).

26. Interview with Louise M. Parent, Executive Vice President and General Counsel, American Express Company (Nov. 2, 2009).

27. Interview with Daniel Desjardins, Senior Vice President, General Counsel and Assistant Secretary, Bombardier Inc. (May 20, 2011).

ranks, as well as enhancing non-executive employees' trust in, and willingness to approach, the general counsel concerning serious issues.

These efforts are sometimes fruitful in visible ways. According to Parent, "one of the most satisfying moments" she has experienced as general counsel occurred when some junior employees halfway around the world identified her as the only person to whom they would speak to report an issue of concern. She describes the incident as follows:

> We have an ombuds office that people can contact [to report concerns] either with attribution or anonymously. But if they contact the ombuds office with attribution, the ombuds office will try to encourage the person to come forward and bring the complaint to somebody in senior management so that we can actually deal with the issue.
>
> Many years ago we had some people in a mid-eastern country who were very concerned about the conduct of some of their senior people. They were [non-senior] people in that country and they were speaking to our ombuds office in England. Personnel in that office said, "the concerns that you raise seem to be serious and we would like you to at least discuss them with somebody in New York so that they can be dealt with." But the people reporting the concerns said, "the only person we'll talk to is the general counsel."
>
> So, I felt: God bless this person for calling me across the world and for having trust and confidence that somebody in headquarters could help them. I thought it was just a huge endorsement. I felt very grateful. In fact, we actually did get to the bottom of what was going on without identifying that employee as the source of the information that led us to be concerned. And we actually ended up firing his boss who was eventually prosecuted for insider trading.
>
> You preach the gospel and you are never sure [it is received]. This person took an incredible risk because his boss was a pretty domineering kind of person. It is halfway around the world and it was just as likely that his boss would figure out what was up and he would get canned or worse. But instead he had the courage to explain what was going on.
>
> That was really one of the most satisfying moments I have had as general counsel.[28]

Thus, the general counsel is and should be a model for, promoter of, and a resource for ethical conduct throughout the company. Not only must she be one of the persons responsible for establishing and maintaining the

---

28. Interview with Louise M. Parent, Executive Vice President and General Counsel, American Express Company (Nov. 2, 2009).

company's code of business conduct and ethics,[29] but also she must person-ally adhere to the rules of professional responsibility that are imposed on her. In short, the CLO must teach by personal example.

B. ETHICS AND PROFESSIONAL CONDUCT RULES GOVERNING IN-HOUSE COUNSEL

The chief legal officer is a lawyer and a member of the bar. As such, she has taken an oath, which in essence is to uphold the integrity of the profession. If one scans the ABA Model Rules of Professional Conduct,[30] one can see a sampling of what compliance with the rules of the lawyer's jurisdiction may entail. Moreover, in the case of lawyers involved in public company filings with the Securities and Exchange Commission (SEC), there are additional

---

29. *See, e.g.,* New York Stock Exchange Listed Companies Manual § 303A.10 ("Listed companies must adopt and disclose a code of business conduct and ethics for directors, officers and employees, and promptly disclose any waivers of the code for directors or executive officers."), http://nysemanual.nyse.com/LCMTools/ PlatformViewer.asp?searched=1&selectednode=chp%5F1%5F4%5F3%5F1&CiRestric tion=303A&manual=%2Flcm%2Fsections%2Flcm%2Dsections%2F.

30. The Model Rules of Professional Conduct are promulgated by the American Bar Association (ABA). They are the official, recommended rules of the ABA, approved by the House of Delegates. The Model Rules are normally used as a template (often with changes) by each state supreme court in adopting and promulgating the official ethics rules of each of the states. The ethics rules adopted by the state supreme court where the general counsel or other in-house or outside corporate lawyer is admitted are the rules that apply to the particular lawyer. We use the Model Rules here as examples of provisions that might be applicable to a particular general counsel for purposes of her state ethical compliance. Norman Veasey, one of the co-authors of this book, was chair of the Commission to Evaluate the Model Rules of Professional Conduct ("Ethics 2000") during the period 1997 to 2003. The House of Delegates of the ABA approved in 2001 and 2002 most of the recommendations of Ethics 2000. Significantly, the form of Rule 1.6 (Confidentiality), which enabled lawyers in certain circumstances to report wrongdoings to prevent significant financial harm, as recommended by Ethics 2000, was not accepted in the 2001 vote of the House of Delegates. But it was ultimately accepted in 2003 as a result of Enron and other scandals of 2001–2002. A report by another ABA committee, chaired by James H. Cheek, III (the "Cheek Commission"), demonstrated the need for the Ethics 2000 provisions in 1.6(b)(2) and (3) to permit lawyers to disclose client confidences if reasonably necessary to prevent, mitigate, or rectify financial harm under certain circumstances. The Cheek Commission also rec-ommended changes to strengthen Model Rule 1.13 relating to the corporate lawyer's ethical responsibilities when the client is an organization, such as a corporation. The House of Delegates approved the recommendations of the Cheek Commission in 2003. The official name of the Cheek Commission is The American Bar Association Task Force on Corporate Responsibility, and its *Report of the American Bar Association Task Force on Corporate Responsibility* is published in 59 Bus. Law. 145 (2003).

requirements of professional responsibility. We turn first to state-based ethics rules.

1. State Rules of Professional Conduct

The ethical conduct directly and explicitly required of the chief legal officer and her in-house subordinates as members of the legal profession includes:

- being "a public citizen having special responsibility for the quality of justice;"[31]
- providing "competent representation" to the client, using "the legal knowledge, skill, thoroughness and preparation reasonably necessary for the representation;"[32]
- acting diligently, promptly, and, within legal and ethical parameters, "with commitment and dedication to the interests of the client and with zeal in advocacy upon the client's behalf," "despite opposition, obstruction or personal inconvenience to the lawyer;"[33]
- not counseling the client "to engage, or assist a client, in conduct that the lawyer knows is criminal or fraudulent," with the understanding that the lawyer "may discuss the legal consequences of any proposed course of conduct with a client and may counsel or assist a client to make a good faith effort to determine the validity, scope, meaning or application of the law;"[34]
- continually assessing whether a client's activity is criminal or fraudulent and whether the lawyer is assisting in any such conduct;[35]
- engaging in prompt and open communication with the client, including with respect to ethical issues;[36]
- protecting the confidentiality of information relating to the representation of the client, except to prevent death or substantial bodily harm or to prevent the client from committing substantial crimes or frauds (or prevent, mitigate, or rectify substantial injury from a client's

---

31. MODEL RULES OF PROF'L CONDUCT preamble (2010).
32. *Id.* R.1.1.
33. *Id.* R.1.3; R.1.3 cmt. 1.
34. *Id.* R.1.2; *see also id.* R.1.2 cmt. 9 ("There is a critical distinction between presenting an analysis of legal aspects of questionable conduct and recommending the means by which a crime or fraud might be committed with impunity.").
35. *See id.* R.1.2. cmt. 10 ("A lawyer may not continue assisting a client in conduct that the lawyer originally supposed was legally proper but then discovers is criminal or fraudulent.").
36. *See id.* R.1.4.

commission of a crime or fraud) in furtherance of which the client has used or is using the lawyer's services;[37]

- avoiding conflicts of interest;[38]
- exercising "independent professional judgment" and rendering "candid advice" that is not limited to narrow legal technicalities, but instead refers as well to relevant "moral, economic, social and political factors,"[39] even if the advice is "unpalatable";[40]
- being truthful, including to persons other than the client;[41]
- withdrawing from a representation that is facilitating a client's crime or fraud, and giving notice of the withdrawal or disaffirming an opinion, document, or affirmation, if necessary;[42]
- ensuring that lawyers over which she has direct supervisory authority conduct themselves in an ethical manner;[43]
- avoiding misconduct, including:
  - violating the Rules of Professional Conduct or knowingly assisting or inducing another to do so;
  - committing a criminal act that "reflects adversely on the lawyer's honesty, trustworthiness or fitness as a lawyer in other respects";
  - engaging in "conduct involving dishonesty, fraud, deceit or misrepresentation";
  - engaging in "conduct that is prejudicial to the administration of justice";
  - stating or implying an ability to improperly influence a government agency or official; or
  - knowingly assisting a judicial officer in conduct that violates applicable rules of judicial conduct or other law.[44]

37. *See id.* R.1.6; *see also id.* R.1.6 cmt. 2 (discussing how confidentiality fosters the client-lawyer relationship and facilitates open communication and the effective provision of legal advice); *id.* R.1.6 cmt. 3 (describing the differences between client-lawyer confidentiality and the attorney-client privilege and the work-product doctrine); *id.* cmts. 7, 8 (expounding upon the crime-fraud exception to the confidentiality rule).
38. *See id.* R.1.7.
39. *See id.* R.2.1.
40. *See id.* R.2.1 cmt. 1; *see also id.* R.2.1. cmt. 2 ("Advice couched in narrow legal terms may be of little value to a client, especially where practical considerations, such as cost or effects on other people, are predominant. Purely technical legal advice, therefore, can sometimes be inadequate. It is proper for a lawyer to refer to relevant moral and ethical considerations in giving advice. Although a lawyer is not a moral advisor as such, moral and ethical considerations impinge upon most legal questions and may decisively influence how the law will be applied.").
41. *See id.* R.4.1.
42. *See id.* R.4.1 cmt. 3.
43. *See id.* R.5.1.
44. *See id.* R.8.4.

Rule 1.13 of the Model Rules applies when the client is an organization, and thus always applies to the chief legal officer, her in-house subordinates, and outside counsel. Key features of the application in the corporate context include:

- the client is the corporation, acting through its duly authorized representatives (its officers, directors, employees and shareholders);[45]
- a communication between an officer, director, employee, or shareholder communicating in that person's corporate capacity with a corporate lawyer is protected by client-lawyer confidentiality. This protection is for the corporation's benefit, and the person should not become a client of the lawyer;[46]
- a corporate lawyer who knows that someone associated with the corporation is violating a legal obligation to the corporation or engaging in a violation of law that reasonably might be imputed to the corporation, and that is likely to result in substantial injury to the corporation, must "proceed as is reasonably necessary in the best interest" of the corporation, including referring the matter to higher authority within the corporation and even up to highest authority in the corporation (generally the board of directors or the independent directors);[47]
- if the board fails to address the issue in a timely and appropriate manner, the lawyer may—but is not required to—reveal confidential

45. *Id.* R.1.13(a); *id.* R.1.13 cmt. 1.
46. *Id.* R.1.13 cmt. 2.
47. *Id.* R.1.13(b); *id.* R.1.13 cmt. 5; *see also id.* R.1.13 cmt. 4 ("[T]he lawyer should give due consideration to the seriousness of the violation and its consequences, the responsibility in the organization and the apparent motivation of the person involved, the policies of the organization concerning such matters, and any other relevant considerations. Ordinarily, referral to a higher authority would be necessary. In some circumstances, however, it may be appropriate for the lawyer to ask the constituent to reconsider the matter; for example, if the circumstances involve a constituent's innocent misunderstanding of law and subsequent acceptance of the lawyer's advice, the lawyer may reasonably conclude that the best interest of the organization does not require that the matter be referred to higher authority. If a constituent persists in conduct contrary to the lawyer's advice, it will be necessary for the lawyer to take steps to have the matter reviewed by a higher authority in the organization. If the matter is of sufficient seriousness and importance or urgency to the organization, referral to higher authority in the organization may be necessary even if the lawyer has not communicated with the constituent. Any measures taken should, to the extent practicable, minimize the risk of revealing information relating to the representation to persons outside the organization. Even in circumstances where a lawyer is not obligated by Rule 1.13 to proceed, a lawyer may bring to the attention of an organizational client, including its highest authority, matters that the lawyer reasonably believes to be of sufficient importance to warrant doing so in the best interest of the organization.").

information to the extent the lawyer reasonably believes necessary to prevent substantial injury to the corporation;[48]

- unless the "reporting up" or "reporting out" rules apply, "[w]hen constituents of the organization make decisions for it, the decisions ordinarily must be accepted by the lawyer even if their utility or prudence is doubtful. Decisions concerning policy and operations, including ones entailing serious risk, are not as such in the lawyer's province";[49]
- if the corporation's interests are adverse or may become adverse to one or more of the corporation's constituents, the lawyer should advise the relevant constituent that the lawyer cannot represent the constituent and that independent representation may be desirable.[50]

2. SEC Rules for Lawyers Involved in Public Company Filings

In addition to state rules of ethics, when a public company is required to provide SEC filings, the chief legal officer, her subordinate in-house lawyers, and outside counsel involved in work related to those filings must comply with Part 205 of the SEC rules adopted pursuant to Section 307 of the Sarbanes-Oxley Act.[51] Pursuant to the Act, Part 205 establishes "minimum standards of professional conduct for attorneys appearing and

---

48. *Id.* R.1.13(c). Note that Model Rule 1.6(c)(2) and (c)(3) permit revealing a client's confidence in this context only if the lawyer's services are being used as part of the misconduct. But Model Rule 1.13(c) does not contain that limitation, and therefore it trumps Rule 1.6 in this context.

49. *Id.* R.1.13 cmt. 3.

50. *Id.* R.1.13 cmt. 10.

51. 17 C.F.R. pt. 205. Section 307 of the Sarbanes-Oxley Act of 2002 mandates that the Commission:

> shall issue rules, in the public interest and for the protection of investors, setting forth minimum standards of professional conduct for attorneys appearing and practicing before the Commission in any way in the representation of issuers, including a rule –
>
> (1) requiring an attorney to report evidence of a material violation of securities law or breach of fiduciary duty or similar violation by the company or any agent thereof, to the chief legal counsel or the chief executive officer of the company (or the equivalent thereof); and
>
> (2) if the counsel or officer does not appropriately respond to the evidence (adopting, as necessary, appropriate remedial measures or sanctions with respect to the violation), requiring the attorney to report the evidence to the audit committee of the board of directors of the issuer or to another committee of the board of directors comprised solely of directors not employed directly or indirectly by the issuer, or to the board of directors.

15 U.S.C. § 7245.

practicing before the Commission in the representation of an issuer."[52] The rules set forth in Part 205 "supplement applicable standards of any jurisdiction where an attorney is admitted or practices."[53]

The standards in Part 205 are in some ways similar to Rule 1.13 of the Model Rules of Professional Conduct. For example, section 205.3(a) provides that an attorney representing an issuer "owes his or her professional and ethical duties to the issuer as an organization. That the attorney may work with and advise the issuer's officers, directors, or employees in the course of representing the issuer does not make such individuals the attorney's clients."[54] Similar to Model Rule 1.13, Part 205 of the SEC rules is centered on the "reporting up" requirement and a "reporting out" option.

As noted, Part 205 applies to lawyers "appearing and practicing before the Commission" and is a densely written and very exacting set of detailed rules. This broad definition seems to encompass any lawyer who participates in developing or approving almost any information that ends up in an SEC filing.[55] The CLO and her subordinate in-house lawyers need to understand fully the intricacies of the entirety of Part 205. Part 205, while focusing on many of the same goals as Model Rule 1.13, uses some significantly different terms, many of which are defined in the lengthy definition section.[56] For example, Model Rule 1.13 imposes an up-the-ladder reporting requirement on a lawyer who "knows" of potential wrongdoing.[57] The SEC rules impose their version of the up-the-ladder reporting requirement

52. 17 C.F.R. § 205.1. See *infra* note 55 for the definition of "appearing and practicing before the Commission."

53. 17 C.F.R. § 205.1.

54. *Id.* § 205.3(a).

55. *Id.* § 205.2(a)(1)(iii) (defining "[a]ppearing and practicing before the Commission" as "[p]roviding advice in respect of the United States securities laws or the Commission's rules or regulations thereunder regarding any document that the attorney has notice will be filed with or submitted to, or incorporated into any document that will be filed with or submitted to, the Commission, including the provision of such advice in the context of preparing, or participating in the preparation of, any such document").

56. *Id.* § 205.2.

57. MODEL RULES OF PROF'L CONDUCT R.1.13(b) ("If a lawyer for an organization knows that an officer, employee or other person associated with the organization is engaged in action, intends to act or refuses to act in a matter related to the representation that is a violation of a legal obligation to the organization, or a violation of law that reasonably might be imputed to the organization, and that is likely to result in substantial injury to the organization, then the lawyer shall proceed as is reasonably necessary in the best interest of the organization. Unless the lawyer reasonably believes that it is not necessary in the best interest of the organization to do so, the lawyer shall refer the matter to higher authority in the organization, including, if warranted by the circumstances, to the highest authority that can act on behalf of the organization as determined by applicable law.").

on any covered corporate lawyer who "becomes aware of evidence of a material violation."[58] The terms applicable in this context are defined, as well.[59] The foregoing is only one example of the language differences between the Model Rules and the SEC rules.

We refer the reader to an excellent, succinct, and understandable explication in plain English of the essence of the rules. We quote below the description of the SEC rules by Fox and Martyn in their excellent book on the ethics of lawyers when representing organizations:

> Obligations of Lawyers under SEC Regulations Adopted Pursuant to Sarbanes-Oxley
>
> A Lawyer who provides advice to any client with respect to any matter described or that should have been described in an SEC filing, who becomes aware of credible evidence that a material violation (violation of any federal or state securities law or material breach of fiduciary duty under federal or state law) has likely occurred by the issuer or officers, directors, employees or agents of issuer shall report evidence of the violation to the CLO (Chief Legal Officer) or CLO and CEO of the issuer.
>
> CLO or CEO shall investigate whether a violation has occurred.
>
> Unless the lawyer reasonably believes that CLO or CEO has made an appropriate response that no violation has or is about to occur, that reasonable remedial measures have been undertaken, or with board approval an investigation has been undertaken that will result in either remedial action or a colorable defense to the matter can be asserted, within a reasonable time, lawyer shall report violation to:
>
> An audit committee of the board of directors, or
>
> A committee of outside directors, or
>
> The entire board of directors, or
>
> A qualified legal compliance committee of the board (QLCC).

---

58. 17 C.F.R. § 205.3(b) ("*Duty to report evidence of a material violation.* (1) If an attorney, appearing and practicing before the Commission in the representation of an issuer, becomes aware of evidence of a material violation by the issuer or by any officer, director, employee, or agent of the issuer, the attorney shall report such evidence to the issuer's chief legal officer (or the equivalent thereof) or to both the issuer's chief legal officer and its chief executive officer (or the equivalents thereof) forthwith. By communicating such information to the issuer's officers or directors, an attorney does not reveal client confidences or secrets or privileged or otherwise protected information related to the attorney's representation of an issuer.").

59. *Id.* § 205.2(e) ("Evidence of a material violation means credible evidence, based upon which it would be unreasonable, under the circumstances, for a prudent and competent attorney not to conclude that it is reasonably likely that a material violation has occurred, is ongoing, or is about to occur.").

Except where the lawyer has reported to a QLCC, the lawyer has an obligation to assess whether the issuer has appropriately responded. A lawyer who does not reasonably believe that the issuer has made an appropriate response within a reasonable time shall explain his or her reasons therefore to the CLO, CEO and the directors, and may disclose confidential information to the SEC to the extent the lawyer reasonably believes necessary:

To prevent material violations likely to cause substantial injury to the financial interest or property of the issuer or investors;

To prevent the issuer from committing perjury or acts likely to perpetrate a fraud upon the Commission;

To rectify the consequences of a material violation by the issuer that may cause substantial injury to the financial interest or property of the issuer or investors, in furtherance of which the lawyer's services were used.

Subordinate lawyers (those who appear or practice before the SEC under the direct supervision or direction of another lawyer) comply by reporting evidence of a material violation to their supervising lawyer, and may take the steps permitted or required above if the subordinate lawyer reasonably believes that the supervisory lawyer to whom he or she has reported has failed to comply with the regulatory requirements.

Violation of these regulations can result in discipline by the SEC, including disbarment. The regulations also provide that lawyers who comply cannot be held civilly liable or disciplined under any inconsistent state rule, though this grant of immunity has not been tested to date.

Lawyers who are fired for complying with the good regulations may report the firing to the Board of Directors.

The SEC has threatened, but to date never decided, to impose mandatory disclosure obligations on lawyers when they do not believe that the entity has made an appropriate response.[60]

Fox and Martyn also include in their book an excellent table comparing Model Rule 1.13 with Part 205.[61]

The chief legal officer, as an attorney who supervises the work of other lawyers, is generally subject to the duties and obligations set forth, in a manner similar to the Model Rules, in Part 205.[62] Part 205 explicitly states that "[t]o the extent a subordinate attorney appears and practices before the Commission in the representation of an issuer, that subordinate

60. Lawrence J. Fox & Susan R. Martyn, The Ethics of Representing Organizations 258–60 (2009).
61. *Id.* at 260–61.
62. 17 C.F.R.§ 205.4(a).

attorney's supervisory attorneys also appear and practice before the Commission."[63] The obligations of supervisory attorneys include making reasonable efforts to ensure that subordinate attorneys comply with the rules established by Part 205[64] and fulfilling the duties of the supervisory and subordinate attorney in the "reporting up" context.[65]

All of the foregoing having been said about the general counsel and her in-house lawyers being the guardians of corporate integrity, there is a caveat involving human nature to consider. Is there sometimes an incentive for counsel to overlook, rationalize, or fail to press other actors in corporate management when potential wrongdoing is not clear, but shrouded in shades of gray? Are section 307 of SOX and the SEC Part 205 rules strong enough to provide lawyers with incentives to be diligent in respecting their up-the-ladder obligations? Or, do they impair or chill appropriate candor between lawyers and their corporate constituents who may be skeptical and chary of frank communications with the corporation's lawyers? Consider the following interesting observations from Professor Stephen Bainbridge:

> The nature of the legal market gives lawyers—both in-house and outside counsel—strong incentives to overlook management wrongdoing. As to the former, even if the board of directors formally appoints the in-house general counsel, his tenure normally depends mainly on his relationship with the CEO. . . . Consequently, despite an attorney's overarching legal obligations to report misconduct, he might be inclined to intentionally or subconsciously "overlook" marginal conduct. . . . As to both [in-house and outside counsel], moreover, although their ultimate duty is owed to the corporation itself, their daily responsibilities involve dealing with management and they thus often develop a de facto loyalty to management that trumps their de jure duties.
>
> . . . . Because the management-attorney relationship tends to become the focus of the attorney's relationship with the firm, however, lawyers have strong incentives to help management control the flow of information to the board of directors.
>
> Worse yet, attorneys may be tempted to turn a blind eye to managerial misconduct or even to facilitate such misconduct. . . .
>
> . . . . By enlisting legal counsel as aides of the board, Sarbanes-Oxley sought properly to help shift the *de facto* balance of power between boards and managements towards the *de jure* model of director primacy. But will it work?

---

63. *Id.* § 205.4(b).
64. *Id.*
65. *Id.* § 205.4(c), (d).

. . . .

. . . . Under Part 205, an attorney should only go up the ladder where management has failed to properly address or remedy the situation. In practice, this approach means that only a fraction of reports will ever make it beyond the CEO/CLO stage.

. . . .

. . . . It typically is personally beneficial for lawyers to refrain from antagonizing the corporate managers who hire and fire them. The claim is not that lawyers are pervasively co-opted or immoral. The claim is only that lawyers have both economic incentives and cognitive biases that systematically incline them to stay on the good side of the corporation's managers. Hence, absent the proverbial smoking gun, we can expect lawyers to turn a blind eye to indicia of misconduct by those managers. Section 307 does too little to change those incentives.

. . . .

As many commentators complained during the regulatory process, the Part 205 Regulations nevertheless still may have a chilling effect on attorney-client communication. Even corporate managers not engaged in actual misconduct will not welcome the investigation that an attorney's reporting up would engender, especially where there is a possibility that counsel will go over their heads. Managers therefore may withhold information from counsel, so as to withhold it from the board, especially when the managers are knowingly pursuing an aggressive course of conduct. . . .

. . . .

The SEC was quite reticent in exercising its authority under § 307. Consistent with the spirit of Sarbanes-Oxley the SEC might have been even more aggressive in pressing lawyers to communicate with the board of directors. The SEC might have required, for example, that the audit committee and/or the board meet periodically with the general counsel outside the presence of other managers and inside directors.

. . . .

There is a very real risk that the new post-SOX legal ethics rules will make the lawyer-client relationship more adversarial and less productive. Such a deterioration in the lawyer-client relationship would be most unfortunate. Corporate lawyers are one of [the] basic categories of advisors who play a critical role in virtually all corporate transactions. . . .

At the end of the day, § 307—warts and all—was necessary to break the organized bar's resistance to legal ethics reforms intended to reduce the managerialist bias of the rules of professional conduct. Corporate counsel work for the board, not management. Only by threatening lawyers who fail to report up-the-ladder with discipline could the balance of power be shifted in favor of directors relative to managers.

.... In consultation with the audit committee, the general counsel and principal outside counsel should develop a written policy for identifying and reporting violations. The board members, CEO, and CFO should be briefed on their legal obligations with respect to reports, but also encouraged to view a report as a potential win-win situation rather than a zero-sum or adversarial game. Up-the-ladder reporting can give the firm an opportunity to cut off potential violations before they mature into a legal or public relations nightmare, but only if counsel and managers are willing to trust one another.[66]

One could reasonably argue that Congress and the SEC did, in fact, go far in mandating proper lawyer conduct in the corporate governance arena. Nevertheless, there is room, consistent with Professor Bainbridge's observations above and the Cheek Report,[67] to encourage some private ordering. That is, the general counsel and the board of directors might consider having the board adopt a stated corporate policy that the audit committee or the independent directors meet routinely and periodically—rather than episodically—with the general counsel outside the presence of other managers and insider directors. That way, it will not be only a special occasion that will trigger such a meeting, raising suspicions and, potentially, hackles.

In fact, general counsel may want to share with the board some of the suggested policies advanced by the Cheek Report:

[M]any corporate boards have developed a culture of passivity with respect to senior executive officers, in which those officers are not subject to meaningful director oversight. Direct legislative action or the imposition of legal sanctions to change this culture may produce a confrontational climate in the board room which would have undesirable consequences. The Task Force believes, rather, that desirable changes in attitude can most effectively be encouraged by a variety of structural and procedural reforms.

....

1. The board of directors of a public corporation must engage in active, independent and informed oversight of the corporation's business and affairs, including its senior management.

....

4. Providing information and analysis necessary for the directors to discharge their oversight responsibilities, particularly as they relate to legal compliance

---

66. BAINBRIDGE, *supra* chapter I, note 2, at 293–95, 301–02, 305–07, 310–11, 314–15.
67. Cheek Report, *supra* chapter III, note 45 (establishing recommended policies of corporate governance for companies to follow).

matters, requires the active involvement of general counsel for the public corporation.

. . . .

7. Public corporations should adopt practices in which:

   a. The selection, retention, and compensation of the corporation's general counsel are approved by the board of directors.

   b. General counsel meets regularly and in executive session with a committee of independent directors to communicate concerns regarding legal compliance matters, including potential or ongoing material violations of law by, and breaches of fiduciary duty to, the corporation.

   c. All reporting relationships of internal and outside lawyers for a public corporation establish at the outset a direct line of communication with general counsel through which these lawyers are to inform the general counsel of material potential or ongoing violations of law by, and breaches of fiduciary duty to, the corporation.[68]

There may, however, be some general counsel who would regard a practice of regular meetings between the CLO and the independent directors as uncomfortable, as it may imply that there is a need for the directors to discuss with the CLO, *in camera*, their observations about the CEO. "Corporate America" should be assured that the general counsel is expected not only to live up to the high moral and ethical standards embodied in her responsibilities as a member of the bar, but also that there are unique expectations by virtue of her position as chief legal officer of the corporation.[69]

Indeed, the theme of this book focuses on expectations. As noted throughout this book, we place heavy emphasis on the unique concept that the CLO is the "partner-guardian." So, as she "labors" in the business "vineyard" with the CEO, CFO, COO, and other officers and senior executives in the C-Suite, she must practice and preach the highest principles of ethics and integrity in that milieu. Significantly, as well, she must do so when she counsels the directors as their principal legal advisor.

The vast majority of general counsel fulfill these duties and exhibit strong leadership in promoting an integrated ethical culture throughout the corporation. These general counsel employ certain qualities of mind— creativity, constructiveness, persuasive articulation, an ability to balance fairly competing values, strong capacity for risk assessment (but not risk

---

68. *Id.* at 159–60 (footnote omitted).

69. *See generally* FOX & MARTYN, *supra* note 60 (providing an excellent discussion of ethical issues facing the lawyer for the corporation or other entity).

aversion), skills for practical implementation of rules, political savvy, cooperation, an interdisciplinary understanding, a global worldview—as well as a values-driven mindset to guide their institutions to ethical results.[70]

C. DEMONSTRATING OPENNESS AND COMMUNITY INVOLVEMENT

1. Corporate Citizenship

As part of the general counsel's role in creating and fostering an ethical corporate culture, she may also be called upon to contribute to, or even oversee, the company's efforts regarding corporate citizenship (also known as "corporate social responsibility" or "CSR"). As a general matter, corporate citizenship or CSR "is a business concept pursuant to which companies seek to address social and environmental issues through support for international legal norms and sustainable business practices."[71]

One of the goals of a corporate citizenship program is to ensure that the company follows internationally-adopted standards relating to such issues as labor conditions and environmental practices, which may not be adequately implemented by regulators in certain locales.[72] Thus, corporate citizenship efforts bolster the rule of law through self-enforcement of international standards that may be in place but not enforced in some areas.[73] Because these issues lie at the intersection of law, business, public relations, and risk management,[74] the general counsel is well situated to be a leader among the key players in a company's corporate social responsibility initiatives.[75]

---

70. Heineman, *supra* note 2, at 6.

71. Interview with Gare A. Smith & Daniel F. Feldman, *Corporate Social Responsibility: Mitigating Legal and Reputational Risk in the Global Arena*, METRO. CORP. COUNSEL (Oct. 2006).

72. *Id.*

73. *Id.*

74. *See* Interview with Michael R. Levin, *Risk Management Requires Legal and Compliance Officers to Focus on Corporate Social Responsibility*, METRO. CORP. COUNSEL (May 2007) [hereinafter *Focus on Corporate Social Responsibility*] (discussing the role of corporate social responsibility in risk management, and the difference between corporate social responsibility and corporate philanthropic initiatives).

75. *See id.* ("CSR lends itself well to corporate risk reduction, and as such, should be overseen by those with the tools to manage such risks—the Chief Legal Officer or the Chief Compliance and Ethics Officers. Increasingly, we see individuals with the title Corporate Responsibility Officer (CRO). Individuals holding this title tend to work toward creating overall corporate strategy incorporating CSR principles which is critical. As part of this strategy, Chief Legal and Chief Compliance Officers should play

Corporations have a variety of social responsibilities as participants in, and beneficiaries of, society. As articulated by John G. Ruggie, Special Representative of the UN Secretary-General on Business and Human Rights, "in addition to compliance with national laws, the baseline responsibility of companies is to respect human rights. . . . The responsibility exists even where national laws are absent or not enforced because respecting rights is the very foundation of a company's social license to operate."[76]

In addition to a general duty to behave as socially responsible participants in society, conducting corporate affairs in a socially responsible manner makes good business sense and may even be a matter of compliance or liability.[77] The Report of Weil, Gotshal & Manges LLP for the U.N. Corporate Law Project of the Special Representative of the Secretary-General (SRSG) on the Issue of Human Rights and Transnational Corporations and Other Business Enterprises explains:

> Apart from abiding by laws and regulations, corporations owe no specific duty to society. However, they are permitted to use corporate resources for public welfare, humanitarian, educational or philanthropic purposes where consistent with the interests of the company and its shareholders. They are encouraged by a variety of forces to act ethically and in socially and environmentally responsible ways above the requirements of law and regulation. It is common for

a part."); *see also* Interview with Kristin Campbell, Senior Vice President and General Counsel, Staples, Inc. (Oct. 28, 2009) ("I am one of Staples's cultural officers, both because I am the Compliance Officer and because I am responsible for oversight of much of our CSR work. Our outreach to shareholders not only addresses our responsiveness to shareholders on issues like majority voting; it also addresses what we are doing for the environment and what we are doing in the community. In my view, that is part of corporate governance.").

76. Report of Weil, Gotshal & Manges LLP for the U.N. Corporate Law Project of the Special Representative of the Secretary-General (SRSG) on the Issue of Human Rights and Transnational Corporations and Other Business Enterprises 3 (Aug. 2010) [hereinafter *Ruggie Report*], *available at* http://www.reports-and-materials.org/Corp-law-tools-USA-Weil-Gotshal-Manges-for-Ruggie-Aug-2010.pdf. "[T]he corporate responsibility to respect human rights . . . in essence means to act with due diligence to avoid infringing on the rights of others." *Id.* at 2.

77. *See id.* at 3 ("[C]ompanies may face non-compliance with corporate and securities laws where they fail to adequately assess and aggregate stakeholder-related risks, including human rights risks, and thus may be less likely to effectively disclose and address them, as may be required."); *see also id.* at 5, 7 (noting that implementing an effective compliance and ethics program may help to minimize potential liability under the United States Federal Sentencing Guidelines and discussing disclosure requirements relating to such issues as human rights violations or environmental damage).

corporations in the U.S. to engage in such activities because, in part due to reputational interests, it is often good business sense to do so.[78]

Joe W. (Chip) Pitts III, former chief legal officer of Nokia, Inc. and Chair of Amnesty International USA, has identified the key business-related drivers of corporate social responsibility efforts as "brand/reputation assurance, business productivity, risk management, [and] employee recruitment and retention."[79] The practical, business- and reputation-driven effects are likely to be enhanced as technology rapidly increases the public visibility and transparency of corporate actions around the world.[80]

Good corporate citizenship creates a symbiotic relationship of benefit for communities and corporations. An example of the social and corporate benefits that arise can be found in PepsiCo's program of buying corn and sunflowers directly from small local farmers in an area near two PepsiCo plants in Mexico.[81] In contrast to the system formerly in place—in which the farmers had to sell their crops to middlemen—PepsiCo's upfront price guarantees enable the farmers to obtain credit, which allows them to buy seeds, fertilizer, crop insurance, and equipment.[82] PepsiCo achieves direct business benefits—reduced transportation costs and access to crop varieties best suited to its needs—as well as indirect benefits in the form of goodwill.[83] The social and environmental benefits reportedly include higher educational and nutritional standards among participating farmers, positive

78. *Id.* at 4–5, 10; *see also, e.g.,* GE 2009 CITIZENSHIP REPORT, RENEWING RESPONSIBILITIES 5 (July 2010) ("Citizenship is not a spectator sport. Companies with global reach and impact like GE must set commercial priorities to increase shareholder value while recognizing that our business foundation rests on forward progress on public policy imperatives. GE is making a dedicated effort to develop its business strategy so that its products and services have a positive human impact and produce long-term business success."), http://www.ge.com/citizenship/.

79. Joe W. (Chip) Pitts III, *Corporate Social Responsibility: Current Status and Future Evolution,* 6 RUTGERS J.L. & PUB. POLICY 334, 337 (2009); *see also* Cathleen Flahardy, *Refreshing Communities,* INSIDE COUNSEL, May 2011, at 91 (describing the Coca-Cola legal department's community service initiatives and stating that "[w]hether in-house lawyers are doing traditional pro bono work or other community service, [the chair of Coca-Cola's pro bono committee] believes these efforts improve overall morale within the legal department. 'They feel the work they do in the community is valued,' she says. 'It's a win-win for everyone.'").

80. *See* Pitts, *supra* note 79, at 335–37 (discussing the "historically unprecedented degree of technology-driven transparency, scrutiny, and accountability" relating to corporate social impacts and stating that this trend "is likely the most important and enduring of all the drivers for [corporate social responsibility principles]").

81. Stephanie Strom, *When Business Is Good,* N.Y. TIMES, Feb. 22, 2011, at B1.

82. *Id.*

83. *Id.* at B8.

impacts on illegal immigration to the United States, environmental benefits, increased community cooperation, market stabilization, and perhaps even a reduction in marijuana production.[84]

Discourse concerning corporate citizenship sometimes evokes "a debate over the duties of corporate fiduciaries with respect to the maximization and distribution of wealth owned by the corporation and the opportunities available to the corporation."[85] In that vein, many states' corporation laws include "other constituency" statutes, provisions that expressly permit the board of directors to consider the impact of a decision on a variety of constituents or social factors—such as employees, customers, suppliers, creditors, the community, social interests, and the economy of the state and the nation—in determining the best interests of the corporation.[86]

Although Delaware does not have such a statute, Delaware jurisprudence leaves room for the directors to take into account, in certain circumstances, the interests of stakeholders (such as creditors) other than stockholders when consideration of such interests is in the corporation's best interests.[87] Similarly, the American Law Institute's *Principles of Corporate Governance* state that the corporation and its fiduciaries may take into account ethical considerations when evaluating the corporation's best interests, even if they are not tied directly to any economic gain.[88] Examples of such actions

84. *Id.*
85. Robert Ashford, *The Socio-Economic Foundation of Corporate Law and Corporate Social Responsibility*, 76 TUL. L. REV. 1187, 1190 (2002).
86. *Ruggie Report, supra* note 76, at 10, 13–14. As a general matter, these provisions are designed to enable takeover defenses rather than to express altruistic motives. *See generally* Roberta Romano, *What Is the Value of Other Constituency Statutes to Shareholders?*, 43 U. TORONTO L.J. 533, 533–36 (1993).
87. *See, e.g.*, Trenwick Am. Litig. Trust v. Ernst Young LLP, 906 A.2d 168 (Del. Ch. 2006), aff'd sub nom Trenwick Am. Litig. Trust v. Billett, No. 496, 2007 WL 2317768 (Del. Aug. 14, 2007); Production Resources Group LLC v. NCT Group, Inc., 863 A.2d 772 (Del. Ch. 2004); Credit Lyonnais Bank Nederland N.V. v. Pathe Commc'ns Corp., No. 12150, 1991 Del. Ch. LEXIS 215 (Del. Ch. Dec. 30, 1991); E. Norman Veasey, *Counseling the Board of Directors of a Delaware Corporation in Distress*, AM. BANKR. INST. J., June 2008, at 1, 64 (discussing *Credit Lyonnais, Production Resources*, and *Trenwick*).
88. *See* 1 AMERICAN LAW INSTITUTE, PRINCIPLES OF CORPORATE GOVERNANCE § 2.01 & cmt. h ("The ethical considerations reasonably regarded as appropriate to the responsible conduct of business necessarily include ethical responsibilities that may be owed to persons other than the shareholders with whom the corporation has a legitimate concern, such as employees, customers, suppliers, and members of the communities within which the corporation operates."); *id.* § 4.01 & cmt. d (1994) ("There are, of course, instances when § 2.01 would permit the corporation to voluntarily forgo economic benefit—or accept economic detriment—in furtherance of stipulated public policies. This could happen, for example, when the corporation takes account of ethical considerations that are reasonably regarded as appropriate to the responsible conduct of business or devotes resources to public welfare, humanitarian, educational,

may include those "aimed at maintaining the confidence of business organizations with which the corporation deals [or] fostering the morale of employees."[89] Additionally, some states' corporation statutes include provisions permitting a corporation's charter to authorize or direct the corporation to conduct its business in a socially and environmentally responsible manner.[90]

In addition to the fact that corporate fiduciaries generally are permitted to consider matters other than pure stockholder wealth maximization, a wide range of statutes and regulations impose on corporations specific obligations—whether affirmative or prohibitive—relating to social or environmental issues or concerns. For example, the Dodd-Frank Wall Street Reform and Consumer Protection Act[91] requires companies to report, in accordance with SEC regulations promulgated under the Act, their use of "conflict minerals" originating in the Democratic Republic of the Congo.[92] The key focus of directors and officers must be the best interests of the corporate entity, and compliance with statutory or regulatory requirements is an essential component of determining those best interests. The point here, however, is that corporate social responsibility efforts often far exceed any obligations imposed by law or regulation, and the general counsel often is one of the leaders of those efforts.[93]

A CSR initiative tends to fit well within the framework of existing corporate efforts surrounding compliance and ethics. The steps, as a general matter, are

- assembling the appropriate team, which often includes the general counsel, ethics and compliance officers, and corporate-citizenship-dedicated officers;
- identifying potential trouble spots and the company's most significant corporate citizenship risks and opportunities;

---

or philanthropic purposes. Such actions, even though they may be inconsistent with profit enhancement, should be considered in the best interests of the corporation and wholly consistent with the obligations set forth in § 4.01." (citations omitted)).

89. *Ruggie Report*, *supra* note 76, at 11.

90. *E.g.*, OR. REV. STAT. § 60.047(2)(e).

91. Pub. L. No. 111–203, 124 Stat. 1376 (2010).

92. Pub. L. No. 111–203, § 1502; *see also* 15 U.S.C. § 78(m) (codifying the reporting requirement).

93. *Cf.* Ashford, *supra* note 85, at 1192 ("The questions of corporate fiduciary duties, corporate social responsibility, and lawyers' professional responsibility all connect in the role of general counsel of a large corporation. . . .").

- setting the tone at the top by communicating to (and training, as applicable) employees, suppliers, investors, and customers the company's corporate citizenship commitments;
- tracking global standards and verifying the company's conformance to those standards and the effectiveness of the corporate citizenship efforts;
- reporting results to stakeholders.[94]

As a general matter, U.S. companies are not required to report or disclose their corporate social responsibility efforts, except to the extent that specific issues implicate particular disclosure rules, such as the duty under the federal securities laws to inform investors of material information, including material foreseeable risks.[95] Some other governments, such as France, South Africa, and Australia, do require companies to include CSR information in their annual reports.[96] A number of U.S. companies elect to disclose information regarding their corporate social responsibility initiatives, even where the information is not material and disclosure is not otherwise required by law. Microsoft, ExxonMobil, GE, and Starbucks are just some examples of companies that voluntarily produce corporate social responsibility reports.[97]

2. Diversity

General counsel have also taken the lead in fostering diversity and inclusion efforts within their corporations. U.S. public companies must disclose whether and the extent to which their nominating committees consider diversity in selecting director candidates.[98] But "[m]ost corporate boards

94. *Focus on Corporate Social Responsibility, supra* note 74.
95. *See Ruggie Report, supra* note 76, at 16. See also, for example, the discussion, *supra* note 92 & accompanying text, of the Dodd-Frank Act provision requiring disclosure regarding conflict minerals.
96. *Focus on Corporate Social Responsibility, supra* note 74.
97. *Ruggie Report, supra* note 76, at 16.
98. *See* 17 C.F.R. § 229.407(c)(2)(vi) ("Describe the nominating committee's process for identifying and evaluating nominees for director, including . . . whether, and if so how, the nominating committee (or the board) considers diversity in identifying nominees for director. If the nominating committee (or the board) has a policy with regard to the consideration of diversity in identifying director nominees, describe how this policy is implemented, as well as how the nominating committee (or the board) assesses the effectiveness of its policy[.]"); *see also Ruggie Report, supra* note 76, at 20 (discussing this requirement).

recognize the value that diverse experiences and skill sets bring to board decision making, and many recognize the specific value in diversity reflective of customers and employees."[99] Therefore, many companies are designing and implementing diversity programs and efforts that far exceed—in both scope and quality—this reporting requirement. In a recent article in *Metropolitan Corporate Counsel*, Tom Sager, General Counsel of DuPont, articulated some of the value derived from promoting diversity:

> From DuPont's perspective, to succeed in today's highly competitive global marketplace our company must have an employee base and a law firm network that is as diverse as the customers who buy our products, the shareholders who purchase our stock, the vendors who supply us with goods and services, and the judges and juries who hear our cases. It long ago became clear to us that juries, judges, regulators and policy makers were becoming increasingly diverse and this trend impacted our ability to connect with these segments of the legal and business world. So besides valuing people of all races, ethnicities, and genders, diversity efforts also became a business imperative. It has proven critically important in a number of cases. One of them allowed us to find an alternative solution to a lawsuit against former lead pigment and paint manufacturers.[100]

The corporate programs aimed at expanding diversity can be quite creative. For example, Rhonda McLean, deputy general counsel of Time, Inc., has described a unique program at Time that facilitates contact between senior executives and lower-level employees who might not otherwise have access to members of senior management:

> We've initiated a unique program that has been very well-received. In order for people to get exposure to the executives regardless of demographic, race or gender, and be able to ask how to become a CFO or the COO, we started what we call speed career dating. We get 20 or 30 very senior people throughout our organization to commit to spend two hours with us where they each sit at a table. Junior people then can sign up for an eight-minute date with these executives. So while you're not interviewing for a job, you are talking about your career trajectory, and asking questions on how did you get to do what you're doing, what are your responsibilities, etc?

99. *Ruggie Report*, *supra* note 76, at 20.
100. *MCCA Unlocks Pathways to the Power of Diversity*, Metro. Corp. Counsel, Mar. 2011, at 6 (quoting Tom Sager).

We've done this several times with great success and it's become a great way to involve senior management and get them to see the diversity of people we have on the bottom who are trying to move up.[101]

In-house counsel are at the forefront of developing programs like these, which can promote and encourage the advancement of employees regardless of race, gender, and the like, as well as educate senior management about the benefits of diversity in the company.

The general counsel is often one of the leaders in corporate diversity and inclusion efforts. In 2004, General Mills General Counsel Rick Palmore (then general counsel of Sara Lee) created "A Call to Action," an initiative urging chief legal officers to drive diversity in the legal profession by moving law firms and corporate legal departments to measurable results. The text of the Call to Action reads as follows:

> As Chief Legal Officers, we hereby reaffirm our commitment to diversity in the legal profession. Our action is based on the need to enhance opportunity in the legal profession and our recognition that the legal and business interests of our clients require legal representation that reflects the diversity of our employees, customers and the communities where we do business. In furtherance of this renewed commitment, this is intended to be a Call to Action for the profession generally, in particular for our law departments, and for the law firms with which our companies do business.
>
> In an effort to realize a truly diverse profession and to promote diversity in law firms, we commit to taking action consistent with the referenced Call to Action. To that end, we pledge that we will make decisions regarding which law firms represent our companies based in significant part on the diversity performance of the firms. We intend to look for opportunities for firms we regularly use which positively distinguish themselves in this area. We further intend to end or limit our relationships with firms whose performance consistently evidences a lack of meaningful interest in being diverse.[102]

More than 120 prominent chief legal officers signed on to the Call to Action.[103]

---

101. Aman Singh Das, *"Corporate Citizenship Is a Two-Way Street: If Employees Must Comply, So Should Companies,"* Vault.com, In Good Company: Vault's CSR Blog, June 21, 2010, http://www.vault.com/wps/portal/usa/blogs/entry-detail/index?blog_id=1462 &entry_id=11510.

102. A Call to Action: Diversity in the Legal Profession, *available at* www.acc.com/ public/accapolicy/diversity.pdf.

103. Leadership Council on Legal Diversity, About Us, http://www.lcldnet.org/ about_us_leadership_ roderick_a_palmore.html.

Similarly, in May 2011, a group of general counsel in Canada launched Legal Leaders for Diversity, an initiative that aims to focus general counsel on encouraging diversity and inclusion throughout the legal profession and the Canadian business community.[104] In a "Statement of Support for Diversity and Inclusion by General Counsel in Canada," the Legal Leaders for Diversity signatories "undertake to practice and advance diversity and inclusion by":

- Promoting diversity within our own departments;
- Considering diversity in our hiring and purchasing practices;
- Encouraging Canadian law firms to follow our example;
- Promoting diversity initiatives at all levels in the legal and business community;
- Measuring the effectiveness of our efforts.[105]

In a speech at an inaugural event for the Legal Leaders for Diversity initiative, The Honourable David C. Onley, Lieutenant Governor of Ontario, stressed the importance of leadership from the legal community in promoting civil rights.[106] Through initiatives such as Legal Leaders for Diversity and A Call to Action, general counsel can share ideas, enhance accountability, and generate increased momentum for diversity efforts.

Amy Schulman, Senior Vice President and General Counsel, Pfizer Inc., describes her role as one of the executive leaders of Pfizer's diversity program as follows: "I have long been a champion for women in the profession and that hasn't changed now that I have this seat. I'm one of the executive sponsors of Pfizer's robust diversity and inclusion effort, and I chair the women's component of that effort. We have measurable and accountable goals, and we're working with our outside firms to ensure that they understand the centrality of diversity at Pfizer. This is a big priority for me and continues to be a focus of my attention."[107]

Including the legal department at the helm of a company's diversity efforts makes sense. In-house counsel are well positioned to understand

104. Julius Melnitzer, *GCs Launch Diversity Initiative*, FIN. POST, May 9, 2011, http://business.financialpost.com/2011/05/09/gcs-launch-diversity-invitiative/; Legal Leaders for Diversity, A Statement of Support for Diversity and Inclusion by General Counsel in Canada (on file with authors).

105. Legal Leaders for Diversity, A Statement of Support for Diversity and Inclusion by General Counsel in Canada (on file with authors).

106. The Honourable David C. Onley, Lieutenant Governor of Ontario, Remarks at the Launch of the Legal Leaders for Diversity (May 11, 2011) (on file with authors).

107. Interview with Amy W. Schulman, Senior Vice President and General Counsel, Pfizer Inc. (Mar. 17, 2010).

the effects of discriminatory employment practices, and they have the analytical and persuasive skills to improve diversity and inclusiveness throughout the corporation.[108]

In addition to promoting diversity within their own organizations, many corporate legal departments are using their buying power to influence diversity at law firms. General counsel have identified a range of methods by which they monitor the diversity efforts of the outside counsel they hire. These methods include communicating an interest in diversity to engagement and managing partners, tracking the number of hours billed by minority lawyers relative to the total number of hours billed by a firm, including diversity-related feedback in the company's annual performance evaluation of its outside counsel, and terminating relationships with firms that fail to demonstrate diversity values in line with the company's values.[109] Chief legal officers are also conscious of the power of making a particular person in a law firm the billing partner on a matter—outside firms may need to prove the success of their diversity efforts by being able to assign diverse billing partners and not just by identifying diverse lawyers to be part of the legal team serving the client.[110]

Many law departments are also recognizing the importance of "pipeline" efforts. Through pipeline programs, lawyers are "address[ing] diversity by reaching out to minority and low-income students throughout their educations. The idea is that by working with kids in their communities, lawyers are also investing in the profession with the hope that some of the young people will go on to law school and become lawyers where previously that might have been a distant goal—if it appeared on their radar screens at all."[111] Pipeline programs include mentoring, programs through which lawyers engage with elementary through high school students about legal subjects such as constitutional rights or intellectual property law, and academic- and career-choice programs.[112]

Tom Sager, General Counsel of DuPont, has described the successful pipeline program that DuPont has developed in collaboration with Georgetown University Law Center's Street Law Inc. program:

---

108. Judith L. Turnock, *Proactive Attorneys Driving Corporate Diversity*, DIVERSITY AND THE BAR, Mar./Apr. 2003, http://mcca.com/index.cfm?fuseaction=page.view page&pageid=1027.

109. Veta T. Richardson, *General Counsel Collaborate to Advance Diversity*, METRO. CORP. COUNSEL, Mar. 2004, http://www.metrocorpcounsel.com/current.php?artType= view&artMonth=February&artYear=2011&EntryNo=271.

110. *Corporate Counsel: Taking Stock*, ARIZ. ATTORNEY, Nov. 2003, at 12, 21 (Tim Eigo, moderator).

111. Melissa Maleske, *Pipeline Priority*, INSIDE COUNSEL, May 2011, at 50.

112. *Id.* at 52–57.

In my 34 years as a DuPont attorney, we have been working to increase the number of attorneys of color and women in our law department and the legal community. Approximately ten years ago, we realized that we had to put more emphasis on starting with high school students to fill the pipeline with young minorities interested in the practice of law. In 2006, we formed a partnership with Street Law Inc. Our legal Street Law and Diversity Pipelines initiative is conducted at Howard High School of Technology in downtown Wilmington [Delaware]. It is the only predominantly black high school in the state of Delaware. Howard High School has a career track legal administrative assistant program, and students in the track learn about the basics of the law and administrative skills to work in a law firm or legal department. Our lawyers go into the classes to teach students basic legal subjects as well. In addition, DuPont also brings students to its offices for instruction, mentoring and, in some cases, paid internships. I am pleased to say that the vast majority of these disadvantaged youngsters go on to college.[113]

Of course, the general counsel's role in promoting diversity throughout the corporation and its suppliers (including outside counsel) often begins by promoting diversity within the legal department.[114] To do this, the general counsel must both build a diverse team of legal, paralegal, and administrative staff, and manage the team with the goal of reaping the rewards of a diverse team.[115] In a 2010 article in *Inside Counsel*, Thomas Lalla, Senior Vice President and General Counsel of Pernod Ricard USA, described the following components of effective management to achieve the benefits of a diverse legal team:

- encouraging inclusion and collaboration in decision making, particularly with respect to department policies impacting the department overall and its interaction with other facets of the business;
- maintaining an open mind and recognizing that no one—including the general counsel—has all the answers;

---

113. *MCCA Unlocks Pathways to the Power of Diversity, supra* note 100, at 6.

114. *See* Thomas Lalla, *The Importance of Diversity in Corporate Legal Departments*, INSIDE COUNSEL, July 2010, http://www.insidecounsel.com/Issues/2010/July-2010/Pages/The-Importance-of-Diversity-in-Corporate-Legal-Departments.aspx ("Every corporate legal department needs to set the gold standard for diversity in the workplace. The general counsel can't ask other executives of the company to develop diverse functional teams without first building a diverse legal department that demonstrates the values of diversity in the workplace.").

115. *See id.* ("When properly managed, a diverse group will demonstrate increases in creativity and productivity, new attitudes among the department members, and the development of new processes and solutions.").

- building project teams that reflect the diversity of the department, including diversity of background and experience;[116]
- promoting successful results to others, within and beyond the department.[117]

Success in promoting and achieving diversity goals in recent years may be reflected in diversity among the individuals rising to general counsel positions, as a more diverse pool of qualified candidates is created and developed.[118]

3. Pro Bono

General counsel have also led the way in formalizing corporate pro bono programs that benefit communities, enhance corporate reputation, and provide personal and professional satisfaction to in-house lawyers.[119] The ABA's Standing Committee on Pro Bono and Public Service and the Center for Pro Bono have articulated a range of benefits achieved by corporate pro bono programs.[120]

The Standing Committee has identified the following "essential elements" to creation of a successful corporate pro bono program:

- committed leadership from the general counsel, including public participation by the general counsel in the program;

116. *See id.* ("Form project teams consisting of members from diverse backgrounds to handle special matters. It might seem the easier solution to build a project team that consists of members with the same background or previous experience with the matter. This group might be able to complete the project quicker but may do so by employing the same, previously used methods. Break that pattern: Construct a team of people and encourage them to use their different views and backgrounds to approach the matter in a new and better way. This will reduce or even eliminate the tendency to resort to getting the job done the same old way.").

117. *Id.*

118. *See Diversity Among Top Women General Counsel Hits All-Time High*, NAT'L JURIST, July 21, 2010, http://www.nationaljurist.com/content/diversity-among-top-women-general-counsel-hits-all-time-high (highlighting survey by Minority Corporate Counsel Association finding highest-ever level of women general counsel of Fortune 500 companies, as well as increased racial diversity among those general counsel).

119. *See e.g.*, Cathleen Flahardy, *Pro Bono Push*, INSIDE COUNSEL, Mar. 2011, at 67 (reporting American Airlines general counsel Gary Kennedy's leadership in formalizing the company's pro bono initiative).

120. ABA Standing Committee on Pro Bono & Public Service and the Center for Pro Bono, Corporate Counsel, http://apps.americanbar.org/legalservices/probono/corporate_counsel.html (last visited Feb. 21, 2011).

- a formalized structure, with a pro bono policy and a coordinator or committee;
- active identification of opportunities, facilitating participation by in-house counsel;
- substantive training and support in areas of law implicated by the pro bono opportunities presented.[121]

A strong focus on pro bono efforts within corporate legal departments may also have a positive impact on pro bono efforts in the legal community more generally, as law firms develop and expand their pro bono programs in order to parallel the efforts of their corporate clients and potential clients (among the many other reasons for, and benefits of, pro bono programs).

Many corporate legal departments have found partnering with legal services organizations in their communities or with their outside law firms to be an effective way of jumpstarting their pro bono initiatives and getting their lawyers involved.[122] Moreover, resources abound for general counsel or other corporate counsel who may be interested in setting up or developing best practices for their corporate pro bono programs, benchmarking their companies' programs with other companies' programs, or identifying pro bono opportunities. Corporate Pro Bono, a partnership of the Association of Corporate Counsel and the Pro Bono Institute, offers a range of resources, including free consultation services.[123] The Corporate Counsel Section of the New York State Bar Association has drafted a model pro bono policy for use by corporate legal departments.[124]

D. KEY TAKEAWAYS FOR THE GENERAL COUNSEL IN LEADING THE ETHICAL CHARGE

It is axiomatic that the general counsel's job is to "do the right thing" and lead the other corporate constituents to that goal as well. To achieve that

---

121. *Id.*
122. *See, e.g.*, Cathleen Flahardy, *Refreshing Communities*, Inside Counsel, May 2011, at 91 (discussing the Coca-Cola legal department's partnership with the Atlanta Volunteer Lawyers Foundation, the Pro Bono Partnership of Atlanta, and Street Law, and the "Wills on Wheels" partnership between the Coca-Cola legal department and King and Spalding).
123. http://corporateprobono.org.
124. Corporate Counsel Section of the New York State Bar Association, Model Pro Bono Policy, New York State Bar Association, http://www.nysba.org/AM/Template. cfm?Section=Corporate_Pro_Bono_Model.

goal, the general counsel has to identify the "right thing" not only for purposes of her own personal integrity and the ethical duties of her subordinates, but also, of course, to keep herself and her colleagues out of trouble. She must also identify the right thing for her client, the corporation.

We begin with the plain fact that the chief legal officer and her subordinates in the legal department are lawyers. As such, each lawyer is governed by the rules of the highest court in the state of his or her admission to the bar. In addition, some federal ethical rules, such as those adopted by the SEC pursuant to the Sarbanes-Oxley Act, may also apply. In-house lawyers must abide by all these rules to keep their "tickets" to practice law.

The general counsel, in particular, and subordinate in-house counsel, to an extent, have responsibilities beyond protecting their own ethical hides. They are expected to do what they can to ensure that their clients—the corporations they serve—focus on and implement goals like integrity, diversity, pro bono activities, and corporate citizenship.

Both the general counsel's personal reputation and also that of the corporate client are worth protecting and burnishing. Why? Because it is the right thing to do as a noble personal and societal goal. It is also good for the client's business and the lawyer's future.

First comes the personal goal of ethical conduct. The CLO has a dimension to her life that is unique in the C-Suite and the boardroom. That is her status as a member of the bar. One "ticket" to keeping her job as the most senior in-house lawyer for the corporate client is remaining a lawyer. If she loses that status, she can no longer operate as general counsel.

Second comes the derivative impact of ethical behavior. Solidifying her position as a member of the bar of the highest court of her state of admission takes the general counsel to the derivative plateau of ethical leadership for the corporate client. The fact that in-house counsel must report wrongdoing up the ladder to satisfy both state and federal ethics rules demonstrates not only the corporate curative effect but also the deterrent effect of infusing ethical behavior throughout the enterprise.

Doing the right thing does not stop with ethical compliance. More and more general counsel are leading the charge beyond compliance with rules of professional conduct. There is a significant uptick in leadership by CLOs in areas of corporate citizenship, social responsibility, diversity in corporate departments, insistence on diversity in outside counsel firms, and robust pro bono activities. CLOs lead this charge not only because they know it is good for the company's business success but also because it is the right thing to do.

CHAPTER 5
Advising the Board on Corporate Law and Other Laws

A. CORPORATE LAW AND CORPORATE GOVERNANCE UNDER STATE LAW[1]

1. Introduction

We write about corporate law here to a greater extent than other laws, for this reason: corporate law is the overarching law; it is the elephant in the C-Suite and the boardroom in many discussions of strategy, risk, and a broad spectrum of legal consequences. The chief legal officer is called upon to counsel management and directors on their fiduciary duties as they navigate legal concepts. To be sure, the CLO and her department must advise the corporate constituents with respect to other laws (such as antitrust, environmental, foreign corrupt practices, insider trading, employment, criminal laws, etc.). But, at the end of the day, corporate law, corporate governance, and securities laws (particularly disclosure obligations) often predominate the conversation in the executive suites and may be the analytical framework for the consideration of other laws.

For example, when considering strategy, opportunity, and risk, officers and directors may have to focus on antitrust concerns. Although counsel will inform management and the board about antitrust law and evaluate

---

1. For additional discussion of some of the topics discussed in this chapter, see E. Norman Veasey with Christine T. Di Guglielmo, *What Happened in Delaware Corporate Law and Governance from 1992–2004: A Retrospective on Some Key Developments*, 153 U. PA. L. REV. 1399 (2005).

the risks of contemplated corporate action, the fiduciary duties of due care and loyalty will often guide the discussion in this area. Similarly, the duties of care and loyalty, as well as various standards of judicial review, will often come into play in a merger context in evaluating the risks and opportunities of a specific decision, in deciding how to handle crises, and in numerous other applications. Or, the board may find it necessary to consider the business judgment of breaching a contract that may be more problematic to honor than to suffer damages liability for breach.[2] Thus, we focus on the fiduciary duties of due care and loyalty, with particular emphasis on the good faith component of the duty of loyalty.

As noted above, the general counsel is often a central figure in the boardroom, interacting with the entire board of directors, committees of the board, and individual directors. As part of these interactions the general counsel advises the corporate constituents on their fiduciary duties, which form the undergirding of discussions in many legal or ethical contexts.

2. Overview of Fiduciary Duty

It is important here to set forth an overview of corporate law and corporate governance. In the pages that follow, we attempt to go "back to basics" on those topics, because corporate counsel is often obliged to refer back to basics in advising management and the directors in various contexts. In counseling the directors, in particular, corporate counsel needs to be certain that the directors fully understand the landscape and the issues involving their duties and responsibilities under corporate law and corporate governance and other laws.

The introductory issue is: What do we mean when we use the term "corporate governance"? In its broadest sense it is used to define the structure, relationships, norms, control mechanisms, and objectives of the

2. *See In re* Tyson Foods, Inc. Consol. S'holder Litig., 919 A.2d 563, 601 (Del. Ch. 2007) ("A director might well breach a contract without violating any fiduciary duty."); *id.* at 601 n. 109 ("Indeed, to the extent that a contract may be rationally and efficiently breached, a director might believe that he is *obligated* by his fiduciary duties to do so.") (emphasis in original); *see also* E.I. duPont de Nemours & Co. v. Pressman, 679 A.2d 436, 445 n. 18 (Del. 1996) (stating that "[o]ur system . . . is not directed at compulsion of promisors to prevent breach; rather it is aimed at relief to promisees to redress breach," thus providing "considerable freedom to breach" contracts); *see also* Restatement (Second) of Contracts 16 Introductory Note (1981) ("The traditional goal of the law of contract remedies has not been compulsion of the promisor to perform but compensation of the promisee for the loss resulting from the breach").

corporate enterprise.[3] The objective of the firm is to maximize corporate growth and profitability for the benefit of stockholders by seeing that the corporation attracts capital, performs efficiently and profitably, and complies with the law.

Corporate law is the law governing the internal affairs of corporations, and is based in state law, often Delaware law. Corporate law is related to—but is not perfectly coextensive with—corporate governance. State enabling acts, such as the Delaware General Corporation Law (DGCL), are part of the corporate law. They create only a skeletal framework of mandatory requirements, however, and they leave room for private ordering by directors and common law decisions by the courts on the fiduciary duties of directors and officers.[4]

The "flesh and blood" of corporate law is judge-made. It is the common law formulation of principles of the fiduciary duties of care and loyalty, articulated on a case-by-case basis. In addition to fiduciary principles, a variety of other norms, expectations, and aspirational standards influence corporate governance. For an extremely comprehensive treatment of the subject, see Steve Radin's book *The Business Judgment Rule*, now in its sixth edition.[5] The detailed table of contents of that treatise reflects the range of issues presented; it is reproduced as Appendix B to this book.

Because fiduciary duty law is judge-made, some scholars say it is "far from clear and predictable" and therefore "demonstrates a degree

---

3. Professor Hillary Sale offers one definition:

> The term "corporate governance" is widely used to refer to the balance of power between officers, directors, and shareholders. Academics often discuss it in the context of regulating communications and combating agency costs where corporate officers and directors have the power to control the company, but the owners are diverse and largely inactive shareholders. Good corporate governance, then, allows for a balance between what officers and directors do and what shareholders desire. The term implies that managers have the proper incentives to work on behalf of shareholders and that shareholders are properly informed about the activities of managers.

Hillary A. Sale, *Delaware's Good Faith*, 89 CORNELL L. REV. 456, 460 (2004) (footnote omitted).

4. For a concise overview of the corporate law of fiduciary duties, see Ira M. Millstein et al., Fiduciary Duties Under U.S. Law, American Bar Association Section of Business Law, Corporate Governance Committee, International Developments Subcommittee, Multinational Comparative Analysis Project (Mar. 15, 2011), *available at* http://www2. americanbar.org/calendar/section-of-international-law-2011-spring-meeting/ Documents/Wednesday/Fiduciary%20Duties%20for%20Directors%20and%20Office rs/ABA%20Fiduciary%20Article_March%2015_2011.pdf.

5. STEPHEN A. RADIN, THE BUSINESS JUDGMENT RULE (6th ed. 2009).

of indeterminancy."[6] But importantly, any indeterminacy found in the Delaware law of fiduciary duty does not outweigh the benefits produced by flexible, fact- and context-specific, case-law development. Professor Fisch observes that "Delaware lawmaking offers Delaware corporations a variety of benefits, including flexibility, responsiveness, insulation from undue political influence, and transparency."[7] A flexible regime, such as that in Delaware, is distinct from the type of rigid codification system that prevails in many systems outside the United States.[8] That is part of the "genius of American corporate law."[9]

Life in the boardroom is not black and white. Directors and officers make decisions in shades of gray all the time. The general counsel, in advising the board, must help them navigate those shades of gray. A "clear" law, in the

---

6. Jill E. Fisch, *The Peculiar Role of the Delaware Courts in the Competition for Corporate Charters*, 68 U. CIN. L. REV. 1061, 1063, 1074–75 (2000) (footnotes omitted). *But see* Edward B. Rock, *Saints and Sinners: How Does Delaware Corporate Law Work?*, 44 UCLA L. REV. 1009, 1017 (1997) (arguing that "despite the fact-specific, narrative quality of Delaware judicial opinions, over time they yield reasonably determinate guidelines"). Even if the Delaware common law process resembles the legislative process in some ways, the Delaware courts do exercise restraint to avoid judicial legislation. *See, e.g.*, Williams v. Geier, 671 A.2d 1368, 1385 (Del. 1996) ("If we were to engraft here an exception to the statutory structure and authority in order to accommodate Williams' objection to this result, we would be engaging in impermissible judicial legislation."); Nixon v. Blackwell, 626 A.2d 1366, 1377 (Del. 1993) ("If such corporate practices were necessarily to require equal treatment for non-employee stockholders, that would be a matter for legislative determination in Delaware. There is no such legislation to that effect. If we were to adopt such a rule, our decision would border on judicial legislation.").

7. Fisch, *supra* note 6, at 1064.

8. *See* E. Norman Veasey, *The Judiciary's Contribution to the Reform of Corporate Governance*, 4 J. CORP. L. STUD. 225, 239–40 (2004) (comparing the American corporate law regime with the systems in the U.K. and the E.U.). The American Bar Association Section of Business Law, Corporate Governance Committee, International Developments Subcommittee has undertaken a Multinational Comparative Analysis Project with respect to the law of fiduciary duties in various jurisdictions around the world. The papers, as they are released, will provide an interesting comparative perspective on the subject. *E. g.*, Ira M. Millstein et al., Fiduciary Duties Under U.S. Law, American Bar Association Section of Business Law, Corporate Governance Committee, International Developments Subcommittee, Multinational Comparative Analysis Project (Mar. 15, 2011), *available at* http://www2.americanbar.org/calendar/section-of-international-law-2011-spring-meeting/Documents/Wednesday/Fiduciary%20Duties%20for%20Directors%20and%20Officers/ABA%20Fiduciary%20Article_March%2015_2011.pdf.

9. See ROBERTA ROMANO, THE GENIUS OF AMERICAN CORPORATE LAW 1 (1993) ("The genius of American corporate law is in its federalist organization . . . . Firms . . . can particularize their charters under a state code, as well as seek the state whose code best matches their needs so as to minimize their cost of doing business."); E. Norman Veasey, *The Defining Tension in Corporate Governance in America*, 52 BUS. LAW. 393, 393 (1997) ("[T]he 'genius of American corporate law' is its state-oriented federalism and its flexible self-governance . . . .").

sense of one that is codified, is simply not a realistic expectation in American business. There can be no viable corporate governance regime that is founded on a "one-size-fits-all" notion. Fiduciary law is based on equitable principles in specific factual settings. Thus, it is both inherently and usefully indeterminate, because it allows business practices and expectations to evolve. And it enables courts to review compliance with those evolving practices and expectations.

The judicial articulation of fiduciary duty law in Delaware is constantly evolving and has developed over about nine decades of court decisions. It is the quintessential application of the common law process.[10] Directors and officers are fiduciaries, duty-bound to protect and advance the best interests of the corporation. When those interests conflict—or may conflict—with the personal interests of the fiduciaries, the personal interests of the fiduciary must be sublimated to those of the corporation. The evolution of fiduciary principles occurs not only because courts must decide only the cases before them,[11] but also because business norms and mores change over time. Thus, corporate law concepts develop or acquire more defined content and doctrinal status over time as cases emerge addressing new business dynamics, and as judges and others ruminate on the law in extrajudicial contexts.[12]

---

10. *See* Randy J. Holland, *Law, Politics and the Judiciary: Statutory Enactments and the Common Law*, DEL. LAW., Fall 2003, at 22 (describing the relationship and interactive development of judicial common law and legislative statutes).

11. *See* Paramount Communications Inc. v. QVC Network Inc., 637 A.2d 34, 51 (Del. 1994) ("It is the nature of the judicial process that we decide only the case before us.").

12. *See* Melvin A. Eisenberg, *The Duty of Good Faith in Corporate Law*, 30 DEL. J. CORP. L. 1, 30 (2006) ("The life of the law, including the life of corporate law, is in a constant state of change in response to social changes. Circumstances change, the social norms applicable to the conduct of business change, business practices change, concepts of efficiency and other issues of policy applicable to corporate law change."); Myron T. Steele & J.W. Verret, *Delaware's Guidance: Ensuring Equity for the Modern Witenagemot*, 2 VA. L. & BUS. REV. 189 (2007) (examining how Delaware judges' participation in extrajudicial activities such as speeches, articles, dicta, and participation in bar association activities and committees reduce indeterminacy in corporate law); E. Norman Veasey, *Musings on the Dynamics of Corporate Governance Issues, Director Liability Concerns, Corporate Control Transactions, Ethics, and Federalism*, 152 U. PA. L. REV. 1007, 1014 (2003) ("Although, as judges, we give speeches and write articles raising academic issues and exhorting directors to adopt best practices, we do not reach out and make *ex cathedra* pronouncements on reformulating our jurisprudence or forecasting how certain fact situations should be decided."); Thomas A. Roberts, et al., Director Liability Warnings from Delaware, Bus. & Sec. Litigation, Feb. 2003, at 1, *available at* http://www.weil.com/wgm/cwgmhomep.nsf/Files/BSLFeb03/$file/BSLFeb03.pdf (citing judicial speeches as signaling the court's focus on corporate governance issues).

For example, the concept of good faith in the fiduciary duty context has undergone significant jurisprudential development in recent years. In the famous *Disney* case[13] involving the hiring and termination of Michael Ovitz, the Delaware Supreme Court, affirming the Court of Chancery's decision after trial, articulated good faith as part of the duty of loyalty. Specifically, the court held (as had the Court of Chancery) that one way of understanding what constitutes lack of good faith is that directors and officers may be held liable for an intentional disregard of a known responsibility. The court made clear that the liability-producing concept of good faith differs from gross negligence, which ordinarily does not result in personal liability for directors,[14] because of the element of intent, analogous to mens rea in criminal law.

The *Disney* case articulated the good faith concept in the context of decision-making by the board of directors. The court held that the directors were protected by the business judgment rule, despite a sloppy process, in making a series of decisions about hiring and terminating Michael Ovitz as president—decisions that ultimately cost the company in excess of $130 million.

Later in 2006, the Supreme Court in *Stone v. Ritter*[15] applied the same good faith/loyalty concept in connection with a claim in a stockholder derivative suit challenging the board's alleged lack of oversight—a so-called *Caremark*[16] claim. *Stone* involved a derivative suit against the directors of AmSouth Bancorporation for damage to the corporation due to criminal activities by low-level employees in running a "Ponzi scheme." The court held that the complaint failed to allege a lack of good faith by the directors excusing demand because it did not allege facts supporting the contention that the directors had intentionally and utterly failed to establish and monitor an effective compliance system.[17]

There are at least seven normal expectations that a stockholder should have of a board of directors. Although others may apply in some situations, the stockholders expect at least that (i) the stockholders will have a right to cast a meaningful and informed vote for the members of the board of directors and on fundamental structural changes, such as mergers; (ii) the board of directors will actually *direct and monitor* the management of the

---

13. *In re* Walt Disney Shareholder Litigation, 906 A.2d 27 (Del. 2006).
14. By statute in Delaware, the certificate of incorporation may provide for the exoneration of directors for due care violations but not for lack of good faith. DEL. CODE ANN. tit. 8, § 102(b)(7).
15. 911 A.2d 362 (Del. 2006).
16. *In re* Caremark Int'l Inc. Deriv. Litig., 698 A.2d 959 (Del. Ch. 1996).
17. *Stone*, 911 A.2d at 372–73.

company, including strategic business plans, risk assessment, and fundamental structural changes; (iii) the board will see to it that competent and honest business managers and general counsel are hired; (iv) the board will understand the business of the firm, develop a business plan, assess risks in the context of strategy, and monitor the managers as they carry out the business plan and the operations of the company; (v) when making a business decision, the board will develop a reasonable understanding of the transaction and act in good faith, on an informed basis, and with a rational business purpose; (vi) the board will carry out its basic fiduciary duties of care and loyalty; and (vii) the board will take good faith steps, under the guidance of corporate counsel, to ensure that the company complies with the law.

The tension between deference to director flexibility in decision-making and the need for judicial oversight is often a defining tension.[18] The complexity of the issues and the variety of highly textured fact situations require that courts practice a delicate balance in fiduciary duty jurisprudence.[19] Moreover, it is incumbent upon the chief legal officer, other in-house counsel, and outside counsel to deal with and counsel other fiduciaries on these highly textured fact situations.

3. Standards of Conduct and Standards of Liability

Standards of conduct are distinct from standards of liability.[20] Standards of conduct include not only conduct that is required of directors by the legal and regulatory regimes, but also the aspirational goals expectations for directors to achieve best practices.[21] Standards of liability, also referred to as standards of review, govern whether directors or officers will be held liable or a transaction set aside as a result of particular director conduct

---

18. *See* Veasey, *supra* note 9, at 402 (describing the role of independent decision-making and judicial oversight in corporate governance).

19. E. Norman Veasey, *An Economic Rationale for Judicial Decisionmaking in Corporate Law*, 53 BUS. LAW. 681, 682, 694–95 (1998).

20. *See* Melvin A. Eisenberg, *The Divergence of Standards of Conduct and Standards of Review in Corporate Law*, 62 FORDHAM L. REV. 437 (1993); MODEL BUS. CORP. ACT §§ 8.30, 8.31.

21. *See* Eisenberg, *supra* note 20, at 437 ("A *standard of conduct* states how an actor should conduct a given activity or play a given role."). In the context of professional counseling of boards of directors, the *Corporate Director's Guidebook* is a very helpful framework in the quest for best practices. CORPORATE LAWS COMMITTEE, AMERICAN BAR ASSOCIATION, CORPORATE DIRECTOR'S GUIDEBOOK (6th ed. 2011).

or inaction.[22] These concepts are implied in Delaware jurisprudence and developed in speeches and articles, but are not expressly stated as such in the Delaware cases. These concepts are expressly stated as such, however, in the statutory law in states that have adopted those provisions of the Model Business Corporation Act (MBCA).[23] It makes sense that these concepts are consonant with, though not expressly stated in, Delaware jurisprudence.[24]

When considering standards of conduct, one begins with the duties and responsibilities of directors. Directors must *direct* the management of the corporation.[25] They also have a vital oversight role in monitoring management without micromanaging corporate operations. They must carry out their responsibilities in accordance with principles of fiduciary duty, specifically the duty of care and the duty of loyalty. The business judgment rule is a standard of review, and these duties are embodied in the rule itself. That is, directors are expected to act—indeed are presumed to act, unless the presumption is rebutted—"on an informed basis, in good faith, and in the honest belief that the action taken was in the best interests of the company."[26]

22. *See* Eisenberg, *supra* note 20, at 437 ("A *standard of review* states the test a court should apply when it reviews an actor's conduct to determine whether to impose liability or grant injunctive relief."); E. Norman Veasey, *A Historical Peek at the Model Business Corporation Act and the American Law Institute Principles Through the Delaware Lens*, 74 LAW & CONTEMP. PROBS. 95, 98 (2011) (noting the distinction between standards of conduct and standards of review).

23. MODEL BUS. CORP. ACT §§ 8.30, 8.31.

24. Former Delaware Chancellor William Allen, Justice (then-Vice Chancellor) Jack Jacobs, and Vice Chancellor (now Chancellor) Leo Strine have ventured another useful definition:

> A judicial standard of review is a value-laden analytical instrument that reflects fundamental policy judgments. In corporate law, a judicial standard of review is a verbal expression that describes the task a court performs in determining whether action by corporate directors violated their fiduciary duty. Thus, in essential respects, the standard of review defines the freedom of action (or, if you will, deference in the form of freedom from intrusion) that will be accorded to the persons who are subject to its reach.

William T. Allen, Jack B. Jacobs & Leo E. Strine, Jr., *Function over Form: A Reassessment of Standards of Review in Delaware Corporation Law*, 56 BUS. LAW. 1287, 1295 (2001); *see also id.* ("There exists a close, but not perfect, relationship, between the standard by which courts measure director liability (the 'standard of review') and the standard of behavior that we normatively expect of directors (the 'standard of conduct').").

25. DEL. CODE. ANN. tit. 8 § 141(a) (stating that the business and affairs of the corporation "shall be managed by or under the direction of a board of directors").

26. This formulation is taken from the oft-quoted 1984 Supreme Court decision in *Aronson v. Lewis*, 473 A.2d 805, 812 (Del. 1984).

When discharging their duties, directors shall properly inform themselves and act in good faith. In *Aronson*, the court articulated the fiduciary duty of due care as follows:

> [To] invoke the rule's protection directors have a duty to inform themselves, prior to making a business decision, of *all material information reasonably available* to them. Having become so informed, they must then act with requisite care in the discharge of their duties. While the Delaware cases use a variety of terms to describe the applicable standard of care, our analysis satisfies us that under the business judgment rule director liability is predicated upon concepts of gross negligence.[27]

The italicized language is important for the chief legal officer and other corporate lawyers to keep in mind when counseling the board: Directors and officers[28] must inform themselves of "all material information reasonably available" to them.[29] The basic responsibilities of the board of directors stem from the operative Delaware statute, requiring the board to provide direction. The noun "direction," like the verb "to direct," is defined in the dictionary as a proactive concept, implicating strategic control and goal orientation. The very plain and forceful dictionary meaning of the noun "direction" is "guidance or supervision of action, conduct, or operations, . . . something that is imposed as authoritative instruction or bidding . . . an explicit instruction."[30]

As noted, the root "direct" in this statutory mandate for directors has two components: directors must (1) determine policy in their decision-making function and (2) guide and supervise in their oversight function. Thus, directors are not merely the group that hires and fires the CEO and is expected simply to advise management. They must be proactive in *directing* the management. Accordingly, the role of the chief legal officer is to ensure that all of this is carried out properly.

---

27. *Id.* at 812 (emphasis added; footnote omitted); *see also* Smith v. Van Gorkom, 488 A.2d 858 (Del. 1985).

28. Officers are subject to the same fiduciary duties as directors, but do not necessarily have the same protections from liability. *Gantler v. Stephens*, 965 A.2d 695, 708–09 & n. 37 (Del. 2009).

29. This expectation became a reality in *Smith v. Van Gorkom*, 488 A.2d 858 (Del. 1985) (holding directors personally liable for a due care violation in not becoming sufficiently informed before deciding on a merger transaction). This harsh result was later mitigated in 1986 by the Delaware legislature in the enactment of Section 102(b)(7) of the DCGL permitting corporations in their charters to exculpate directors for due care violations.

30. WEBSTER'S THIRD NEW INTERNATIONAL DICTIONARY 650 (3d ed. 2002).

Principles of corporate law and governance continue to develop the expectation that directors will seek to engage in best practices. The best practices expectation creates an aspirational standard of conduct and also provides a source of guidelines for directors to consider and potentially follow when engaged in a certain activity or faced with a particular type of decision. Failure to adhere to best practices will not necessarily result in liability, as the Delaware Supreme Court made clear in the first phase of the *Disney* case, in *Brehm v. Eisner*:[31]

> This is a case about whether there should be personal liability of the directors of a Delaware corporation to the corporation for lack of due care in the decision-making process and for waste of corporate assets. This case is not about the failure of the directors to establish and carry out ideal corporate governance practices.
>
> All good corporate governance practices include compliance with statutory law and case law establishing fiduciary duties. But the law of corporate fiduciary duties and remedies for violation of those duties are distinct from the aspirational goals of ideal corporate governance practices. Aspirational ideals of good corporate governance practices for boards of directors that go beyond the minimal legal requirements of the corporation law are highly desirable, often tend to benefit stockholders, sometimes reduce litigation and can usually help directors avoid liability. But they are not required by the corporation law and do not define standards of liability.[32]

The interesting conundrum, going forward, is whether or not certain aspirations of best practices will some day become the norm. And if they do, will it become necessary to consider the extent to which the failure to adhere to certain norms will become liability-producing acts or omissions? Judge-made law, at least in Delaware, is not static. It is dynamic, but should be reasonably predictable, so that corporate planners will not be unduly surprised.[33]

---

31. 746 A.2d 244 (Del. 2000).

32. *Id.* at 255–56. In *Brehm*, the court also noted that there is a director-protective statute in Delaware, which provides that directors shall be "fully protected" if they rely "in good faith" on corporate documents, reports, and experts chosen with due care. DEL. CODE ANN. tit 8, section 141(e).

33. *See* Veasey, *supra* note 22, at 97 ("[T]he judge-made law must not be of a free-wheeling or ad hoc quality. It must involve a disciplined and stable *stare decisis* analysis based on precedent and a coherent economic rationale."); Veasey, *supra* note 19, at 694 ("As I see it, the courts have at least seven key obligations. They are: (i) be clear; (ii) be prompt; (iii) be balanced; (iv) have a coherent rationale; (v) render decisions that are

As a matter of prudent counseling, the CLO and other corporate lawyers may wish to keep in mind and impart to the board that its conduct may be measured not only by the evolving expectations of directors in the context of Delaware common law fiduciary duty and in the context of developing business realities, but also by other standards, at least with respect to their oversight duties. The Sarbanes-Oxley Act,[34] the Dodd-Frank Act,[35] the rules of the Securities and Exchange Commission (SEC), and the listing requirements of self regulatory organizations (SROs) such as the New York Stock Exchange (NYSE) and NASDAQ can be relevant in state courts in certain contexts. For example, Dodd-Frank may increase the directors' oversight responsibilities.

Thus, adherence to best practices is advisable, whether or not expressly required as a matter of state fiduciary duty law.[36] Indeed, it is clearly the Delaware law that directors do not have to adhere to best practices in order to be protected by the business judgment rule. But adhering to best practices may be in the nature of a safe harbor.[37] Some of the requirements and evolving best practices in the New Reality present serious challenges for corporate counsel in shepherding their clients.

4. The Business Judgment Rule

The conduct of directors of Delaware corporations in their decision-making role in most circumstances[38] continues to be reviewed under the business judgment rule, which is alive and well in Delaware corporate jurisprudence. In fact, one goal for corporate counselors often is to achieve business judgment review, should director conduct be challenged in litigation. Because of the mandate that directors manage or direct the management of the business and affairs of the corporation, the focus of the business judgment

---

stable in the overall continuum; (vi) be intellectually honest; and (vii) properly limit the function of the court.").

34. Sarbanes-Oxley Act of 2002, Pub. L. No. 107–204, 116 Stat. 745 (codified in scattered sections of 11, 15, 18, 28, 29 U.S.C.).

35. Pub. L. No. 111–203, 124 Stat. 1376 (2010) (codified in scattered sections of 7, 12, 15, 18, 31 U.S.C.).

36. *See* William B. Chandler III & Leo E. Strine, Jr., *The New Federalism of the American Corporate Governance System: Preliminary Reflections of Two Residents of One Small State*, 152 U. PA. L. REV. 953, 957 (2003).

37. See Brehm v. Eisner, 746 A.2d 244, 256 (Del. 2000).

38. The circumstances where the business judgment rule may not apply include a board's decision to fend off a hostile takeover attempt (*Unocal*) or to sell control of the company (*Revlon*). These and others are discussed at chapter V.A.5.

rule remains on the *process* that directors use in reaching their decisions.[39] The business judgment rule will normally protect the decisions of a board of directors reached by a careful, good faith process. It is axiomatic that courts will not examine or second guess the substance of a board's decision in such circumstances.[40]

This approach is consistent with the Delaware doctrine that the business judgment rule is a presumption that courts will not interfere with, or second guess, decision-making by directors.[41] This is true unless the presumption is rebutted or unless a more exacting standard of review, such as entire fairness, applies because of the nature of the transaction before the court.[42] The business judgment rule applies not only to protect the decision (transactional justification) but also to protect directors and officers from personal liability, unless a different standard of judicial review is implicated.

Sometimes the standard of review for transactional justification purposes may diverge from the standard of review for purposes of determining when directors may be held personally liable in damages. For example,

---

39. *See, e.g.,* R. Franklin Balotti & James J. Hanks, Jr., *Rejudging the Business Judgment Rule*, 48 BUS. LAW. 1337, 1344 (1993). Balotti and Hanks point out:

> It is in the effort to impose liability for *decisions*—as opposed to *process*—that plaintiffs' efforts to hold directors liable for money damages have encountered the greatest difficulty. . . . A different rubric, however, should be employed to determine whether to impose liability for a judgment that later turns out to be erroneous than for an act that was not performed properly. Thus, the deference given to the judgments of the directors—i.e., the substantive aspect of the business judgment rule—prohibits courts from overturning judgments of the directors.

Id.

40. *See* Brehm v. Eisner, 746 A.2d 244, 264 n. 66 (Del. 2000) (explaining the deference courts give a board's decision). In *Brazen v. Bell Atlantic Corp.*, the court explained:

> The business judgment rule is a presumption that directors are acting independently, in good faith and with due care in making a business decision. It applies when that decision is questioned and the analysis is primarily a process inquiry. Courts give deference to directors' decisions reached by a proper process, and do not apply an objective reasonableness test in such a case to examine the wisdom of the decision itself.

695 A.2d 43, 49 (Del. 1997) (footnotes omitted).

41. *See* FRANK H. EASTERBROOK & DANIEL R. FISCHEL, THE ECONOMIC STRUCTURE OF CORPORATE LAW 93, 98–99 (1991) (asserting that courts must continually strive to stay out of business decisions and keep the business judgment rule alive and well).

42. *See Paramount Commc'ns Inc. v. QVC Network Inc.*, 637 A.2d 34, 45 (Del. 1994), as an example of enhanced scrutiny when selling control. Various forms of enhanced scrutiny are discussed at chapter V.A.5.

when the business judgment rule does not protect directors because they did not act on an informed basis, they may nevertheless be protected from personal, monetary liability by a provision in the corporate charter adopted pursuant to a state's corporate statute, such as Section 102(b)(7) of the DGCL (and comparable statutes in other states), which exonerates directors from personal liability.[43] But the transaction they approved may nevertheless be set aside or enjoined due to the directors' violation of the duty of care.[44] Section 102(b)(7) does not bar an injunction of a prospective transaction that is the result of a board's breach of their duty of care. Nor does it exonerate officers from personal liability.[45]

Section 102(b)(7) provides, in essence, that the certificate of incorporation of a Delaware corporation may contain a provision eliminating or limiting personal liability of a director, except for a breach of a director's duty of loyalty, acts or omissions not in good faith or which involve intentional misconduct or a knowing violation of law, improper dividend, or improper personal benefit. Thus, if the director's conduct goes beyond gross negligence (which may be exonerated from liability under section 102(b)(7)) into the realm of self-dealing or bad faith, for example, such conduct may violate the duty of loyalty and will not be exonerated.

Perhaps the most interesting analysis, which has been developed by the Delaware courts in the early twenty-first century, is the concept of good faith as part of the duty of loyalty. In short, good faith requires adherence to positive law, and lack of good faith is principally articulated to be an intentional disregard of a known responsibility.[46] This applies to decision-making as well as oversight.[47]

---

43. For discussion of Delaware General Corporation Law section 102(b)(7) provisions and their implications, see *Malpiede v. Townson*, 780 A.2d 1075 (Del. 2001).

44. *See* Hanson Trust PLC v. ML SCM Acquisition Inc., 781 F.2d 264 (2d Cir. 1986) (granting a preliminary injunction enjoining the exercise of a lock-up option based on directors' breach of the duty of care); *see also* RADIN, *supra* note 5, at 507–10 (discussing the *Hanson* case).

45. *See* Gantler v. Stephens, 965 A.2d 695, 709 n. 37 (Del. 2009); McPadden v. Sidhu, 964 A.2d 1262, 1273, 1275–76 (Del. Ch. 2008). But in some states, such statutory exoneration provisions do apply to officers. *E. g.*, LA. REV. STAT. ANN. § 12:24(C)(4).

46. In re Walt Disney Co. Deriv. Litig., 906 A.2d 27 (Del. 2006).

47. Stone v. Ritter, 911 A.2d 362 (Del. 2006). As previously noted, there is an outstanding and extremely comprehensive, richly documented exposition of corporate law in many dimensions, well beyond the business judgment rule, in a four-volume treatise by Stephen A. Radin. RADIN, *supra* note 5. This treatise is a valuable resource for the chief legal officer and others. The reader can get some perspective on the range of topics covered in that treatise by viewing its table of contents, reprinted in Appendix B of this volume.

The business judgment rule functions to protect the policies underlying corporate law, including maximization of stockholder value. Stockholders benefit from owning the equity of a profitable company—one that can attract capital and one that has expanding earnings and earning potential. Stockholders expect that the company will be overseen by a board that knows the business, is smart, honest, hard working, has a good percentage of independent directors, and, of particular note in the new reality, is not risk-averse but is risk-aware. That is, in the new reality, the general counsel must be attuned to very specific counseling on risk assessment and risk management.[48]

Substantial academic literature has discussed the concept of "hindsight bias," the human tendency to view decisions as having been obviously poor ones after having learned that the outcome was poor.[49] Hindsight bias is a hot topic in behavioral law and economics, as well as in the empirical work of certain psychologists and sociologists. Psychological research on hindsight bias strongly suggests the wisdom of the traditional Delaware approach, with its emphasis on protecting the substance of business judgments from after-the-fact scrutiny and condemnation, while allowing critiques based on disloyalty, lack of adequate process, and the like.[50]

An interesting example of the Delaware courts' refusal to second-guess a costly business judgment made by the board in the context of risk and the "new reality" of the economic meltdown of 2008–2010 is former Chancellor Chandler's decision in the *Citigroup* case.[51] In *Citigroup*, the plaintiffs argued that the directors did not act in good faith when they allegedly failed to heed "red flags" concerning the losses occurring in the bank's portfolio of securities involving sub-prime mortgages that failed. The Chancellor held that the thrust of the plaintiffs' case was not really a failure of oversight, but really related to the business decisions to invest in those mortgage-backed securities in the first place. Those decisions were held to be protected by the business judgment rule.

48. *See* Veasey, *Maelstrom, supra* chapter I, note 36; Bainbridge, *supra* chapter III, note 29.
49. *See, e.g.,* DAVID G. MYERS, INTUITION: ITS POWERS AND PERILS 89–93 (2002) (introducing the phenomenon of hindsight bias).
50. *See* Jeffrey J. Rachlinski, *A Positive Psychological Theory of Judging in Hindsight,* 65 U. CHI. L. REV. 571, 574 (1998) (observing that the law "must tolerate biased assessments of liability or create some form of immunity for potential defendants," and discussing the business judgment rule as an example).
51. *In re* Citigroup, Inc. S'holder Litig., 964 A.2d 106 (Del. 2009).

Investor interests will be advanced if corporate directors and managers honestly assess risk and reward, cost and benefit. In their strategic vision, directors should pursue with integrity the highest available risk-adjusted returns that exceed the corporation's cost of capital. But directors may tend to be risk-averse if they must assume a substantial degree of exposure to personal risk relating to ex post claims of liability for any resulting corporate loss occasioned by a business decision gone bad. They need not worry under Delaware law about mistakes of judgment—even "stupid" ones. They should not worry about liability if they exercise loyalty in the good faith pursuit of the best interests of the corporation. Indeed, courts should not equate a bad outcome with bad conduct.[52] It is difficult to summarize on a practical level how one should, as general counsel, help management and the board exercise best practices in their process that will be viewed as acceptable to a court in a prevailing set of circumstances. But a cornerstone to counseling best practices is to encourage the board to be proactive and to engage in penetrating questioning of management and invigorating collegial board discussions.[53]

5. Enhanced Scrutiny

Aside from the business judgment rule that applies in most day-to-day decision-making settings, other standards of review involving various gradations of judicial scrutiny apply in certain circumstances. As noted in the preceding section, if the business judgment rule applies, courts will not second guess directors or even question whether a business decision is "reasonable." But the takeover era of the 1980s, culminating in the watershed year of 1985, led to more and increasingly complicated standards of review. The Delaware Supreme Court has set forth differing review mechanisms to be applied in various contexts. The various forms of enhanced scrutiny range from testing the reasonableness and proportionality of the

---

52. *See* Stone v. Ritter, 911 A.2d 362, 373 (Del. 2006) ("With the benefit of hindsight, the plaintiffs' complaint seeks to equate a bad outcome with bad faith. The lacuna in the plaintiffs' argument is a failure to recognize that the directors' good faith exercise of oversight responsibility may not invariably prevent employees from violating criminal laws, or from causing the corporation to incur significant financial liability, or both . . . .").

53. In many respects, but particularly in the area of risk assessment and risk management, the types of questions the board should ask are set forth *infra* chapter V.B.2b.

directors' resistance to a takeover under the *Unocal*[54] standard, to the "entire fairness" test under *Weinberger*,[55] to the "best price on sale of control" standard under *Revlon*[56] and *QVC*,[57] to the "compelling justification" standard for interference with a stockholder vote under *Blasius*.[58]

Numerous cases have been decided in the early twenty-first century under Delaware law concerning constituency directors,[59] companies in distress,[60] mergers, acquisitions, and going-private transactions,[61] raising various issues. They are too numerous to list and are constantly increasing and expanding. The chief legal officer and her in-house lawyer staff must be continually alert to new developments in the case law. The cases involving fiduciary duties of directors may have an overarching effect on legal advice to directors on an ongoing basis.[62] The job of evaluating the circumstances facing a company and relating them to the case law, as well as advising the directors with respect to how the standard of review regime impacts board decisions and processes, are major challenges for the general counsel.

---

54. Unocal Corp. v. Mesa Petroleum Co., 493 A.2d 946, 958 (Del. 1985); *see also* Unitrin Inc. v. Am. Gen. Corp., 651 A.2d 1361, 1372 (Del. 1995).

55. *See* Weinberger v. UOP, Inc., 457 A.2d 701, 710 (Del. 1983) (holding that in a transaction involving conflicted insiders, those who are conflicted have the burden to satisfy the court that the transaction is entirely fair to stockholders or the corporation, both as to fair price and fair process).

56. Revlon, Inc. v. MacAndrews & Forbes Holdings, Inc., 506 A.2d 173, 182 (Del. 1985).

57. Paramount Communications, Inc. v. QVC Network, Inc., 637 A.2d 34, 43 (Del. 1994).

58. Blasius Indus., Inc. v. Atlas Corp., 564 A.2d 651, 661 (Del. Ch. 1988).

59. Directors who have been elected to the board by a particular constituency (such as preferred stockholders in certain situations) nevertheless owe fiduciary duties to the entire enterprise and thus all stockholders. *See* E. Norman Veasey & Christine T. Di Guglielmo, *How Many Masters Can a Director Serve? A Look at the Tensions Facing Constituency Directors*, 63 Bus. Law. 761 (2008) (exploring the constituency director phenomenon).

60. *E. g.*, N. Am. Catholic Educational Programming Found., Inc. v. Gheewalla, 930 A.2d 92 (2007); Trenwick Am. Litig. Trust v. Ernst Young LLP, 906 A.2d 168 (Del. Ch. 2006), *aff'd sub nom* Trenwick Am. Litig. Trust v. Billett, No. 496, 2007 WL 2317768 (Del. Aug. 14, 2007); Production Resources Group LLC v. NCT Group, Inc., 863 A.2d 772 (Del. Ch. 2004); Credit Lyonnais Bank Nederland N.V. v. Pathe Commc'ns Corp., No. 12150, 1991 Del. Ch. LEXIS 215 (Del. Ch. Dec. 30, 1991); *see also* Veasey, *supra* chapter IV, note 87, at 1, 64 (discussing cases).

61. *In re* CNX Gas Corp. S'holders Litig., 4 A.3d 397 (Del. Ch. 2010).

62. For a comprehensive review of the myriad cases and issues, the reader is referred to the four-volume treatise STEPHEN A. RADIN, THE BUSINESS JUDGMENT RULE (6th ed. 2009). As noted previously, the detailed table of contents of this treatise is set forth in Appendix B of this volume.

B. THE CLO'S ADVICE ON OTHER LAWS AND ISSUES

1. Other Laws

We have, so far, discussed the general counsel's key role in advising officers and directors of their fiduciary duties in the corporate law realm. But the general counsel, her subordinates, and outside counsel must also advise the directors and officers on myriad other laws. These occasions for advice—which may arise in either a preventive or reactive mode, or both—range from securities laws (e.g., what must we disclose and when?) to antitrust laws (e.g., may we implement a certain merger or not?); employment law (e.g., what employment policies are legal, ethical, and competitive?) to intellectual property law (e.g., is our patent protection adequate?); and so forth. We cannot begin to catalog the innumerable aspects of the general counsel's advice to the board and management on substantive and procedural law. There is a wealth of resources on each particular subject, written by experts in those subjects. Many general counsel have experts in particular specialized areas on their legal staff, if the specific circumstances of their companies warrant that, or draw on the expertise of outside counsel with specialties in the applicable area of the law who can provide guidance and advice.

Either way, it is important to recognize that the legal, and related quasi- or extralegal, issues presented can be quite complex and specialized. Directors and senior executives must understand that the general counsel cannot be an expert in every area of the law, and they must be prepared to ensure that the general counsel has available the budget necessary to obtain the required resources (through internal hiring or retention of outside counsel). The necessity of obtaining adequate resources within the legal department budget is a key goal and challenge of the chief legal officer, and is discussed in greater detail in chapter VI.A.

2. Other Issues

a. Compliance

Senior management and the board of directors are, or should be, intimately involved in compliance issues. Management has the primary responsibility for establishing compliance programs. Since the 1996 Delaware Court of Chancery decision in *Caremark*,[63] it has been established and reaffirmed in

---

63. *In re* Caremark Int'l, Inc. Deriv. Litig., 698 A.2d 959 (Del. Ch. 1996).

the 2006 Delaware Supreme Court decision in *Stone v. Ritter*[64] that both management and the board must set up information systems to ensure that reasonable efforts are applied to seeing that laws are followed, financial controls are in place, and red flags indicating potential problems are heeded. The utter failure to do so could, in some circumstances, result in liability for directors.[65]

Moreover, Section 404 of Sarbanes-Oxley[66] and the federal sentencing guidelines[67] have reinforced this doctrine and brought to bear federal incentives and sanctions to have effective compliance systems and to monitor them on an ongoing basis. The general counsel has a responsibility, either directly or by working in conjunction with other compliance-oriented executives in the company, to ensure that these steps are taken. The board of directors must effectively monitor those steps. Many companies have a Chief Compliance Officer (CCO) who has this management responsibility. The CCO may report to the CLO, the CFO, the CEO, or the audit committee of the board of directors. Regardless of what the formal reporting structure is, however, the general counsel and the compliance function should be closely linked and coordinated in most instances.[68]

b. Risk Assessment and Management

The responsibilities of management and the board for risk assessment and management are somewhat analogous to those involved in establishing and monitoring compliance systems.[69] Risk assessment and management

64. 911 A.2d 362 (Del. 2006).

65. *Id.* at 369.

66. 107 Pub. L. No. 107–204, § 404, 116 Stat. 745, 789 (codified as amended at 15 U.S.C. § 7262).

67. *See* U.S. Sentencing Comm'n, 2010 Federal Sentencing Guidelines Manual 496, 504–09 (Nov. 1, 2010) (stating that "[t]he two factors that mitigate the ultimate punishment of an organization are: (i) the existence of an effective compliance and ethics program; and (ii) self-reporting, cooperation, or acceptance of responsibility," and setting forth guidelines for a compliance and ethics program that will be effective in mitigating criminal punishment), http://www.ussc.gov/Guidelines/2010_guidelines/ToC_PDF.cfm.

68. *See* Ben Heineman, *Don't Divorce the GC and Compliance Officer*, Corp. Counsel, Dec. 2010, op. ed. (discussing various reporting relationships and responsibilities of chief compliance officer and general counsel), http://belfercenter.ksg.harvard.edu/publication/20612/dont_divorce_the_gc_and_compliance_officer.html.

69. *See* Veasey, *Maelstrom, supra* chapter I, note 36, at 8–16 (comparing the board's role in compliance and risk management); *see also* Bainbridge, *supra* chapter III, note 29, at 968 ("Risk management and law compliance differ only in degree and not in kind.").

have been in the forefront of public discourse in the context of the 2008–2010 financial meltdown and the ensuing Dodd-Frank Act.

The National Association of Corporate Directors (NACD) in 2009 issued a Blue Ribbon Commission (BRC) Report on risk.[70] The principal theme of the report is that risk taking and risk assessment are intimately tied to—and necessary components of—business strategy. And the GC operates in the center of the action in that regard, as the general counsel we interviewed have made clear:

> If you didn't take on any risk, you'd never get anything done. Certainly the management looks to the GC for that purpose, and I've often seen the board do the same thing: that is, [evaluating with the GC] whether or not what we're doing falls within the parameters of what we think are acceptable levels of risk.[71]
>
> * * * * *
>
> The GC role has evolved to the point where risk management is absolutely the top calling for the GC's office.[72]
>
> * * * * *
>
> Risk management is one of my top three priorities in any given year. The CFO and I co-own enterprise risk which is different, of course, from any kind of episodic risk issue. We have a systematic look at enterprise risk. We tackle the top five issues, and we own them. It doesn't mean that I'm responsible for each and every enterprise risk. Proactive risk assessment, responding to a specific risk, and helping the company plan to avoid risk are all responsibilities that I certainly hold myself accountable for and that others do as well.[73]

In short, it is axiomatic that a business must take risks. In doing so, however, the business must engage in risk assessment that is (a) prudent and (b) actively overseen and undertaken by the senior management and the entire board of directors.

How the board organizes the role of overseeing and managing risk depends on the company's operating environment and culture. Guidance from the general counsel to both management and the board is essential.

---

70. BLUE RIBBON COMMISSION, NATIONAL ASSOCIATION OF CORPORATE DIRECTORS, RISK GOVERNANCE: BALANCING RISK AND REWARD (2009) [hereinafter NACD, RISK GOVERNANCE].

71. Interview with Gary Kennedy, Senior Vice President, General Counsel, and Chief Compliance Officer, American Airlines, Inc. (Nov. 10, 2009).

72. Interview with Thomas L. Sager, Senior Vice President and General Counsel, E.I. du Pont de Nemours & Co. (Nov. 9, 2009).

73. Interview with Amy W. Schulman, Senior Vice President and General Counsel, Pfizer Inc. (Mar. 17, 2010).

There is no one-size-fits-all approach. Companies do not necessarily need to assign risk review to a single "risk committee" of the board. Some corporate boards do use a risk committee, while others use the audit committee or other committees to organize risk assessment and management. In the end, however, regardless of committee structure, the entire board of directors must be involved in risk assessment and risk management.[74] David Leitch, General Counsel of Ford, explained his company's approach this way:

> Our view is that different committees of the board manage different risks and that the full board has overall responsibility for ensuring that risks are appropriately considered and accounted for.
>
> The audit committee monitors one type of risk and that's pretty clear. We have a sustainability committee thinking about what are we doing for new technologies that we'll need to be advancing in the way cars are powered: What are the government regulations going to tell us about how that has to happen and what are our competitors doing in that space? So that's certainly a risk to our business but it wouldn't go through our audit committee. It would go through our sustainability committee on up to the full board.
>
> The compensation committee manages risks when they decide what the compensation programs are going to be. There's risk for employee retention. There's risk for public perception. So in the world of comp these days there are lots of risks that go with the job of setting comp in various programs for employees.
>
> For Ford, to put it all in one committee as a "risk committee" would really segregate in an unhealthy way the risk that all the committees should be thinking about within their jurisdiction on up to the full board.[75]

In the area of evaluating the corporation's appetite for, and management of, risk, the general counsel might be well advised to encourage the directors to ask management and each other these kinds of questions:

1. What are we aiming to accomplish, and how (corporate strategy)?
2. What alternative strategies have been considered/explored?
3. Do the directors receive risk material which adequately distills vast quantities of risk information into prioritized, actionable summaries?

---

74. NACD, RISK GOVERNANCE, *supra* note 70.
75. Interview with David G. Leitch, General Counsel and Group Vice President, Ford Motor Company (Feb. 1, 2010).

4. Are the risks associated with business units presented to the board in a comprehensive, holistic manner?

5. How do the losses which have occurred compare to the risks which have been identified? Are the losses consistent in magnitude and frequency with what one could expect given the risk profile presented to the board?

6. Can management and the board tie profits, as well as losses, to the presented risk profile?

7. How actively are resources—capital, balance sheet, talent— redeployed? Does the organization consistently, and on a timely basis, feed its winners and starve its losers?

8. What could go wrong or derail our strategy? For example, could multiple problems arise simultaneously or sequentially (the "perfect storm")?

9. Has management been forthcoming about any differences among senior leadership regarding material strategic recommendations and decisions?

10. What assumptions underlie our strategy, and which of those assumptions could change/be wrong?

11. What processes did management use to develop strategy and identify risk?

12. Have we achieved a common understanding of what triggers bring an issue to the board's attention?

13. What capabilities are required to address risks? Where do we have capability gaps?

14. Is there a common understanding among management, the board, and board committees about their respective roles, responsibilities, and accountabilities on strategy and risk oversight?

15. Does the board have a clear understanding of where strategy and risk oversight are delegated and what processes are used within management and among business units?

16. Do the board and committees discuss risk appetite with management?

17. How can this discussion become a part of the board's regular routine?

18. Is the board and are the appropriate committees meeting regularly with a chief risk officer (CRO)?

19. If there is a CRO, has the board ensured that the CRO and general counsel have a adequate resources and appropriate reporting lines to bring any changes in material risks to the board's attention?

20. Does the board have the appropriate committee structure for its significant oversight obligations in the risk area?

21. Does the board have sufficient personnel (including advisors) and financial resources in place to enable it to fulfill its risk engagement responsibilities?
22. Has the board adopted a board leadership structure that ensures that the independent directors have a clearly defined leader?
23. Do the board and appropriate committees have access to the information they need to provide oversight in troubled financial times?
24. Has the board and have the appropriate committees reviewed the incentive structure with strategy and risks in mind?
25. Has the board and have the appropriate committees reviewed board composition and director skill sets in relation to up-to-date competencies for oversight of the company's strategy, business lines, and material risks?[76]

These kinds of questions and the robust process inherent in the kind of discussion, consideration, and analysis that they will prompt will help not only the optics of the company's process but also will enhance the quality of board decisions and oversight.

c. Crisis Preparation, Management, and Internal Investigation

We do not here undertake a full, comprehensive exposition or manual detailing the complex steps and considerations that the chief legal officer should take when the company is in, or preparing for, a crisis mode, investigation, or serious litigation. Instead, we simply touch the highlights of investigation and litigation issues.

As a matter of crisis management preparation, the general counsel is the key player in ensuring that on a "clear day" a crisis management plan is in place. When the crisis hits, the general counsel should normally be intimately involved in executing that plan, absent a potential conflict of interest. Then, if, despite corporate counsel's best preventive efforts, the specter of corporate misconduct arises, an internal investigation may be necessary in order to uncover and deal with wrongdoing within the corporation, ensure compliance with the law or the public interest, or minimize the long-term criminal and civil liability of the corporation.[77]

76. NACD, RISK GOVERNANCE, *supra* note 70, at 24–25 (app. B).
77. *See* Sarah H. Duggin, *Internal Corporate Investigations: Legal Ethics, Professionalism and the Employee Interview*, 2003 COLUM. BUS. L. REV. 859, 938. For excellent, comprehensive overviews and recommendations relating to internal investigations,

The pursuit of these goals brings many conflicting forces to bear on counsel. A lawyer must deal with management, governmental agencies, employees, and other third parties while acting in the best interests of the corporation. Most significantly, in this context counsel may take on the role of corporate "cop," effectively acting as internal law enforcement agents.[78] Also, there are many occasions when conflicts or allegations of misconduct at high levels of the corporation require that the board undertake its own investigation through a standing committee (such as the audit committee) or a special committee of independent directors who must hire its own counsel.

An internal investigation may advance the objective of minimizing corporate liability, but it also presents risks. It may lead to unintended adverse consequences, corral facts supporting corporate liability, or chill employees' willingness to disclose problems.[79] Furthermore, the results of an internal investigation might ultimately be disclosed to third parties.[80] These issues may affect the attorney-client privilege as well as airing the corporation's "dirty laundry," thus enhancing liability or reputational risk. As a result, a general counsel who is considering an internal investigation faces a complex risk/benefit calculus.[81]

In certain cases, the decision to undertake an internal investigation is not difficult. A whistleblower, an impending government investigation, a conflict transaction, or a private lawsuit often compels an internal investigation.[82] Close questions place counsel in a more difficult position. Prosecutors increasingly expect counsel to be proactive in ferreting out

see INTERNAL CORPORATE INVESTIGATIONS (Barry F. McNeil & Brad D. Brian eds. 3d ed. 2007); Robert S. Bennett et al., *Internal Investigations and the Defense of Corporations in the Sarbanes-Oxley Era*, 62 BUS. LAW. 55 (2006).

78. *See* William R. McLucas et al., *The Decline of the Attorney-Client Privilege in the Corporate Setting*, 96 J. CRIM. L. & CRIMINOLOGY 621, 639 (2006) ("[P]rivate lawyers are effectively 'deputized' in many internal investigations, and the government obtains the facts of their inquiry through waiver of attorney-client privilege."). For additional discussion of various models of in-house counsel, as "cops," "gatekeepers," or "persuasive counselors," see *infra* chapter VII.A.

79. *See* Theodore R. Lotchin, Note, *No Good Deed Goes Unpunished? Establishing a Self-Evaluative Privilege for Corporate Internal Investigations*, 46 WM. & MARY L. REV. 1137, 1149 (2004).

80. *See* McLucas et al., *supra* note 78, at 630–32.

81. *See* Christopher A. Wray & Robert K. Hur, *Corporate Criminal Prosecution in a Post-Enron World: The Thompson Memo in Theory and Practice*, 43 AM. CRIM. L. REV. 1095, 1144 (2006).

82. *See* Brad D. Brian & Barry F. McNeil, *Overview: Initiating an Internal Investigation*, *in* INTERNAL CORPORATE INVESTIGATIONS 1, 6 (Brad D. Brian & Barry F. McNeil, eds., 2d ed. 2003).

"culture problems," even when no clear triggering event has occurred.[83] To accomplish this, in-house counsel must leverage their familiarity with corporate culture to make a legal judgment that may put them at odds with their close colleagues.

Once the decision to undertake an investigation is made, corporate counsel must decide or recommend who should conduct the investigation. In-house counsel's superior familiarity with corporate operations and culture are an asset in the management of an internal investigation.[84] But reliance on insiders may undermine the real or perceived independence of the investigation,[85] thereby leading the general counsel or a special board committee to consider whether outside counsel should be engaged to conduct the investigation.

The use of outside counsel does not, by itself, guarantee that law enforcement (nor, certainly, public opinion) will credit an internal investigation with independence, however. Prior relationships between the company and outside counsel may limit the extent to which the investigation is perceived as independent.[86] Moreover, outside counsel's mandate must afford a sufficiently broad scope of review,[87] and management must not exert control on the investigation while it is in progress.

Finally, as discussed in greater detail above,[88] the whistleblower provisions enacted as part of the Dodd-Frank Act and SEC regulations thereunder raise new challenges for the general counsel in this context. The provisions create financial incentives for individuals who voluntarily provide to the SEC "original information" leading to the successful enforcement of the

83. *See* Christopher A. Wray, Remarks at the 22nd Annual Corporate Counsel Institute, Georgia State Bar, *available at* http://www.usdoj.gov/criminal/press_room/speeches/2003_2986_rmrk121203Corprtconslinst.pdf (Dec. 12, 2003).

84. *See* H. Lowell Brown, *An Overview of Internal Investigations from the In-house Perspective, in* INTERNAL CORPORATE INVESTIGATIONS 449, 458 (Brad D. Brian & Barry F. McNeil, eds., 2d ed. 2003).

85. *See* Securities and Exchange Commission, Report of Investigation Pursuant to Section 21(a) of the Securities Exchange Act of 1934 and Commission Statement on the Relationship of Cooperation to Agency Enforcement Decisions [hereinafter SEC Investigation Report], at ¶ 10 (Oct. 23, 2001), *available at* http://www.sec.gov/litigation/investreport/34-44969.htm; *see also* Gabriel L. Imperato, *Internal Investigations, Government Investigations, Whistleblower Concerns: Techniques to Protect Your Health Care Organization*, 51 ALA. L. REV. 205, 209–10 (1999).

86. *See* SEC Investigation Report, *supra* note 85, at ¶ 10.

87. *See id.* at ¶ 10; *cf. also* Sung Hui Kim, *The Banality of Fraud: Re-Situating the Inside Counsel as Gatekeeper*, 74 FORDHAM L. REV. 983, 1000–01 (2005) (discussing the limitations imposed on the scope of Vinson and Elkins's investigation into whistleblower allegations at Enron).

88. See *supra* chapter I.C.3, where the whistleblower provisions of Dodd-Frank and the implementing SEC rules are discussed in detail.

securities laws.[89] Thus, they effectively "deputiz[e] every employee of a public company to be a watchdog,"[90] potentially undermining internal compliance programs and encouraging premature disclosure to the government.[91]

Even before the enactment of Dodd-Frank and the implementing whistleblower provisions, corporate disclosure to the government of wrongdoing[92] has been the subject of intense scrutiny and debate in light of the evolution of government guidelines for the investigation and prosecution of corporate crimes from the 2003 memorandum, by then-Deputy Attorney General Larry Thompson (the Thompson Memorandum),[93] through the guidelines as modified by the McNulty Memorandum,[94] to the current policy established in 2008 by the Filip Memorandum, which amended the United States Attorneys' Manual.[95] The Principles of Federal Prosecution of Business Organizations that were added to the U.S. Attorney's Manual in August 2008 establish, among other things, guidelines for the Department of Justice in determining whether a corporation has cooperated with the government, which can impact the DOJ's decision whether to bring criminal charges or how to resolve them.[96] The manual states that waiver of the attorney-client privilege and work-product protection are not "a prerequisite under the Department's prosecution guidelines for a corporation to be viewed as cooperative" and directs prosecutors not to seek such waivers.[97] Instead, according to the manual, "[t]he critical factor [in determining corporate cooperation with the government] is whether the corporation has provided the facts about the events."[98]

---

89. Dodd-Frank Wall Street Reform and Consumer Protection Act, Pub. L. No. 111–203, §§ 922–24, 124 Stat. 1376, 1841–50 (2010); Implementation of the Whistleblower Provisions of Section 21F of the Securities Exchange Act of 1934, 17 C.F.R. pts. 240, 249 (2011).

90. Sue Reisinger, *When the Whistle Blows*, CORP. COUNSEL, Nov. 2010, at 78.

91. *See supra* I.C.3.d (discussing the anticipated effects of the whistleblower provisions).

92. *See* Lotchin, *supra* note 79, at 1140. Disclosure is sometimes required by law. *See* Thomas E. Holliday & Charles J. Stevens, *Disclosure of Results of Internal Investigations to the Government or Other Third Parties*, *in* INTERNAL CORPORATE INVESTIGATIONS, *supra* note 77, at 279, 281–85; Imperato, *supra* note 85, at 223–24.

93. Larry D. Thompson, Principles of Federal Prosecution of Business Organizations (Jan. 20, 2003), *available at* http://www.usdoj.gov/dag/cftf/corporate_guidelines.htm.

94. Paul J. McNulty, Principles of Federal Prosecution of Business Organizations (Dec. 12, 2006).

95. United States Attorneys' Manual, Principles of Federal Prosecution of Business Organizations §§ 9.28.100–.1300 (added Aug. 2008), http://www.justice.gov/usao/eousa/foia_reading_room/usam/title9/28mcrm.htm#9–28.1300.

96. *Id.* § 9–28.700.

97. *Id.* § 9–28.710.

98. *Id.*

Managing the process of government investigations and the accompanying tensions has become a significant challenge for corporate counsel. Commentators and courts have observed that the emphasis on "cooperation" creates possibilities for overbroad and coercive government investigations.[99] These problems have been ameliorated somewhat at the DOJ and SEC, but perhaps not in other government agencies with investigatory powers.

There had been another important concern relating to counseling the company with respect to paying legal fees of corporate employees who may be swept up in a government investigation. Judge Lewis Kaplan forcefully dealt with this issue in the *KPMG* case. In that case, Judge Kaplan castigated the government for pressuring KPMG to cut off legal fees of employees, thereby violating their constitutional rights.[100] As corporate counsel—and now, under the expanded whistleblower provisions of Dodd-Frank, employees throughout the corporate organization—are more commonly used as arms of law enforcement, the natural tensions that attend an internal investigation are likely to become more disruptive. The Filip Memorandum may have partially alleviated this problem as far as the U.S. Department of Justice is concerned. But there are other agencies to consider. In short, general counsel must continue to confront significant challenges in this area.[101]

---

99. *See* McLucas, *supra* note 78, at 639 (observing that use of private lawyers to perform investigations lessens the importance of governmental budget constraints, giving agencies "nearly unlimited opportunity . . . to find misconduct at a public corporation").

100. *See* United States v. Stein, 435 F. Supp. 2d 330, 336 (S.D.N.Y. 2006) (recognizing that the government's prosecution strategies under the Thompson Memorandum, whereby prosecutors "held the proverbial gun to [KPMG's] head," causing KPMG to "cut off all payments of legal fees and expenses" to indicted employees, violated the employees' constitutional rights). The Second Circuit affirmed. *See* United States v. Stein, 541 F.3d 130, 136 (2d Cir. 2008) ("We hold that KPMG's adoption and enforcement of a policy under which it conditioned, capped and ultimately ceased advancing legal fees to defendants followed as a direct consequence of the government's overwhelming influence, and that KPMG's conduct therefore amounted to state action. We further hold that the government thus unjustifiably interfered with defendants' relationship with counsel and their ability to mount a defense, in violation of the Sixth Amendment, and that the government did not cure the violation.").

101. Before the Filip Memorandum and the accompanying changes to the U.S. Attorney's Manual, there had been concern among corporate counsel that abusive practices were rampant among DOJ lawyers. This led to a report by Norman Veasey that was presented to the U.S. Senate in connection with pending legislation. *See* E. Norman Veasey, Report to the Senate Judiciary Committee Hearings on S. 186 (Sept. 13, 2007) *available at* http://www.acc.com/public/coalition-statement.pdf.

C. KEY TAKEAWAYS FOR THE GENERAL COUNSEL IN ADVISING ON CORPORATE LAW AND OTHER ISSUES

Corporate law and corporate governance form an overarching framework for directors and officers to know and heed when engaged in their corporate duties. This is because issues relating to other laws, business issues, and litigation must be analyzed by the corporate constituents within a process framework that is governed by corporate law.

In this chapter, we have touched on other issues only briefly, not because they are unimportant, but because this book is not a "how to" manual intended to cover every legal concept that impacts general counsel. For example, securities laws are a cousin to corporate law, but have highly specialized nuances that are too numerous to catalog here. Antitrust laws on which general counsel and outside counsel must advise directors and officers are also highly specialized. Likewise, risk assessment, management, internal investigations, and the like are extremely important issues for general counsel. All of these issues must be evaluated in light of the particular circumstances facing a company in the context of a certain decision or action. Much current material has been written on these subjects, and we attempt merely to direct the reader to some of those writings.

Fiduciary duties of directors and officers. Many consultations between general counsel and directors and officers are framed by an analysis of fiduciary duties under corporate law. General counsel are steeped in this analysis and often are expected to impart and/or repeat this advice not only in the boardroom but also in the C-Suite.

Director liability is key but is not the only concern. It has been our experience and that of many general counsel we have interviewed that directors are very concerned about personal liability. This concern shapes many corporate law and corporate governance discussions, whether or not there is adequate D&O insurance. The general counsel should see to it that adequate D&O insurance is in place in the applicable categories, given the particular company's situation and the risk exposure of directors, officers, and the corporation.

Other issues implicating fiduciary duties. There is much more to the topic of fiduciary duties than liability. For example in a merger or large acquisition, there are corporate law/governance overlays, and fiduciary duties and the applicable standard of judicial review must be thoroughly understood, analyzed, and applied so as to sustain the transaction, for example, or to justify strategies and tactics that the directors and officers may employ in defending against a hostile takeover.

Framework for analyzing other laws. Fiduciary duty law often frames the discussion on securities laws, antitrust laws, FCPA concerns, environmental laws, and many other laws that directors and officers must consider. The same considerations apply to managing special board committees and internal investigations.

Framework for analyzing other issues. In addition to legal issues of liability and transactional justification that come before boards of directors, fiduciary duty concerns and motives to "do the right thing" abound. The most prominent and topical of those are compliance and risk assessment/management. These may be among the most important matters that the directors and officers—and therefore general counsel—must deal with on a regular basis.

CHAPTER 6
Managing the Legal Department

A. NEED FOR ADEQUATE RESOURCES

As head of the legal department, the chief legal officer has the responsibility to ensure that the department is equipped with adequate resources to carry out the mission. First and foremost is the need for an adequate and well-compensated in-house staff. That means good lawyers, paralegals, and assistants in sufficient numbers to fulfill routine and crisis responsibilities. Beyond that is the need for up-to-date technology and other equipment.

The legal department's budget should have sufficient capacity to retain outside counsel when needed. This is often seen as a significant challenge on many levels. The budgetary issues facing the in-house legal department are an important component of this chapter. But first we turn to the issue of how the CLO structures the legal department—whether the legal functions of the company are centralized or decentralized—in order to enable the department to be optimally effective.

B. COMPARTMENTALIZATION AND DECENTRALIZATION

One of the general counsel's many important roles in the corporation is functioning as the overall manager of the company's legal department. The general counsel's leadership in setting an ethical tone and encouraging the independent exercise of professional judgment[1] in the legal department

---

1. *See supra* chapter III.B.1 (discussing the general counsel's independence). See also *infra* VI.C for a discussion of the absence of attorney-client privilege accorded in-house counsel in certain EU member states, per the decision of the European Court of Justice

can serve as the foundation for her role in promoting a legal and ethical culture throughout the organization.[2]

In the role of legal department manager, the CLO should carefully consider the structure of the legal department and evaluate whether the department's organization is optimal for serving the needs of the client—the corporate entity. Over-compartmentalization of legal tasks, as well as over-decentralization and dissipation of legal staff, may have contributed to the problems at Enron and other companies.[3]

When deciding how to structure the mechanisms for providing legal services to discrete business units of the company, the general counsel should focus on how particular structural features of the organization may impact the lawyers' ability to identify issues, seek the views of colleagues, and solve problems or bring them to the attention of the appropriate corporate agents. An individual lawyer or team of lawyers that is assigned a single piece of a complex deal (compartmentalization) may not know enough about the transaction's overall structure to recognize problems.[4] Susan Hackett, former Senior Vice President and General Counsel, Association of Corporate Counsel, has articulated this problem, as well as the approach that counsel should take when problems arise:

> Sometimes an in-house counsel receives a request from someone in the organization for advice on whether or not [a particular, narrowly defined] project can be done and how it should be done. The counsel who is not operating as a gatekeeper

---

in the *Akzo* case. The court's decision was predicated on in-house counsel's supposed lack of independence.

2. *See* Interview with Larry D. Thompson, Senior Vice President, Government Affairs, General Counsel and Secretary, PepsiCo (Dec. 9, 2009) ("I think the general counsel, especially with his or her team, needs to set the tone. In addition to expecting your people to be very good lawyers and to be professional, you expect them to be independent. The gatekeeper role does come into play here, because you do want your people to know that they are guardians of the company's reputation and matters that deal with values. I think the general counsel has to set the tone and to communicate it frequently and periodically to his or her people.").

3. *See* Regan, *supra* chapter III, note 55, at 1153 ("Enron's decentralized entrepreneurial culture of multiple fluid project teams provided little systematic oversight by superiors in a conventional organizational hierarchy. Formal review processes were in place, but were buffeted by influences from both above and below in favor of moving deals forward. The project teams themselves were populated by financial whiz kids who ostensibly were creating a new era of capitalism, and who therefore had little patience for those who failed to understand the intricacies of their transactions."); *see also* DeMott, *supra* chapter I, note 24, at 970 (discussing challenges that may arise in a decentralized legal department).

4. *Cf.* Regan, *supra* chapter III, note 55 (discussing how such assignment of isolated legal tasks might have contributed to lawyers' failure to spot or address the issues at Enron).

figures out how to answer that question and hands it back. The person who is a gatekeeper says: "All right, explain to me what this project is about. I don't wish to work on what would constitute less than the full alphabet of this project. If I don't understand A through Z, I can't give you advice. I need to understand the context in which my advice is being used. Unless I have enough information to figure out both whether it's legal and whether it's stupid, we won't do it."

"Legal but stupid" is one of my favorite phrases when we talk about these issues. For the lawyer who wasn't a gatekeeper, so long as she was being asked the question, "is this legal," "can we do it," or "how do we do it" and she could answer those questions without violating professional malpractice standards, it was considered OK or defensible [to answer those narrow questions]. That's indefensible in a gatekeeper role. It doesn't matter only if it's legal. It matters if it's stupid.[5]

A variety of factors or motivations may lead corporate managers to over-compartmentalize legal work. These factors may include inadvertence, a desire to reduce costs, a desire to seek particular legal expertise, social ties, or misfeasance (for example, to enable a deal by avoiding any lawyer's knowing "too much").[6] In this context, lawyers working on individual legal issues must carefully consider how much they should know about the matter as a whole in order to perform a legal task that the client limits in scope.[7] The general counsel must also consider—and communicate—how the legal staff should address ethics and policy issues—in the field or through "headquarters."

General counsel should monitor the company's use of legal services for signs of compartmentalization and determine whether it raises any red or yellow flags indicating gaps or misfeasance or whether it could lead to problems or unintended consequences in the future. Undertaking such monitoring may tend to strain the relationship with management and implicate

5. Interview with Susan Hackett, Senior Vice President and General Counsel, Association of Corporate Counsel (Sept. 2, 2009).

6. *See, e.g.*, Nicholson, *supra* chapter III, note 7, at 559–600 ("The practice of spreading fragments of the business around to different outside law firms and different lawyers internally makes it easier for corporate managers to shop around for compliant lawyers who will approve complex transactions with little more than verbal assurances from the managers. . . . Some have argued that this fragmentation also leads to a lack of accountability on the part of the lawyers since no one ever would be fully informed about how his or her legal advice fits into the company's overall plans.").

7. *Cf.* Regan, *supra* chapter III, note 55, at 1199–1201, 1212 (querying how lawyers should determine how much they need to know about a transaction in order to perform a specific legal task).

the tension between counsel's role as advisor/advocate and her role as gatekeeper/"watchdog."

By the same token, some in-house legal departments in major multinational corporations are organized in a partially-centralized and partially-decentralized structure. In such a model, far-flung business units will have their "own in-house counsel" who report to the business heads of those units on legal matters of the units and report administratively to the general counsel. It is the general counsel who manages the tenure, compensation, assessment, and assignment of subordinate lawyers, as well as having a responsibility to "back up" and support the independence of the lawyers in the field.

Lawyers in the field are often able to develop specialized skills to serve the particular needs of the business units in which they work. As noted, it has been suggested that excessive decentralization may have contributed to the situation at Enron,[8] raising the question of the need for the general counsel to maintain an active role in managing all of the company's legal affairs, including, in particular, its relationships with outside counsel as well as the selection and management of in-house counsel. The lawyers operating within the business units should report to the general counsel. In turn, the general counsel and her centralized staff must stand up for those lawyers and ensure that they maintain their professional independence while providing the specialized legal services that their client requires.

Business unit leaders, senior in-house lawyers, and the general counsel should work together to create a culture that encourages inclusion of lawyers early on in any strategy, deal, or transaction. One practical way of doing this is for management routinely to meet presentations of new ideas with the question, "where are the lawyers on this?"[9] "The culture has to come from management, essentially making sure that [subordinates know] that [superiors] want things done correctly, with legal assistance and with a good compliance role."[10] Another practical step to drive a culture of early inclusion of legal guidance is to assign lawyers to particular business groups so that they are readily accessible to the business people, and to charge the

8. DeMott, *supra* chapter I, note 24, at 979; *see also id.* at 977–79 (discussing "decentralization, distance, and mismatched expertise" in the legal department as contributing to Enron's situation); Kelley, *supra* chapter III, note 31, at 1197 ("[P]ressures . . . exist in decentralized legal departments, where lawyers in the field usually find their principal reporting responsibility, in fact if not in structure, to be to an operating officer rather than to the general counsel.").

9. Interview with Charles Matthews, General Counsel, Exxon Mobil Corporation (Sept. 1, 2009).

10. *Id.*

legal expenses to the business units whether they use them or not, rather than on a usage basis.[11] David Leitch, General Counsel and Group Vice President, Ford Motor Company, articulated how the general counsel can partner with the business unit leaders to ensure that the company's in-house lawyers are appropriately "empowered, evaluated, and developed":

> We have moved steadily—without paying a lot of attention to work charts and dotted lines and things like that—toward having a more cooperative relationship between me and the head of a business unit in trying to make sure that the lawyer is appropriately empowered, evaluated, and developed.
>
> In terms of overseeing our lawyers, I make myself as aware as I can of what they are doing, the job that they are doing, and the satisfaction that people have with it. I get out and see them in their environment, see how they are plugged in with the team where they are located, and talk face-to-face with the business unit leaders about how the lawyers are doing. I also let the lawyers know that I am a resource for them. One of the most important things I do as a general counsel, not just for lawyers located elsewhere but also for lawyers at headquarters, is to advocate for their role to see to it that they are in the right meetings and empowered to do their jobs.
>
> I let all the lawyers around the world know that I have an open door. If there is something that the lawyer is not having success with that the lawyer thinks is a real concern, bring it to me. I will not necessarily go straight to the business leader and say, "Hey, Frank tells me you won't listen to him." But I can work with the lawyer to figure out together how to work out those problems.
>
> It is all about relationships with those lawyers out there. So, I try to let them know they have a business unit father and a skill team mother. That is, let them know that they work for a business unit but they are also part of a skill team, and those are both important relationships. I try to build relationships with them where they know they can count on me to help accomplish what they need to accomplish if necessary.[12]

Striking the correct balance between centralization and decentralization, in-house and outside counsel, is not an easy task. Richard Gruner has highlighted the difficulties encountered in tackling this organizational function. In particular, he has emphasized the challenges inherent in achieving a desirable balance between the "concentrated expertise" of

11. *Id.*
12. Interview with David G. Leitch, General Counsel and Group Vice President, Ford Motor Company (Feb. 1, 2010).

centralized lawyers and the "superior operating contacts" of field attorneys.[13] As Gruner observes, "[i]n this and other legal department design choices, the best organizational solution will often be determined only after experimentation with several work allocation and attorney assignment strategies."[14]

Chief legal officers are often faced with the challenge of budget constraints limiting their ability to staff the legal department or to retain outside counsel in a manner they believe to be optimal in the best interests of the corporation.[15] Counsel must resist budget pressures that have the effect of denying needed legal advice to some operations or issues. General counsel may have a duty in certain circumstances to assert persuasive "lobbying" with the CFO and the CEO and, if necessary, take the matter up with the board. It may also be important to inform the board of directors, if necessary, that some needed legal advice has not been provided because of budget constraints.

The organizational hurdles may be difficult to maneuver, but it seems clear that the chief legal officer is in the best position to find the balance that will best serve the corporation's interests. And most of the ones we know do just that.

C. GLOBAL CHALLENGES

Globalization is now a driving force for many public companies' businesses, and it has a particularly strong impact on the life of the general counsel. Bruce Sewell, Senior Vice President and General Counsel of Apple, highlighted for us some of the ways that globalization impacts the general counsel role:

> A critical event—a sort of environmental change—that's occurring for large publicly-traded companies is the globalization of business and the fact that increasingly over the past 5 to 7 years large companies have seen more and more of their revenue derived from outside of the United States. As a result, the need to understand international regulation and international legal systems has exploded.

---

13. Gruner, *supra* chapter III, note 25, at 1148–49.
14. *Id.* at 1149.
15. *See infra* chapter VI.D (discussing the challenges in working within the law department budget).

Correspondingly, the job of the general counsel has gone from being a far more U.S.-centric job ten years ago to being a job that is now much more international in scope. As the general counsel of a U.S.-based company operates farther away from the United States and in less defined, less mature economic societies, the relationship between law and politics gets somewhat blurred.

The general counsel is now an international ambassador who needs a thorough understanding of international regulation, how to deal with international organizations, and, for many general counsel, how to lead the compliance function on an international scale. This has led to an upsurge in the general counsel's involvement in political lobbying, government affairs, and managing the external view of the company—the company's brand and reputation.[16]

Thomas Sager, Senior Vice President and General Counsel of DuPont, expressed a similar view of the impact of globalization on the general counsel:

We are dealing now with an environment in which speed, execution, and global reach and competition have become so intense that it makes it very difficult to focus on all of the various areas, including those outside the U.S., where we're selling more and more product. Two-thirds of our sales now are outside of the United States, and that trend is likely to continue in emerging markets, the so-called BRIC countries: Brazil, Russia, India, and China.

Global reach and a focus outside the U.S. have complicated our world. So the general counsel has to balance the tension between managing risk in the United States, which is quite high, and managing the risks that are unique to facilitating growth outside the U.S., while maintaining the appropriate balance between the resources and focus of the general counsel.[17]

The challenges in dealing with foreign regulators are all over the map, both in becoming familiar with foreign law and cultures and in dealing with personalities in the ex-U.S. regulatory sphere. As for foreign courts, one hopes that judges abroad will adhere to the rule of law. But that is not always the case.[18]

16. Interview with Bruce Sewell, Senior Vice President and General Counsel, Apple Inc. (Nov. 3, 2009).

17. Interview with Thomas L. Sager, Senior Vice President and General Counsel, E.I. du Pont de Nemours & Co. (Nov. 9, 2009).

18. For years, there has been concern here and abroad about judicial independence. Justice Stephen Breyer has often decried "telephone justice" in Russia where government officials order judges to rule a certain way. *E.g.*, Stephen Breyer, *Judicial Independence: Remarks by Justice Breyer*, 95 GEO. L.J. 903 (2007). In fact a Russian

Another significant challenge for global companies is the different approaches to the attorney-client privilege and work product protection taken in other jurisdictions.[19] While some protection remains in the U.K. and some individual European countries, there is virtually no such protection for in-house counsel under European Union (EU) law. In fact, many chief legal officers preach such caution that one should assume the worst— that foreign jurisdictions will deny protection to many attorney-client communications with in-house counsel.

A decision by the European Court of Justice in September 2010 in the *Akzo* case held that there is no legal professional privilege for in-house counsel.[20] The EU court based its decision on its perception of a fundamental difference between the independence of outside counsel, on which the theory of the legal professional privilege rests, and the presumptive lack of independence (in the court's view) of the company-employed lawyer. Because an in-house lawyer is economically bound to his or her employer, that lawyer is more closely linked than outside counsel to the firm's commercial policy, the Court reasoned. Accordingly, the Court concluded that "independence means the absence of any employment relationship between the lawyer and his client."[21]

judge openly admitted recently that he was told how to rule in the case of oil tycoon Mikhail Khodorkovsky. *See* Ellen Barry, *Bosses Pressed Russian Judge, Official Says*, N.Y. Times, Apr. 16, 2011, at 4.

Even in the United States, in states in which judges are elected there may be instances where campaign contributions have so undermined judicial elections that the due process guarantee of an independent judiciary is threatened. *Caperton v. A.T. Massey Coal Co.*, 129 S. Ct. 2252, 2256–57 (2009) (holding that due process required a justice of the West Virginia Supreme Court to recuse himself in a case in which "the Supreme Court of Appeals of West Virginia reversed a trial court judgment, which had entered a jury verdict of $50 million," "[f]ive justices heard the case, and the vote to reverse was 3 to 2," and the justice whose recusal was sought "had received campaign contributions in an extraordinary amount from, and through the efforts of, the board chairman and principal officer of the corporation found liable for the damages").

19. *See* Interview with Kim K.W. Rucker, Sr. Vice President and General Counsel, Avon Products (Jan. 7, 2010) ("I think there are really large, looming issues about how we deal with investigations, including how we deal with international jurisdictions that don't necessarily honor the privilege. There is at least a real perception that regulators are going after and focusing on lawyers. As lawyers get into these more complicated roles of lawyer, business adviser, I do think the complexity and intersections of privilege and how all that falls is pretty important these days.").

20. Case C-550/07 P, Akzo Nobel Chemicals, Ltd. v. European Commission.

21. *Id.* The American Bar Association and the Association of Corporate Counsel (ACC) have sharply criticized this view. The then-general counsel of ACC, Susan Hackett, stated, "In-house counsel are top legal practitioners who are just as capable as their outside counsel counterparts. . . . Since in-house counsel play such a vital role in assuring that companies comply with the law, the ECJ should be promoting—not

As Daniel Desjardins, Senior Vice President, General Counsel and Assistant Secretary of Bombardier, articulated, the *Akzo* decision reflects an outdated view of in-house counsel:

> It is important to recognize that in-house counsel is independent and should be accorded the same status as external counsel when it comes to attorney-client privilege. The *Akzo* case in the EU, holding that in-house lawyers were not independent for purposes of the attorney-client privilege with respect to an antitrust opinion, represents an antiquated view of the role and stature of in-house lawyers.[22]

This presumption of the EU court that in-house counsel are not independent is anathema to the U.S. notion of lawyer independence. As previously noted, Model Rule 2.1 establishes that lawyers are expected to "exercise independent judgment" and render "candid advice."[23] Moreover, the application of the attorney-client privilege is engrained in the U.S. case law and culture.[24] Larry Thompson, then general counsel of Pepsico, emphasized independence as a key characteristic of the general counsel when we interviewed him for this book. He said:

> You need to be more than a technician. The CEO and the board need to respect and trust your judgment, not just your technical legal ability. I think that's very important. You have to be able to say "no" to the board or say "no" to the CEO, but you have to do that in a way that there's a respect there.
>
> CEOs are very strong-willed people. I've worked for two CEOs and when I've had to say "no" or I've had to give them counsel that guided them away from something that they wanted to do, they always challenged me. As they should. But you have to be able to withstand that.[25]

Although EU member states have broadened the reach of the privilege to communications with in-house counsel, the EU court in *Akzo* found that there is no predominant trend toward recognizing the privilege. Nevertheless, the court concluded that denial of the privilege to in-house lawyers

demoting—their capacities." Charles Forelle, *EU Court Rejects Expansion of Attorney-Client Privilege*, WALL ST. J., Sept. 14, 2010.

22. Interview with Daniel Desjardins, Senior Vice President, General Counsel and Assistant Secretary, Bombardier Inc. (May 20, 2011).

23. *See supra* chapter IV.B.1.

24. *See, e.g.,* Upjohn Co. v. United States, 449 U.S. 383 (1981).

25. Interview with Larry D. Thompson, Senior Vice President, Government Affairs, General Counsel and Secretary, PepsiCo (Dec. 9, 2009).

in connection with an investigation by the European Commission into potential anti-competitive practices would not erode legal privilege offered to the same lawyers at member state levels.[26] Thus, it is important, particularly for general counsel, to exercise extreme care in seeking and obtaining legal advice in Europe.

> As government has gotten more invasive, more aggressive, more interested, and more intrusive in its dealings with corporate America, the attorney-client privilege is going to become an increasingly tough battleground. They want what they want, and anything that gets in the way is a problem, something that needs to simply be surmounted, somehow. So the government is either going to ask you to waive it, or they're going to seek judicial decisions that say that it's not privileged in the first place. So, for example, in Europe, in-house opinions on antitrust matters are not considered privileged. You must have an outside lawyer involved in the conversation or it's not privileged. That's an important thing to know.[27]

Aside from denial of the privilege to in-house counsel by the EU court, general counsel managing in-house lawyers abroad must be cognizant of and adhere to foreign rules, cultures, and professional ethics, all of which may vary from the U.S. analog. Many foreign officials and foreign company personnel may have quite different attitudes toward lawyers than those that may be experienced in interactions with U.S. regulators, courts, and company officials. Working closely with foreign nationals, rather than solely with U.S. personnel, in the locations where the company has operations may help the general counsel to navigate this type of issue.

> One of the interesting challenges is being an American GC of a company with a significant non-American management team. I think that a lot of the challenges are, first and foremost, in America. Regulators elsewhere are active. But the risks presented by both the American regulators and the American civil justice system dwarf anything else out there.
>
> Americans also, I think, have a natural understanding and respect for lawyers that people in other countries don't. In particular, it's a serious challenge when you're talking to people who don't have a natural respect for lawyers or understanding of the American legal or regulatory environment.

26. Case C-550/07 P, Akzo Nobel Chemicals, Ltd. v. European Commission.
27. Interview with Adam Ciongoli, General Counsel, Willis Group Holdings, Ltd. (Sept. 4, 2009).

Business people from outside the U.S. often resent what they view as an American system of law that is wholly irrational and culturally-biased. The job of general counsel changes in dealing with executives from other countries who may have a different approach to the whole idea of law.[28]

In some jurisdictions around the world, officials expect bribes as part of the price of doing business. The U.S. Foreign Corrupt Practices Act (FCPA) prohibits, among other things, bribery of foreign officials for the purpose of obtaining or retaining business.[29] General counsel of companies with foreign operations are, of course, familiar with the FCPA and work to ensure that their companies' internal control systems incorporate means of preventing conduct that runs afoul of the FCPA and identifying and appropriately addressing any problematic conduct that does arise.[30]

D. WORKING WITHIN THE LAW DEPARTMENT BUDGET

The law department's output includes tough-to-value products such as wise counsel, risk assessment, risk management, and liability management and avoidance.[31] Some business leaders therefore view the department merely as a cost center,[32] producing intangible, immeasurable, or even

28. Interview with Adam Ciongoli, General Counsel, Willis Group Holdings, Ltd. (Sept. 4, 2009).

29. 15 U.S.C. § 78dd-1 et seq.

30. A useful resource in this regard might be the Organization for Economic Cooperation and Development's Recommendation for Further Combating Bribery of Foreign Public Officials in International Business Transactions and, in particular, Annex II to that document, which "provides guidance concerning internal controls, ethics and compliance programs, and measures for preventing and detecting bribery of foreign public officials in international business transactions." See The OECD Releases Good Practice Guidance on Internal Controls, Ethics, and Compliance to Curb Foreign Bribery, WEIL BRIEFING (Mar. 25, 2010) (summarizing the OECD recommendations), available at http://www.weil.com/news/pubdetail.aspx?pub=9756.

31. See SILVIO J. DECARLI & ANDREW L. SCHAEFFER, THE NEW REALITY: TURNING RISK INTO OPPORTUNITY THROUGH THE DUPONT LEGAL MODEL 32 (2009) ("Under the operational budget, legal services are viewed as protection. . . . Protecting the interests of the Company includes protection of created assets like patents, trademarks and trade secrets, protection from litigation and protection in litigation, and protection of business interests when DuPont files litigation."); cf. Simmons & Dinnage, supra chapter I, note 11, at 110 (discussing assessment of the value of in-house counsel as "not limited to transactions as traditionally envisioned" but as "also encompass[ing] intangible and non-transactional sources of value, such as corporate compliance, which help directors and officers fulfill their oversight duties").

32. See, e.g., Keith Ecker, The Offshore Option, INSIDE COUNSEL, Jan. 2009, at 41 ("[C]orporate executives have historically viewed legal departments as major money pits. . . ."); Thomas Sager & Terri Pepper Gavulic, Let Me Count the Ways, CORPORATE

invisible benefits. Recent economic conditions have resulted in more pressure on general counsel than ever before to control those costs[33] and justify the department's value[34]—pressure that will likely continue even in an improved economy.[35] Kristin Campbell, Senior Vice President and General Counsel, Staples, Inc., articulated the challenges that are inherent in viewing the legal function through the budget lens: "Legal departments really are being required more and more to account for their value. But here is the enigma: How do you prove your value when one of your primary functions is preventing things from happening in the first place? It is like proving a negative."[36]

The pressure does not come only from within the company—there has been significant public backlash concerning attorneys' fees in recent years. But many general counsel have drawn on their seemingly endless powers of innovation to develop new approaches to controlling costs, and even, in some companies, to turn the law department into a revenue center.[37]

COUNSEL, May 2008, at 71 ("Ask any general counsel, and he or she will tell you that his or her department is viewed as an expense to the company, and that therefore they are under enormous pressure to cut costs and operate efficiently.").

33. Chris Johnson, *They're Fed up Too*, CORP. COUNSEL, Nov. 2010, at 18; Marcus Linden, *Effects of the Current Economic Downturn on U.S. Law Departments*, METRO. CORP. COUNSEL, June 2009; Glen Silverstein & Joshua K. Leader, *What Will It Take to Make Non-Hourly Pricing a Real Fee Alternative?*, METRO. CORP. COUNSEL, Jan. 2010; *see also, e.g.*, Ecker, *supra* note 32, at 41; Aric Press, *Calls for New Model of Law Firm-Client Relations at Georgetown Conference*, LAW.COM, Mar. 22, 2010, http://www.law.com/ jsp/article.jsp?id=1202446599915&src=EMC (reporting conference presenters' comments that "the times—and the flow of international capital—demand[] a new model for law firm-client relations," "clients [will] be patient for only another 18 months with their outside firms," and "anyone who [thinks] law firms [don't] understand that a new reality [is] upon them [is] not paying attention to the market"); *see also* Jeff Jeffrey, *Alternative Billing Arrangements Putting down Deep Roots, General Counsel Say*, NAT'L L.J., May 17, 2010, www.nlj.com (noting study conducted by Corporate Executive Board that found that overall "costs to U.S. companies have risen 20 percent over the past decade," while legal costs have increased 75 percent over the same period).

34. *See* Simmons & Dinnage, *supra* chapter I, note 11, at 96 ("[I]nternal legal departments must continually find ways to articulate their value to the business enterprise and justify legal expenditures.").

35. Melissa Maleske & Lauren Williamson, *Budget Blues: Law Departments Tighten up*, INSIDE COUNSEL, Mar. 2009, at 63.

36. Interview with Kristin Campbell, Senior Vice President and General Counsel, Staples, Inc. (Oct. 28, 2009); *see also* Steven Andersen, *Fraud Ascendant*, INSIDE COUNSEL, May 2009, at 40, 41 (explaining that fraud hurts a company's bottom line, and stating that counsel can therefore make financial case for getting the support they need to detect and prevent fraud).

37. *See* Linden, *supra* note 33 ("[I]n-house experts say they are pressed as never before to control legal costs and even to show a return on investment at times."); Andrew L. Schaeffer, Managing Patent Litigation: Successful Results at Reasonable Costs Through the DuPont Legal Model, Presentation at PLI-Patent Litigation 2009,

1. Keeping Work In-House

An increasing number of legal departments—in both the United States and abroad—are managing costs by keeping more work in-house.[38] This trend is enabled by general counsel's ability to "function as sophisticated purchasers by performing aspects of the diagnostic and service functions[,] . . . . tak[ing] some degree of market power and perverse incentives away from outside law firms because outside law firms are no longer exclusively needed to diagnose a legal problem" and improving the client corporation's ability to assess the quality of the legal services that are provided by outside counsel.[39] The general counsel can increase her productivity and the department's ability to handle an increased workload by hiring highly skilled and experienced lawyers who can themselves earn the trust of, and work directly with, senior executives on sensitive issues. Charles Matthews, former General Counsel, Exxon Mobil Corporation, explained how his approach to organization and staffing fostered his department's ability to serve the client corporation and enabled him to focus on substantive matters rather than getting bogged down in department administration:

> Most all of my time is substantive. I have somebody else take care of personnel and administration in the law department with the exception of some of the major decisions that need to be made. I get involved with the final budget and I get involved with some major salary issues. But we have 460 lawyers, so most of the decisions on salary are made by the general counsels of the affiliates, and I don't really get involved in that.
>
> There are a couple of other lawyers on the legal staff who have the respect and stature and experience that I have. They have the expertise over a broad range of business issues in the organization so that our CEO also feels comfortable in talking to them directly. This is a culture that I have created with forethought. I've created a situation where I don't expect the CEO to funnel every question through me.

at 2 (Nov. 16, 2009) (discussing the positive results achieved through the DuPont Legal Model, *see infra* chapter VI.D.2, and noting that "[i]n some years DuPont Legal is a profit center"). See *infra* chapter VI.D.2.b for discussion of the recent shift in some in-house legal departments toward generation of revenue through legal action.

38. Linden, *supra* note 33; Leigh Jackson, *Somebody's Going to Have to Pay*, CORPORATE COUNSEL, Aug. 2008, at 107; Maleske & Williamson, *supra* note 35, at 65; Yesenia Salcedo & Melissa Maleske, *Budget Benchmarks*, INSIDE COUNSEL, Jan. 2008, at 49; *see also* Maleske & Williamson, *supra* note 35, at 64 (describing General Mills's model of "having a robust internal legal department, which reduces the amount of external help we require" (internal quotation omitted)).

39. Simmons & Dinnage, *supra* chapter I, note 11, at 109.

I encourage the CEO to feel free to call one of the other senior members of the law staff any time he has an issue that he wants to talk to them about. Some general counsel may feel threatened in their position if the CEO is calling someone behind their back. But I have confidence in my staff so that when the CEO calls my deputy about a problem that he has heard about and wants some advice on, my deputy will come in and report to me about the conversation and ask if I am in agreement with it. Then the deputy gets back to the CEO. So, there's a strong working relationship here, not only with our CEO but also with our management committee, which is made up of four different people who have different responsibilities throughout the organization.

Let me hasten to add that the expectation of senior management and of the law department is that the legal issues have already been worked along with the business issues before it gets up here. So it's not like somebody up here in headquarters is looking at something and saying "I better get legal advice on this." Legal advice has already been given, and usually what we get involved in is the need for another gray-haired person to look at this and to give comfort about it.[40]

Despite the increase in the workload of the in-house staff driven by a move toward internalization of more legal work, however, in-house staffing has remained fairly stable over time.[41] This means more work for each in-house lawyer, and perhaps a slightly higher hourly cost per in-house lawyer. But these higher per-lawyer costs may be justified by the savings realized on legal costs overall.

In addition to keeping more work in-house, general counsel are also realizing cost savings and efficiencies by evaluating which tasks can be assigned to paralegals or other non-attorney employees, thereby increasing the use of lower-cost employees.[42] Greater paralegal use drives a need for better, more formalized paralegal management, which tends to improve paralegal quality by offering paralegals a strong career-development program.[43]

The legal department can also initiate other, company-wide changes to help manage legal costs. For example, implementation of strict document

40. Interview with Charles Matthews, General Counsel, Exxon Mobil Corporation (Sept. 1, 2009).
41. Salcedo & Maleske, *supra* note 38, at 49, 51; Maleske & Williamson, *supra* note 35, at 65. *But cf. Fulbright Survey Summary: Companies Expect Litigation to Swell in 2010*, LAW OFFICE MGMT. & ADMIN. REPORT, Jan. 2010 (noting survey results indicating an increase in in-house lawyers among large-cap respondents).
42. Schaeffer, *supra* note 37, at 13; Maleske & Williamson, *supra* note 35, at 65.
43. Schaeffer, *supra* note 37, at 13, 19.

retention policies providing guidelines for systematic preservation/destruction can help to decrease future discovery costs.[44] General counsel can also ensure that their companies are leveraging appropriate technology to manage costs, while ensuring that quality is maintained.[45]

2. Managing Outside Costs

Despite the trend toward keeping work in-house, only thirty-five to forty percent of legal department spending is on in-house expenses.[46] General counsel therefore continue to focus on managing outside counsel costs as well, with an emphasis on productivity enhancement and strategic partnering.[47] As they face pressure to control legal costs, they pass some of that pressure through to outside counsel.[48] Thus, general counsel "are getting more serious about stronger outside counsel management programs," including "engaging in convergence and off-shoring work."[49]

In short, "[a]ll the pressure on law departments to change their spending ways results in pressure on law firms to make concessions to hold on to their struggling corporate clients."[50] Thus, alternative billing

44. *Fulbright Survey Summary, supra* note 41.

45. *See* Michael Kozubek, *Automated Accuracy*, INSIDE COUNSEL, Jan. 2011, at 36–37 (evaluating the effectiveness and cost-savings achieved by using electronic review technology for review of electronically stored information in discovery, as compared with attorney review of documents).

46. Salcedo & Maleske, *supra* note 38, at 49; *see also* Johnson, *supra* note 33, at 18 (reporting that Royal Dutch Shell plc spends "half of its legal budget on outside counsel"); Maleske & Williamson, *supra* note 35, at 64 ("On average, 49% of legal department budgets go toward outside counsel.").

47. *See* Veasey, Lawyers' Fees, *supra* Introduction, note 1 ("'The hallmark of these business management programs is that 'everything is on the table' and the focus extends well beyond cost cutting to embrace the far more significant thrust of productivity enhancement and strategic partnering with suppliers and customers.'" (quoting Dan Mahoney of DuPont)).

48. *See* Vanessa O'Connell, *Law Firms Feel Pinch*, WALL ST. J., Mar. 10, 2011, at B8 (discussing corporate clients' efforts to lower outside legal costs).

49. Salcedo & Maleske, *supra* note 38, at 50.

50. Maleske & Williamson, *supra* note 35, at 64; *see also* Sager & Gavulic, *supra* note 32, at 71 ("It is a race, and the first firms to demonstrate to clients that they understand the challenges by presenting effective solutions will win."). *But cf.* Melissa Maleske, *Outside the Box*, INSIDE COUNSEL, Feb. 2011, at 55 (reporting statements by Erik Ramanathan, executive director of Harvard Law's Program on the Legal Profession and former general counsel of ImClone Systems, that "'[t]he process of convergence is mostly played out, and most corporate law departments have a stable network of preferred providers, and those relationships are long-term relationships. . . . There's not much threatening to move on to new law firms—CEO turnover is more significant

arrangements—which enable clients and outside counsel to tailor fee structures based on the characteristics of a specific matter or the values the client desires to incentivize, rather than billing strictly on a hours-spent basis—are receiving increased attention.[51] In increasing numbers, general counsel are partnering with outside counsel to structure billing arrangements that move away from the traditional[52] billable hour and create value for companies and outside counsel alike.[53] And they are using the readily-accessible information available from their electronic billing systems to analyze costs and uncover ways to reduce costs and inefficiencies.[54] These general counsel believe that the move toward alternative fee structures allows the chief legal officer to shift the use of in-house counsel's time away from the role of "fee police," which had become an additional aspect of

than law firms getting fired. We should all be embracing the long-term durability of a law firm relationship and then focusing on strengthening it.'").

51. DECARLI & SCHAEFFER, *supra* note 31, at 34; *Fulbright Survey Summary*, *supra* note 41; Linden, *supra* note 33.

52. Billable hours have only been the standard fee structure for lawyers since about 1958, when the American Bar Association created the Special Committee on Economics of Law Practice. PATRICK J. LAMB, ALTERNATIVE FEE ARRANGEMENTS: VALUE FEES AND THE CHANGING LEGAL MARKET 3–4 (2010). That committee "launched the billable hour revolution" by recommending, as follows, that lawyers engage in hourly billing: "'Time being the lawyer's sole expendable asset, the economic worth of his ability, training and experience is determined by the use made of the hours available for the practice of his profession.'" *Id.* at 4. The committee also observed that "'[t]here are only approximately 1,300 fee-earning hours per year unless the lawyer works overtime.'" *Id.* As Patrick J. Lamb observes: "Lawyers always have been good at finding language they like and ignoring the rest. But think about it—1,300 hours! How things have changed. Today, lawyers who bill only 1,300 hours are likely to be fired." *Id.*

53. *See* Maleske & Williamson, *supra* note 35, at 68 (quoting one subsidiary general counsel as follows: "We are trying to more closely align our firms with rewarding them for value rather than just using the hourly rate, which we don't think is a very good measure of the value of services rendered"); *see also* Sager & Gavulic, *supra* note 32, at 71 ("There are many ways that law firms can help their clients create cost-effective solutions. Most are predicated on the similar principles of risk-sharing, partnership, innovation, and thinking from the client's point of view."); David B. Wilkins, *Team of Rivals? Toward a New Model of the Corporate Attorney-Client Relationship*, 78 FORDHAM L. REV. 2067, 2071 (2010) (describing a modern trend among corporate clients in managing their outside counsel relationships "to move from the 'logic of power,' which emphasizes the ability of stronger actors to gain by coercing their exchange partners into an asymmetric distribution of value, to a 'logic of embeddedness,' which emphasizes the importance of reciprocity and mutual trust for the production of joint gains").

54. Sager & Gavulic, *supra* note 32, at 71; *see also* DECARLI & SCHAEFFER, *supra* note 31, at 33–34 (discussing the matter management and e-billing software used by DuPont's legal department, and noting that one of the key principles of value-based billing is a "focus . . . on how well services are provided, not how long it takes to provide them"); Linden, *supra* note 33 (describing various systems used by legal department managers to track matters, and reporting that a "majority of [interviewees] who tried e-billing said that it provides tighter, more accurate controls").

many in-house counsel's job descriptions, toward better uses of in-house counsel's time, contributing to the corporation's welfare.[55]

A number of prominent general counsel have called for "new models that increase levels of 'cooperation, communication and trust' between the clients and their law firms."[56] Thus, reduced rates frequently are not enough: for many general counsel, "outside counsel efficiency is more important . . . than hourly rates."[57] Amy Schulman, Senior Vice President and General Counsel, Pfizer Inc., has been a strong proponent of eliminating the hourly rate. She has explained the benefits of alternative approaches to structuring—and billing for—the outside counsel relationship:

> I recognize that it is hard to let go of the hourly rate. Yet it is critical to let go of it. We are going to have to change. The hourly rate is responsible for more mischief in our profession than anything else. It is responsible for lawyers who are unhappy. It is responsible for a perverse set of training incentives for young lawyers. It has created an economic paradigm and expectations about compensation for partners in law firms that are completely out of sync with what companies are experiencing.
>
> I have some credibility because I took a pay cut and a not insubstantial one to leave my old job to come to this one. I have very strong feelings that we need to come up with ways of valuing what lawyers contribute that are not tethered to how much time they spend on a matter. So I have done away with hourly billing at Pfizer. I mean that in the most radical sense because I think most people think of alternative fees as a rough approximation for hours billed.
>
> What I have done is say to my few law firms, "Here are the rough areas of work where we think we will use you. Here's all the money we're going to give you this year, and if you really want to take on some other areas you'd better be sure that you're really adding value, because we're not increasing or decreasing your number in a given year. Your fee is not based on hours but on value."
>
> So [the outside firm] is liberated to tell me if [it] really think[s] it can be helpful in a given area because I am not marking to market. And that has actually been great because the law firms are much more strategic about where they are really adding value. Now, why would they do that if their number does not go up? Because I am building long-term relationships; in the following year, their

55. LAMB, *supra* note 52, at 10–11.

56. Press, *supra* note 33 (quoting Trevor Faure, global general counsel of Ernst & Young and former European, Middle East, and Africa general counsel of Tyco).

57. Linden, *supra* note 33; *see also* Maleske, *supra* note 50, at 58 (noting that trust promotes efficiency).

number may in fact reflect a bigger amount for transactional work or task work or employment work or real estate work.

I expect my firms to collaborate. I am not naïve because, from where I sit, everybody looks collaborative. But from where I used to sit in the law firm, I knew some firms really were good at it, and others really were not. I asked the firms in the Pfizer Legal Alliance to rate each other on collaboration. And you might have an incentive to collaborate with a law firm because you are going to get graded on it and because you may well need the firm. You have no disincentive to ask for help from another firm because your number does not go down.[58]

The DuPont legal department has long been recognized as one of the pioneers in structuring alternative fee arrangements and otherwise redefining the company-outside counsel relationship.[59] A DuPont publication describing the DuPont Legal Model[60] explicates the "value-billing" concept and concludes that alternative fee arrangements: (1) "tie law firm billings to value received by the client," (2) "more equitably allocate risks and rewards between the client and outside law firm," and (3) "ideally incorporate incentives for attaining mutually defined client objectives."[61] In other words:

> In [a value-based billing] arrangement, fees are directly related to the value of services rendered, rather than time spent providing legal services. DuPont, like other clients, wants to buy results, not time. Value-based billing is tied to outcomes because it provides performance bonuses to incentivize better results. In other words, if DuPont wins, the firm wins.
>
> Value-based billing is not merely a euphemism for discounts: law firms must be given incentives for obtaining successful results, even if a firm's compensation

---

58. Interview with Amy W. Schulman, Senior Vice President and General Counsel, Pfizer Inc. (Mar. 17, 2010).

59. *See* Veasey, Lawyers' Fees, *supra* Introduction, note 1 (discussing the DuPont model of partnering between lawyer and client and noting DuPont's push for value billing).

60. Schaeffer, *supra* note 37, at 2 ("[The] DuPont Legal Model has evolved into an integrated approach for managing change within the law department and for improving the quality, cost and efficiency of the legal services . . . provided to DuPont.").

61. DECARLI & SCHAEFFER, *supra* note 31, at 35; *see also* LAMB, *supra* note 52, at 14 (arguing that the term "value fees" should be used instead of "alternative fee arrangements," and that the "essential characteristics" of a value fee structure are that (1) "[t]he fee must align with the economic interests of the client and the lawyer," (2) "[t]he fee must create a financial incentive for the lawyer to reduce cost, not increase it," and (3) "[t]he fee structure must create incentives to accomplish a specific, identifiable client objective"); Veasey, Lawyers' Fees, *supra* Introduction, note 1 (discussing a trend toward partnering between clients and lawyers and identifying the "essential ingredients" as "communication, risk/reward sharing and technology").

exceeds what it would have received under straight hourly billing. If the incentives are right, business objectives should be achieved at an optimal transaction cost. Structured fairly, alternative fee arrangements improve overall success, as defined by business objectives.[62]

In the pages that follow, we describe some of the tools that some general counsel have been employing to revolutionize the relationship with outside counsel and manage outside counsel costs. Some outside counsel and general counsel would prefer to continue the practice of hourly billing (at least for some matters and often with agreed discounts and premium arrangements) and would cogently argue that this model is fair and works well for them. Accordingly, we do not here editorialize or express an opinion on what is the "best" model that is fair and efficient for both corporations and outside counsel.

a. New Fee Structure Models

i. Convergence

One method that some CLOs contend reduces outside legal costs while simultaneously strengthening relationships with outside counsel is the use of long-term preferred provider arrangements, also known as "convergence."[63] In the most dramatic examples, some companies have decreased the number of outside firms that they use from hundreds to one.[64] The rise of global law firms has enabled general counsel to employ global convergence.[65] These longer-term, potentially worldwide relationships

62. DECARLI & SCHAEFFER, *supra* note 31, at 35; *see also* Jeffrey, *supra* note 33 (referring to Pfizer's program of reducing the number of outside law firms with which it works, in an effort to encourage the firms "to become 'true partners' of Pfizer's and to encourage 'value-based billing arrangements'"); Press, *supra* note 33 (reporting statements by Susan Hackett, then general counsel of ACC, that there is "pent-up demand for a new definition of quality, namely one 'defined as value, defined by results, not hours,'" and criticizing "some in-house counsel who now find themselves 'in the drivers seat and . . . driving in the wrong direction' toward discounts rather than 'value'").

63. Maleske & Williamson, *supra* note 35, at 64; Rebecca U. Cho, *Law Firms Vie for "Preferred Provider" Status*, L.A. DAILY J., Sept. 15, 2009, at 1.

64. *See* Press, *supra* note 33 (reporting that Tyco's general counsel had led a "massive reorganization of [Tyco's] outside legal counsel in Europe, the Middle East and Africa . . . [by] shift[ing] Tyco's work from 240 firms to one").

65. Johnson, *supra* note 33, at 18 (reporting Finnish communications company Nokia Corporation's 18-month process of "slash[ing] a list of more than 500 law firms worldwide by half").

between outside counsel and client can facilitate cost reductions for clients by encouraging law firms to think in terms of long-term volume instead of focusing on maximizing the payday from an individual matter.[66] They also strengthen relationships between clients and outside counsel, encouraging increased partnership between outside firms and clients.[67]

Advocates for convergence argue that long-term provider relationships can have additional benefits as well. For example, they can allow for the development of fee structures that incentivize more proactive lawyering by outside counsel. Trevor Faure, global general counsel of Ernst & Young and former European, Middle East, and Africa general counsel of Tyco, has suggested that a long-term relationship between a corporate client and outside counsel can allow for development of a "litigation avoidance program," in which the firm "might be paid based on annual reductions in the number of filed suits."[68] Such an arrangement could create incentives for the law firm, which would have greater knowledge of the client on which to base its work, "to find destructive or provocative patterns in a client's behavior, recommend changes and then receive a bonus for the percentage drop in new litigation."[69] Thus, the company "could share most of the savings with a law firm, still come out ahead and have a better relationship with its lawyers."[70] As noted above, in 2007 Tyco reduced its outside law firms from 240 to one, Eversheds.[71] Both Tyco and Eversheds benefited from the arrangement: "The contract . . . includes bonuses and incentives ensuring Eversheds hits Tyco's targets. However, their agreement also imposes caps on the number of hours for which Eversheds can bill."[72]

---

66. Sager & Gavulic, *supra* note 32, at 71; *see also* Cho, *supra* note 63, at 1 ("For the firms that [become preferred providers], they get a steady supply of future work and increased revenue over the long term, even if they are billing less on each individual case."); *id.* at 1–3 (stating that clients with preferred provider lists find that they have "received better quality, more efficient service from firms," because "law firms on a preferred list are in it for the long haul and share the risks with the company"); Jeffrey, *supra* note 33 (stating that convergence efforts "can help to foster long-term relationships between a client and a law firm," increase predictability of legal costs, and encourage customization of billing arrangements).

67. Cho, *supra* note 63, at 1; *see also* DECARLI & SCHAEFFER, *supra* note 31, at 35 (noting that preferred providers and clients can develop "a long-term relationship built on trust").

68. Press, *supra* note 33.

69. *Id.*

70. *Id.*

71. *Trevor Faure Quits Tyco but Leaves Eversheds Legacy*, STRATEGIC LEGAL ADVISOR, Feb. 6, 2009.

72. *Id.*

In addition to promoting trust and adding value to the client-law firm relationship, these long-term relationships between corporate clients and outside firms arguably can also ameliorate the demoralization and related defection of law-firm associates that may result from a dearth of meaningful work and professional development opportunities for law firm associates early in their careers.[73] Given budget constraints and the limited experience and skill sets of new associates, corporations often resist paying "fully loaded rates (salary, bonus, other costs, partner margin)" for the work of new associates with "super-sized" salaries.[74] "But because they do need top-flight senior associates, because they want the firms to train young lawyers, and because they have an obligation to the profession, corporations can work with firms to pay reduced rates for junior lawyers. They can do this if . . . firms have a coherent program of professional development that gives young lawyers increasingly significant work on a systematic basis. The general counsel and senior partners can revise the running rules to open up lawyer-to-lawyer meetings or legal proceedings so that young associates can observe the process (even though the firm will still have to foot the bill as a training cost)."[75] Long-term firm-client relationships can make these investments more worthwhile (and therefore more likely), and can solidify the relationship between firm and client by creating relationships between multiple generations of lawyers at a firm and a client.[76]

ii. Alternative Fee Arrangements

While alternative fee arrangements are not new,[77] there has recently been a large increase in the use of alternative fee arrangements. At least one survey has reported that 75.6% of law departments use them in one form

73. *See* Veasey, Lawyers' Fees, *supra* Introduction, note 1 (identifying some of the problems with lawyers' fees, including "young lawyer dissatisfaction").

74. Ben W. Heineman, Jr. & David B. Wilkins, *The Lost Generation?*, OUTSIDE COUNSEL, Mar. 2008, at 106.

75. *Id.*

76. *Cf.* Amy Miller, *GCs, Law Firms and Flat Fee Arrangements: A Matter of Trust*, LAW. COM, June 9, 2009, http://www.law.com/jsp/tal/PubArticleTAL.jsp?id=1202431310403 (reporting Alston & Bird partner's comments regarding a flat-fee arrangement with a client that "he's not sure the firm makes money on these arrangements, but structuring routine work this way offers young associates valuable work experience and helps the firm solidify its relationship with the client").

77. *See* Veasey, Lawyers' Fees, *supra* Introduction, note 1 (describing in 1995 advances in partnering between clients and lawyers and development of relationships based on "value billing").

or another.[78] Some of the most popular alternatives to hourly billing include blended hourly rates, fixed fees, and task-based billing.[79] The most effective alternatives focus on increasing the predictability of fees and creating incentives for efficiency rather than inefficiency.[80] Several types of alternative fee options are discussed below;[81] they may be used alone or in conjunction with one another. General counsel whose companies have ventured into the alternative fee area stress that these arrangements are limited only by the imagination of general counsel and outside counsel and the ability to structure the arrangements around the unique characteristics of a particular matter and the client-outside counsel relationship.

Blended hourly rates. In a blended hourly rate arrangement, the outside law firm bills all of its lawyer time at the same hourly rate, regardless of the seniority of the lawyer.[82] Blended rates tend to encourage firms to staff matters with less experienced attorneys, which may be undesirable to the client unless development of the less-experienced lawyers is among the client's goals.[83] Critics of blended rates also argue that, by continuing the focus on the billable hour, blended rates do not change the incentives facing law firms or the efficiency with which legal services are delivered.[84]

Fixed fees. Fixed fee agreements, such as a monthly flat fee arrangement, help general counsel manage the cyclical spikes in legal expenses that often occur when several complex, multi-year litigation matters are active at once.[85] "The key element of the fixed fee, whether applied to a case, part of a case, or many cases, is that it gives budget certainty and creates huge incentives for the outside lawyer to reduce the cost of production."[86] At least one study has found that fixed fee arrangements are the most effective alternative fee structure for reducing legal costs.[87]

---

78. Maleske & Williamson, *supra* note 35, at 68.

79. *Id. See generally An Inventory of Creative Billing Arrangements*, LAW OFFICE MGMT. & ADMIN. REPORT, Sept. 2009 (collecting and describing various alternative fee structures).

80. Sager & Gavulic, *supra* note 32, at 71.

81. *See generally* Schaeffer, *supra* note 37, at 9–11 (providing alternative fee scenarios).

82. DECARLI & SCHAEFFER, *supra* note 31, at 36.

83. *Id.*

84. *E.g.*, LAMB, *supra* note 52, at 14; Silverstein & Leader, *supra* note 33.

85. Sager & Gavulic, *supra* note 32, at 71; *see also* Press, *supra* note 33 (identifying "predictability of expense" as one important interest of corporate clients).

86. LAMB, *supra* note 52, at 16.

87. *See* Silverstein & Leader, *supra* note 33 (referring to research by the General Counsel Roundtable).

Fixed fee arrangements can benefit outside counsel when a particular matter is in a lull, and benefit the client during particularly active times.[88] Thus, these arrangements may benefit both client and counsel and mitigate uncertainty in billing.[89] Flat fee arrangements often work best in the context of "routine, repetitive, or predictable types of litigation or legal work."[90]

To mitigate uncertainty and risk, flat fee arrangements can be structured with additional safety measures, such as a "collar" providing that the client will pay fifty percent of any fees that exceed 10 percent more than the flat fee and that the law firm will credit ninety percent of any overage to a future year.[91] Developing a fair and workable flat fee arrangement may also require greater dialogue and information flow—such as detailed information about past legal expenses—between client and counsel while the fee proposal is developed than may be necessary under other fee structures.[92] Maria de Cunha, general counsel of British Airways Plc, explains some of the relationship-driven benefits that can result from fixed fee arrangements: "'I don't want to micromanage my advisers—I'm only interested in the value and the result. . . . [Fixed fee arrangements] require having invested time in a firm and that they've invested time in you, as both sides need to know what they're getting for their money.' But, she added, it also means not worrying 'about things like how many people they send to a meeting. The price is set—it's up to them how they manage the process.'"[93]

A variation on flat fees is a capped fee arrangement, which can encourage efficiency but may impose substantial risk on the law firm if fees are significantly underestimated.[94] As with flat fees, however, the agreement can include provisions that mitigate such risk.[95]

---

88. Sager & Gavulic, *supra* note 32, at 71.
89. *Id.*
90. DECARLI & SCHAEFFER, *supra* note 31, at 35; Miller, *supra* note 76; *cf.* O'Connell, *supra* note 48, at B8 (noting that General Electric has used flat fees or fee caps to manage the uncertainty of fees on the defensive side of patent litigation).
91. Sager & Gavulic, *supra* note 32, at 71.
92. Miller, *supra* note 76; *see also* Silverstein & Leader, *supra* note 33 (noting that alternative fee arrangements require in-house counsel's "willingness to share information that will enable the outside firm to make a fair bid" and "law firm openness regarding how they arrive at alternative fee arrangements").
93. Johnson, *supra* note 33, at 18; *see also* Veasey, Lawyers' Fees, *supra* Introduction, note 1 (noting that the DuPont model works when the client manages the relationship with—but does not micromanage—outside counsel).
94. DECARLI & SCHAEFFER, *supra* note 31, at 36.
95. *Id.*

Contingency fees. The use of contingency fee arrangements, in which a plaintiff's counsel gets paid based on a percentage of a recovery in litigation, by corporations has increased in recent years.[96] In a contingency fee structure, a law firm's interest in taking on a case increases as the likelihood of recovery increases, and vice versa. The law firm's willingness to take on the case, therefore, reflects its assessment of the merits of the case, and thus becomes a gauge for the corporation to assess whether pursuing the case is a good investment of time and resources.[97]

Fixed-fee and contingency arrangements may be combined for even greater flexibility or certainty. For example, a client could complement a lower fixed fee with a contingent fee that is a lower percentage (e.g., ten percent) of the recovery than would be paid in a straight-contingency structure (e.g., thirty percent).[98]

A contingency fee structure may also be used on the defense side of litigation. In a "reverse contingency" arrangement, a client pays its lawyers a percentage of the amount saved vis-à-vis a claim. Modest savings receive a modest percentage of the amount saved, while greater savings receive a higher percentage of the amount saved.[99]

b. Outsourcing and Offshoring

As the prices of domestic legal services in major markets have continued to rise, many general counsel have begun to outsource legal work in order to capture savings from cost-effective labor markets.[100] This trend has included significant growth in "offshoring"—the purchase of legal services in foreign countries with lower labor costs, such as India, the Philippines,

96. LAMB, *supra* note 52, at 19; O'Connell, *supra* note 48, at B8.
97. LAMB, *supra* note 52, at 20; *see also* O'Connell, *supra* note 48, at B8 ("'There's risk associated with [taking cases on a contingency-fee basis] for the firms because it's an uncertain recovery, but businesses like it because they feel it forces law firms to have skin in the game,' said Buckmaster de Wolf, general counsel at GE Global Research Center.").
98. LAMB, *supra* note 52, at 19.
99. *Id.*; *see also* O'Connell, *supra* note 48, at B8 ("Even on the defense side, some big clients such as Cisco Systems Inc., increasingly use what are loosely described as 'contingent' payments to their law firms, in arrangements where payment is contingent on the outcome of the case, said Mark Chandler, general counsel at Cisco.").
100. Ecker, *supra* note 32, at 44; Heineman & Wilkins, *supra* note 74, at 106 ("Given sharp budget constraints, corporations are not going to pay fully loaded rates (salary, bonus, other costs, partner margin) to train green associates earning outsize salaries. (They may look to more experienced contract lawyers in the United States or India to perform basic tasks for less.")).

or Israel.[101] It has prompted law firms to offer certain services at prices that match outside supplier cost structures or to develop vendor relationships that they can offer to clients as a value-added service.[102] And it has even given rise to niche law firms that specialize in providing in-house counsel on demand—providing "an experienced in-house lawyer on site when needed," at fees as low as one-third of the going rate, who "can parachute into a company, even as a C-level executive, and stay for as long or as briefly as needed."[103] Similarly, some general counsel have found that certain types of legal or trial-related services can be performed more cost-effectively by firms that specialize in such services, whether in the United States or offshore.[104]

In addition to cost savings, offshoring sometimes captures other benefits as well. Time zone differences can achieve a work cycle of up to twenty-four hours per day.[105] And the workers at companies providing offshore legal services are generally permanent, not temporary, employees, leading to better education, training, and dedication than their onshore counterparts at outsourcing firms, who tend to be temporary employees.[106]

Some general counsel have found certain types of legal work to be particularly conducive to outsourcing and offshoring. "Increasingly, general counsel are turning to ancillary suppliers as well as contract lawyers and paralegals to help them manage costs in the areas of document management, document collection, coding, imaging, and legal research . . . ."[107] For example, as the number of documents subject to review in litigation has proliferated since the advent of e-discovery, document review has provided fertile ground for experiments with outsourcing and offshoring.[108] Some industry players estimate that offshoring document review can cut document review expenses by eighty to ninety percent.[109] Companies that deal with large numbers of contracts have also found contract review to be an

---

101. Ecker, *supra* note 32, at 44, 46; *cf. also id.* at 45 (noting that the decline in the value of the dollar has decreased the cost-benefit of offshoring, and explaining that decreased hourly rates in secondary U.S. markets, coupled with increasing hourly rates in India, have made it possible to hire U.S. contract attorneys for "pretty close to the wages of an Indian attorney").

102. Sager & Gavulic, *supra* note 32, at 71.

103. Terry Carter, *Outsiders Inside*, ABA JOURNAL, Feb. 2010, at 31 (internal quotations omitted).

104. Schaeffer, *supra* note 37, at 15.

105. Ecker, *supra* note 32, at 45, 46.

106. *Id.* at 45.

107. Sager & Gavulic, *supra* note 32, at 71; *see also* Press, *supra* note 33 (describing a continuum of legal work, with greater price pressure on "more common and regular work" and less on "major litigation, competition and sensitive compliance work").

108. Ecker, *supra* note 32, at 44.

109. *Id.*

area ripe for cost-saving through outsourcing and offshoring.[110] Basic legal research and intellectual property projects also are sometimes conducive to outsourcing.[111] Inherent in the trend toward outsourcing and offshoring "is an understanding that not all legal services warrant high hourly rates and that some portions of legal work are commoditized and need to be performed better, faster, and most of all cheaper."[112]

General counsel who have tried outsourcing and offshoring stress the importance of developing methods of evaluating the quality of the work product provided. Such methods can include programs in which a pilot outsourcing project is conducted parallel to completion of the same project by in-house or regular outside counsel, enabling the outsourced work product to be qualitatively evaluated relative to the "regular" work product.[113] In-house counsel should also diligently evaluate the competence, training, and integration of the people actually conducting the outsourced work, and the hiring practices leading to their involvement with a project.[114] Security is also a concern, and in-house counsel should assess the security of outsourcing providers' physical facilities, information technology systems, and personnel policies.[115]

3. Increasing Recoveries

In addition to managing law department and legal costs, some general counsel have even focused on the generation of revenue through legal action. For example, since 2004, the DuPont Legal Model has included a "global recoveries initiative," focused on asserting the company's rights through legal intervention in order to recoup monetary recoveries or other quantifiable rights and to develop resources to facilitate recoveries in the future.[116] The revenue-generation model may reflect "a big change in emphasis for in-house lawyers, who have tended to be risk-averse and mostly focused on shielding their company from litigation."[117]

110. *Id.* at 45.
111. *Id.* at 46, 47.
112. Sager & Gavulic, *supra* note 32, at 71.
113. Ecker, *supra* note 32, at 44.
114. *Id.*
115. *Id.* at 46.
116. Schaeffer, *supra* note 37, at 16; *cf.* Simmons & Dinnage, *supra* chapter I, note 11, at 126–27 (discussing "proactive" use of litigation "as one of the many instruments used to pursue a broader business strategy").
117. Vanessa O'Connell, *Company Lawyers Sniff out Revenue*, WALL ST. J., May 13, 2011, at B1, B2.

These revenue-generation efforts by in-house legal departments now extend well beyond intellectual property litigation by pharmaceutical and technology companies. Companies such as Ford, Tyco International, and Michelin

> say their lawyers are devoting more time and effort to bringing in extra cash by thinking like plaintiffs. Following in the footsteps of several big drug and technology companies, which have aggressively pursued alleged patent infringers, companies in a range of industries have stepped up legal action, not only in the patent arena but also against suppliers, insurers and even utilities they think have done them wrong or owe them money.[118]

These efforts have paid off in the form of beneficial recoveries by companies, although the recoveries in individual cases generally are not large enough to materially impact the company's bottom line.[119] But they do—particularly when viewed cumulatively—provide general counsel with a dollars-and-cents means of demonstrating to other senior management the value that the legal department provides to the company.[120]

Some of the other changes in the relationship between corporate clients and outside counsel, such as the rise of contingency fees,[121] have influenced in-house counsel's ability to pursue a revenue-generation model. For example, "General Electric Co. recently shifted almost all of its offensive patent litigation to contingency-fee arrangements. Now, GE 'business leaders' are more excited about bringing those cases," according to Buckmaster de Wolf, general counsel at GE Global Research Center.[122] The rise in contingency fees "'changes the dynamics' because 'there's no cost to the business and you end up sharing the spoils, only if you win.'"[123]

---

118. *Id.* at B1.

119. *See id.* ("The sums they win from these 'plaintiff recovery' lawsuits usually aren't big enough to be singled out in earnings statements. Nor do individual cases typically have a material impact on the bottom line.").

120. Schaeffer, *supra* note 37, at 16; *see* O'Connell, *supra* note 117, at B1 ("[T]aken together, they can produce hundreds of millions of dollars in additional revenue for a company in a single year, potentially turning the legal department into a profit maker."); *id.* at B2 (providing examples in which a company's legal recoveries in a specified period, many without requiring litigation, exceeded the company's entire legal costs over the same period).

121. *Supra* chapter VI.D.2.a.ii.

122. O'Connell, *supra* note 48, at B8.

123. *Id.*

4. Litigation Financing

Some companies have also tried third-party litigation financing as a method of managing legal costs or spreading the risk of litigation. In a typical third-party litigation financing arrangement on the plaintiff's side, a financing company provides funding for litigation-related fees, costs, and expenses in return for a share of any damages award or settlement proceeds.[124] The share received by the third-party financer usually is determined by several factors, including the amount of funding provided, the length of time between funding and recovery, the potential value of the case, and whether the case settled or proceeded to trial.[125]

The practice is well-established in some jurisdictions, such as the U.K., and has recently gained traction in the United States, although it is subject to significant criticism as well.[126] In addition to concerns that litigation financing fuels litigation and litigation abuses, questions arise concerning whether attorney-client privilege or work-product protection apply to information that is provided to potential lenders.[127] As a general matter,

---

124. U.S. Chamber Institute for Legal Reform, Selling Lawsuits, Buying Trouble 1–2 (Oct. 2009) [hereinafter Selling Lawsuits]; Richard Lloyd, *The New, New Thing*, Am. Law., May 17, 2010. On the defense side, litigation financing might involve a defendant corporation paying "a third-party financer to assume several million dollars in asbestos liability claims being litigated and carried on the books of the corporation. . . . The funder would, in essence, be betting that it could defend against or settle the claims for considerably less than it was paid to assume the claims, pocketing the difference as profit." Ralph Lindeman, *Third-Party Investors Offer New Funding Source for Major Commercial Lawsuits*, BNA Daily Report for Executives, Mar. 5, 2010, at 3.

125. Selling Lawsuits, *supra* note 124, at 2.

126. For a discussion of the concerns about litigation financing, see *id.* at 4–11. *See also* Steven Garber, *Alternative Litigation Financing in the United States*, Rand Law, Finance, and Capital Markets Occasional Paper (2010) (studying litigation financing and its effects on litigation); Binyanim Appelbaum, *Investors Put Money on Lawsuits to Get Payouts*, N.Y. Times, Nov. 14, 2010 ("A review by *The New York Times* and the Center for Public Integrity shows that the inflow of money is giving more people a day in court and arming them with well-paid experts and elaborate evidence. . . . But the review shows that borrowed money also is fueling abuses, including cases initiated and controlled by investors."); Melissa Maleske, *Hedging Bets: Third-Party Litigation Funding Gains Steam in the U.S.*, Inside Counsel, Dec. 1, 2009 (noting that the practice of litigation financing is well established in the U.K., and discussing some of the criticisms of the practice); Lindeman, *supra* note 124, at 2, 6 (stating that "third-party litigation funding is more prevalent in Europe, particularly in the United Kingdom," noting the practice's "extensive use" in Australia, and discussing pros and cons of the practice).

127. *See* Leader Techs., Inc. v. Facebook, Inc., 2010 U.S. Dist. LEXIS 63507, at *5–7 (D. Del. June 24, 2010) (affirming magistrate's decision that common interest privilege did not protect documents that plaintiff in patent infringement suit provided to potential litigation financers); *see also* Maleske, *supra* note 126 (reporting that there is

some CLOs can see a role for third-party litigation financing, but many remain reluctant to use such arrangements except in unusual cases.[128]

The types of commercial cases that have seen a rise in financing include intellectual property, antitrust, fraud, and breach of contract disputes.[129] Under the right circumstances, litigation financing can offer a way for general counsel to achieve recoveries for their companies on claims that otherwise might have been abandoned because of funding constraints.[130]

E. CHOOSING OUTSIDE COUNSEL

The general counsel has a huge responsibility in choosing outside counsel to represent the corporation generally and for discrete issues.[131] We emphasize

an issue with respect to whether a client waives work-product protection by participating in a potential lender's due diligence process).

128. *See* Lloyd, *supra* note 124 ("In 1997 DuPont brought a case against the U.S. government over the cleanup of company plants that had been owned by the government during World War I, World War II, and the Korean War. 'Funding immediately came to mind on this. I was under pressure, the case had been running for years, and it was approaching $10 million in legal fees,' Sager [General Counsel of E.I. du Pont de Nemours and Company] explains. He [explored the option of funding the litigation with a third-party litigation financer.] Ultimately, [the financer] opted against investing. 'They were troubled by the dynamics of investing in a case against the federal government, which can mean that litigation is dragged out,' Sager says. The suit eventually settled for $51 million in 2008. According to Sager, it was a fairly unusual case where he felt funding might help. (He hasn't since approached a funder about a case.) 'We can only use funding in cases where the cost of pursuing litigation is in the tens of millions,' he says. 'Given the economic climate and our ability to underwrite litigation, those costs [of using outside funders] are difficult to justify.'" (final alteration in original)); *id.* (quoting Jeffrey Carr, general counsel of FMC Technologies, Inc., as "admit[ting] that he can see a market for funders," but expressing that "while 'it might be a useful tool, I'm reluctant to engage in something that feeds the litigation machine'").

129. Maleske, *supra* note 126; *see also* Lindeman, *supra* note 124, at 3 ("Patent litigation, antitrust claims, and international arbitration—along with a smattering of cases involving shareholder disputes, breach of contract, and defaulted debt—are areas of concentration for the [litigation-financing] firms."); Lloyd, *supra* note 124 (noting a litigation finance company's investment in antitrust and patent infringement cases).

130. *See* Lindeman, *supra* note 124, at 5 ("General counsels with big companies have cases that they'd like to bring, but they have to take a backseat because of corporate constraints on funding.'" (quoting James E. Tyrrell Jr., managing partner of Patton Boggs LLP in New York and New Jersey)).

131. There may be times when the independent directors will want their own counsel. In that case those directors might seek recommendations from the general counsel. *Cf.* MCG Capital Corp. v. Maginn, 2010 Del. Ch. LEXIS 87, at *71–72 n.119 (Del. Ch. May 5, 2010). *Compare* Geoffrey C. Hazard, Jr. & Edward B. Rock, *A New Player in the Boardroom: The Emergence of the Independent Directors' Counsel*, 59 BUS. LAW. 1389, 1389 (2004) ("The part-time job of counsel for the occasional special committee of independent directors is about to become a continuing engagement."), *with* E. Norman Veasey,

here that it is the representation of the *corporation* where the general counsel is the primary actor in choosing outside counsel. Where there is a need for a special committee or a standing committee of the board of directors to have its own counsel, the committee must choose its outside counsel and other advisors independently of the general counsel's views. But if asked to do so by the committee, the general counsel may properly provide names for the committee to consider.[132]

There is no established formula for general counsel to consult when selecting outside counsel. There are many and varied practices and circumstances that influence or dictate a choice. Some of those factors include expertise, reputation, collegial partnering experiences, a company's list of preferred counsel, and the like. We do not offer a magic potion to assist general counsel in this area, except to urge extreme care and study when selecting counsel. Knee-jerk decision making can be disastrous.

Of course, outside counsel have the obligation to check conflicts before undertaking a representation. The general counsel (or another senior in-house lawyer) should also consider any potential conflict issues. These may include issues that are of a strategic nature, rather than direct ethical conflicts. Conflicts issues can create time-consuming and expensive sideshows in litigation, and it is important to consider the potential for such issues upfront, if possible.[133]

Separate and Continuing Counsel for Independent Directors: An Idea Whose Time Has Not Come as a General Practice, 59 BUS. LAW. 1413, 1414–15 (2004) ("[T]here should be a presumption that the general counsel is competent, has adequate resources, is ethical, and not conflicted in giving unvarnished advice to all the directors in carrying out their fiduciary duties. That said, the board must have a voice in the selection and retention of the general counsel and must have complete and unfettered access to the legal advice and legal services of the general counsel. Moreover, the directors must have the *authority* to retain separate outside counsel for the independent directors or committees of independent directors when there is a real need to do so. But that need will vary from corporation to corporation and situation to situation and should be invoked only after a careful cost-benefit analysis.").

132. *See In re* W. Nat'l Corp. S'holders Litig., 2000 Del. Ch. LEXIS 82, at *73–75 (Del. Ch. May 22, 2000) (rejecting challenge to special committee's independence based on special committee's retention of counsel that was recommended by management, because management recommended the counsel "for the perfectly appropriate reasons that they were highly qualified and independent").

133. *See* Transcript of Teleconference Ruling of the Court, Air Products & Chems., Inc. v. Airgas, Inc., Civil Action No. 5249-CC (Del. Ch. Mar. 5, 2010) (determining whether Cravath, Swaine & Moore, Air Products's counsel in its attempted hostile takeover of Airgas at issue in the case, should be disqualified from litigation with respect to that transaction based on the firm's previous work of more limited scope for Airgas). Beyond the proceedings in the Delaware Court of Chancery that did not result in the Court disqualifying the Cravath firm, but did involve a distraction, Airgas brought claims in Pennsylvania against Cravath for ethical violations and breach of fiduciary duty.

F. KEY TAKEAWAYS FOR THE GENERAL COUNSEL IN MANAGING THE LEGAL DEPARTMENT

In addition to the many substantive and strategic issues that dominate the life of the general counsel, the CLO also stands at the helm of the in-house law department. This chapter focuses on some of the CLO's management responsibilities in that role, in which she must manage people, resources, and legal functions.

That management responsibility has many dimensions, only a few of which this chapter stresses. One is how the general counsel organizes the department, including what functions are central to the department's operation and when and how a department can be decentralized while still maintaining strong ties to, and supervision by, the central legal office where the general counsel sits. Another is the management of resources, department budgets, and approaches to dealing with legal fees of outside counsel.

The need for resources tops the list. The chief legal officer, particularly of a large public company, needs adequate resources. Sometimes lawyers in a large legal department can number in the hundreds.[134] All these lawyers need good salaries, staff, space, and technology. And there is always the need for outside counsel, either regularly or episodically, particularly when highly specialized expertise is needed.

Organization. The general counsel is head of the legal department, but decisions about how centralized or decentralized the bulk of the lawyers in the department should be for optimal service to discrete business units, without sacrificing centralized oversight, management, and information flow, can be challenging. The general counsel as law-department manager determines what structure and organization will best deliver service throughout the organization, while also ensuring central control and oversight of ethics, training, and professional advancement. Globalization adds an additional layer of complexity, requiring that foreign operations, laws, and cultures be taken into account.

Dealing with outside counsel. The CLO must be the central figure in the process of selecting outside counsel. Factors such as quality, availability,

---

See Airgas, Inc. v. Cravath, Swaine & Moore, LLP, 2010 U.S. Dist. LEXIS 78162 (E.D. Pa. Aug. 3, 2010) (denying Cravath's motion for judgment on the pleadings).

134. *See, e.g.,* Ben W. Heineman, Jr., *Big Isn't Always Best,* OUTSIDE COUNSEL, Nov. 2008, at 94 (noting that General Electric's global law department consists of approximately 1,100 in-house lawyers); Interview with Charles Matthews, General Counsel, Exxon Mobil Corporation (Sept. 1, 2009) (observing that Exxon Mobil employs 460 in-house lawyers).

avoidance of distractions from conflicts, and many others all impact the selection process. Moreover, managing outside counsel fee structures and designing creative solutions for legal fees within the legal department budget have become difficult and time-consuming concerns for CLOs.

Specific focus on outside counsel fees. Many CLOs continue to be comfortable with their outside counsel relationships and their ability to manage those relationships economically and efficiently. Other general counsel have begun to insist on new protocols of counsel selection and compensation. And there are general counsel who are experimenting with some new protocols or blends of the new and the traditional. The takeaway is that there is no one culture or system—one size does not fit all. If the CLO is comfortable with her tried-and-true traditional arrangements, she may conclude, "if it ain't broke, don't fix it." But if she wishes to consider other alternatives, this chapter outlines some of the options that other general counsel have tried.

CHAPTER 7

The General Counsel in the Crosshairs

Exposure to Sanctions, Prosecution, and Liability

Being CLO has substantially higher risks than a lot of other ways to be a lawyer.
                                                        —Adam Ciongoli[1]

General counsel are currently more exposed to the threat of personal liability or ethical sanctions than in the recent past because so many [difficult] decisions come up to the general counsel. What bothers me is that most of this is in the gray area. I very seldom get a black or white issue. The general counsel could make the wrong decision. And I know people are then going to point fingers at the general counsel.
                                                        —Larry D. Thompson[2]

Some general counsel and commentators have expressed concern that over the past decade or so, and particularly in the current regulatory environment, general counsel and other in-house lawyers have increasingly become targets for prosecution, sanctions, and shareholder claims. Although inquiries surrounding some of the Enron-era corporate scandals examined the roles of in-house counsel in the events leading to those scandals, in-house counsel generally were not formally sanctioned.[3] More recent scandals, such as the wave of stock option backdating inquiries, have placed in-house counsel more squarely in the crosshairs, resulting in formal investigations, indictments, plea bargains, and convictions.[4]

---

1. Interview with Adam Ciongoli, General Counsel, Willis Group Holdings, Ltd. (Sept. 4, 2009).
2. Interview with Larry D. Thompson, Senior Vice President, Government Affairs, General Counsel and Secretary, PepsiCo (Dec. 9, 2009).
3. Ben W. Heineman, Jr., *Caught in the Middle*, CORP. COUNSEL, Apr. 2007.
4. *Id.*

In 2007, the Association of Corporate Counsel published a report entitled *In-House Counsel in the Liability Crosshairs.*[5] That report examined the liability environment for in-house counsel and concluded that, following the Enron-Worldcom and other scandals of 2001–2002, "liability has increasingly been imposed or sought against in-house lawyers, particularly by the Securities and Exchange Commission (SEC) and federal prosecutors."[6] But it balanced that conclusion with the observation that "[w]hile the number of suits and other proceedings against in-house lawyers has increased exponentially in recent years and deserves appropriate attention, the absolute number of corporate counsel who have been targeted is still a very small number."[7]

The report also stressed the important point, confirmed by the attitudes and observations of the prominent general counsel that we interviewed when preparing this book, that concern about liability should not be the predominant driver of general counsel's decisions and conduct. Instead, a focus on "doing the right thing" and promoting that goal in others in the general counsel's organization is the best liability prophylaxis. The ACC report put it this way:

> In reality, the fundamentals have not changed: Lawyers are and always have been professionals with a strong ethical creed and a focus on doing the right thing. This important fact partly explains why in-house lawyer roles and attendant "responsibilities" to influence the behavior of others in the corporate structure are under such close scrutiny and increasing demand by stakeholders who want to guarantee better corporate legal compliance.
>
> The result: Heightened scrutiny applied to lawyer behavior leads to a new focus, increased vigilance, and an experiential change in the tone and tenor of daily routines and relationships in the company by corporate counsel the world over, in large and small departments, and in every conceivable industry and specialty. . . .[8]

A. CONCEPTUALIZING THE ROLE: THE GENERAL COUNSEL AS ADVOCATE, GATEKEEPER, OR PERSUASIVE COUNSELOR

The "heightened scrutiny applied to lawyer behavior" relates to a shift in some circles to viewing lawyers—at least those who work for public

---

5. ASS'N OF CORP. COUNSEL, IN-HOUSE COUNSEL IN THE LIABILITY CROSSHAIRS (Sept. 2007).
6. *Id.* at 5.
7. *Id.*
8. *Id.* at 4.

companies—as "gatekeepers." Lawyers serve as both their clients' advisors and their advocates. But the view of lawyers as gatekeepers may shift the understanding of a lawyer's role from that of advisor, protector, and advocate for the client to that of guardian of the public interest. In other words, the gatekeeper view seeks to impose a duty on lawyers to protect public policy or the public interest rather than solely pursuing their clients' interests. As Professor Jack Coffee has put it, gatekeepers work in the securities markets as "independent professionals who pledge their reputational capital . . . to protect the interests of dispersed investors who cannot easily take collective action."[9] The staunchest proponents of the gatekeeper view see the "advocate" view as condoning lawyers who will stop at nothing to pursue their clients' interests—however misguided—including enabling improper dealings.

Indeed, at times a lawyer's best service to the client may be to "just say no."[10] An "autopsy" of the financial crisis, Enron, Worldcom, and many of the other infamous scandals of the early party of the twenty-first century may raise the same questions that District Judge Stanley Sporkin asked in connection with the similarly infamous savings and loan scandals of the late 1980s.[11]

Judge Sporkin's questions are as applicable to the twenty-first century scandals as they were to the savings and loan crisis.[12] Indeed, such sentiments were echoed on the Senate floor during the Sarbanes-Oxley debate

9. John C. Coffee, Jr., *Gatekeeper Failure and Reform: The Challenge of Fashioning Relevant Reforms*, 84 B.U.L. REV. 301, 302 (2004); *see also* Lisa H. Nicholson, *A Hobson's Choice for Securities Lawyers in the Post-Enron Environment: Striking a Balance Between the Obligation of Client Loyalty and Market Gatekeeper*, 16 GEO. J. LEGAL ETHICS 91, 100 (2002) (examining securities lawyers' role as "gatekeepers to the 'level playing fields' of the capital markets"); Sargent, *supra* chapter III, note 21, at 18 ("Lawyers acting in the context of public companies are . . . gatekeepers. They stand at the approaches to the capital markets. As the auditor constrains access to the markets by its power to certify financial statements, and the analyst by its power to make investment recommendations, the company's lawyer has the duty, and at least some power, to constrain unlawful behavior by the company as it seeks to access capital.").

10. Elihu Root, the nineteenth century statesman, suggested in more colorful fashion this gatekeeping role for lawyers: "'About half the practice of a decent lawyer consists in telling would-be clients that they are damned fools and should stop.'" Robert T. Begg, *The Lawyer's License to Discriminate Revoked: How a Dentist Put Teeth in New York's Anti-Discrimination Disciplinary Rule*, 64 ALB. L. REV. 153, 201 n. 252 (2000) (quoting PHILIP C. JESSUP, 1 ELIHU ROOT 133 (1938)).

11. See *supra* chapter I, note 16 & accompanying text for discussion of Judge Sporkin's inquiry in Lincoln Sav. & Loan Ass'n v. Wall, 743 F. Supp. 901, 920 (D.D.C. 1990).

12. *See, e.g.*, Regan, *supra* chapter III, note 55, at 1227, 1238 (discussing the Enron board's waiver of its conflict of interest policy with respect to Enron's CFO's involvement in special-purpose entities).

of 2002. Some senators had their own questions concerning the whereabouts of the lawyers, emphasizing that lawyers are ubiquitous in important corporate matters and thus suggesting that they may be implicated in corporate misfeasance.[13] And the Association of the Bar of the City of New York Report of 2006 (City Bar Report)[14] on the role of lawyers in corporate governance not only focuses on nine scandals of the Enron/Worldcom era, but also contains a detailed and cogent analysis of best practices for corporate lawyers.

Unlike the Enron and Worldcom scandals and their role in catalyzing the adoption of the Sarbanes-Oxley act, the financial crisis of 2008 and beyond did not result—as far as the evidence now shows—from intentional bad acts by lawyers. Yet the financial crisis has similarly led to cries of "where were the lawyers?"[15]

The financial crisis has thus renewed the call by many for lawyers—particularly corporate lawyers—to be gatekeepers. This may be an appropriate role to the extent that a lawyer is asked about the legality of a matter by the board or management or the lawyer is presented with information that should prompt raising a question about legality.[16] But the role of "gatekeeper" may, in certain situations, be either too broad or too narrow, and thus may be misleading or unfocused as an appropriate model for understanding counsel's role.

Professor Coffee has explained that the gatekeeping role for lawyers presents a unique problem of striking an acceptable balance between the lawyer's obligations of client loyalty and advocacy and the purported role of protecting the integrity of the securities markets.[17] Opponents of the concept that the lawyer should act as a gatekeeper argue that the gatekeeping role is akin to the accountant's or auditor's role and is inconsistent with the lawyer's role as advocate, largely because imposing on lawyers a gatekeeping function will chill the attorney-client communication that is essential to good advocacy and forward-thinking, big-picture advice.[18] Coffee has

13. See *supra* chapter I, note 18 and accompanying text for discussion of the statement of Senator Edwards.

14. *Lawyer's Role in Corporate Governance, supra* chapter III, note 5.

15. *See, e.g.*, Sarah Kellogg, *Financial Crisis 2008: Where Were the Lawyers?*, D.C. BAR, Jan. 2010, at 1.

16. *See id.* (discussing structural issues that may prevent individual lawyers from being able to see the big picture or have the information necessary to raise concerns about broader issues, rather than just technical legal issues of a particular matter).

17. Coffee, *supra* note 9, at 346.

18. *See* Sung Hui Kim, *Lawyer Exceptionalism in the Gatekeeping Wars*, 63 SMU L. Rev. 73, 76 (2010) ("[T]he SEC's efforts to impose gatekeeping obligations on lawyers have been fiercely (and almost uniformly) opposed by the bar in highly contentious debates

rejected this argument by distinguishing a litigator's perspective as an advocate from a securities lawyer's role as more like that of auditor, bearing at least some responsibility for due diligence on documents that are drafted and filed with the SEC. He concludes that under this paradigm, the securities lawyer should exercise greater independence from the client, recognize a duty to the public, and employ professional skepticism.[19]

The concerns that drive the gatekeeper model may also drive the treatment of attorney-client privilege with respect to in-house counsel in many jurisdictions outside the United States. Because of the dichotomy that many European jurisdictions perceive between the role of employed in-house counsel and the role of external, independent attorneys,[20] twenty of the twenty-seven member nations of the European Union have rejected attorney-client privilege as between an in-house lawyer and the

---

that I call the "gatekeeping wars. . . ." In those historic battles with the SEC, the bar has repeatedly invoked the powerful rhetoric of "lawyer exceptionalism"—the notion that lawyers' societal function differs from that of all other professionals (such as accountants) who have legal obligations to avert fraud, and that this unique function is so valiant and virtuous that lawyers should be exempt from gatekeeping obligations. The persuasive power of lawyer exceptionalism lies not so much in explicitly reasoned argument but in its implicit invocation of particular images, such as the litigator engaged in zealous advocacy. As natural as that image is, it is exaggerated and deeply misleading in this regulatory context." (footnotes omitted)); Report of the ABA Task Force on Corporate Responsibility, at text accompanying note 26 of the Report, *available at* http://www.abanet.org/leadership/2003/journal/119a.pdf (recommending changes to the model Rules of Professional Conduct); *see also* Interview with Daniel Cooperman, Senior Vice President, General Counsel and Secretary, Apple Inc. (Sept. 1, 2009) ("The increasingly vocal calls for accountability of the general counsel and the obligation of the general counsel to play a policing role has put the general counsel in some respect at odds with the CEO and the members of management in developing the trust that is so important in the relationship. It is an unfortunate development because it does not just jeopardize the relationship between the general counsel and management; it frankly calls into question the sincerity and completeness of the reports and statements that are provided to the general counsel by [management]. They may be reluctant to share everything they could with the general counsel, knowing that the general counsel has this dual role.").

19. Coffee, *supra* note 9, at 360–61; *cf. also* William T. Allen, *Independent Directors in MBO Transactions: Are They Fact or Fantasy?*, 45 Bus. Law. 2055, 2061 (1990) (discussing lawyers' "absolutely crucial" role "in establishing the integrity" of board processes when selling a public company); Peter J. Hennings, *Sarbanes-Oxley Act 307 and Corporate Counsel: Who Better to Prevent Corporate Crime?*, 8 Buff. Crim. L. Rev. 323, 352–53 (2004) (arguing that a gatekeeping role for corporate counsel, imposed through a noisy withdrawal requirement, would not greatly alter the lawyers' roles or the attorney-client relationship).

20. Georgetown Law Corporate Counsel Institute (Europe), Review of General Counsel Roundtable, Project Counsel, *at* http://www.projectcounsel.com/?p=319 (Apr. 24, 2010).

corporate client.[21] This, in turn, further enhances the perceived dichotomy between inside and outside counsel, with potential negative consequences for the corporation.[22] The European Court of Justice upheld this approach in September 2010 in the *Akzo* case, discussed above, basing its ruling on the idea that salaried in-house counsel are unable to exercise the same level of independent judgment as external attorney-advisors.[23] As in the gatekeeper model, concerns about in-house lawyer "capture" by the corporate client drive the approach that many EU jurisdictions take to corporate counsel, leading to an implicit shifting of the lawyer's duties away from the client and toward the public.

The middle ground between the models of lawyers as gatekeepers and lawyers as enablers is that of lawyers as "persuasive counselors."[24] Under the persuasive counselor model, lawyers attempt, through the advice they provide and their personal courage and influence, persuasively to guide their clients to the right course of action. Of course, their ability to do this depends on their receiving the information required to see potential pitfalls, consider issues in the context of the company's bigger picture, and anticipate how matters will be viewed in hindsight. Thus, the general counsel should see to it that the systems and information flow are in place—for both the general counsel and the rank and file of the legal department—that will enable lawyers to fulfill their role as persuasive counselors.

Ben Heineman has described a similar ideal for lawyers—and particularly the modern general counsel—as "lawyer-statesmen."[25] Heineman states

---

21. ASS'N OF CORP. COUNSEL, THE ROLE OF IN-HOUSE COUNSEL: GLOBAL DISTINCTIONS (Sept. 2010).

22. *See* Simmons & Dinnage, *supra* chapter I, note 11, at 82 ("[T]he European courts' negative perception of in-house counsel (i.e., the inability to render independent judgment) has influenced the denial of legal privilege to in-house counsel communications . . . . [T]his narrow perspective forces corporations to undertake less effective and more costly measures through outside counsel, even where the use of in-house counsel would be optimal." (footnote omitted)).

23. Case C-550/07 P, Akzo Nobel Chemicals, Ltd. v. European Commission; *see also* Simmons & Dinnage, *supra* chapter I, note 11, at 82 (discussing *Akzo*).

24. Veasey & Di Guglielmo, *supra* Chapter I, note 8, at 30; *see also* E. Norman Veasey, Chief Justice of the Delaware Supreme Court, Response for the Court at the Delaware Bar Admission Ceremony (Dec. 15, 2003) (on file with authors) ("[T]he best lawyers are the persuasive counselors: those who make the professional effort to see pitfalls that may lie ahead and persuade their clients to change course . . . . [T]he lawyer's responsibility is to be holistic and to eschew tunnel-vision in service to clients and justice."); Lawrence A. Hamermesh, *Who Let You into the House?* 19–20 (Working Paper Nov. 2011) (suggesting reinforcement of the persuasive counselor view as a means of at least partially counteracting any ideological anti-compliance bias among corporate constituents).

25. Heineman, *Lawyer-Statesman, supra* Introduction, note 1.

that the general counsel plays one of the central roles (along with CEOs and other senior executives) in assisting the corporation to achieve a "fundamental fusion" of "high performance with high integrity," which is "the foundation of global capitalism."[26] In fulfilling that role, the general counsel as lawyer-statesman must be "an acute lawyer, a wise counselor and company leader."[27] "The essence of being a lawyer-statesman," writes Heineman, "is to move beyond the first question—'is it legal?'—to the ultimate question—'is it right?'"[28] To do this, the general counsel must exercise "leadership, or shared responsibility, not just for the corporation's legal matters but for its positions on ethics, reputation, public policy, communications, corporate citizenship, country and geopolitical trends."[29]

Proponents of the gatekeeper model likely fear that the persuasive counselor model would allow a lawyer to shirk responsibility for corporate misconduct by arguing that the lawyer gave accurate advice concerning the law and how to comply with it, but executives simply chose not to follow the advice. In essence, it assumes a lack of follow-through, courage, and proactive measures by in-house counsel. Under the persuasive counselor model, however, lawyers go further than simply describing the law and suggesting ways to comply with it. Instead, they affirmatively, proactively, and courageously try to persuade their clients to follow the law, to go beyond mere compliance with the law, and even to "do the right thing" from a moral or ethical perspective.

In many senses, the general counsel is often the "conscience" of the corporation. The directors should understand that a principal role of corporate counsel is to serve the board in ensuring that the board's and management's best efforts are devoted to achieving the proper "tone at the top." Yet it could be argued that the concept of setting up the general counsel as the "conscience" of the corporation places a target on her back. That is, the argument goes, if things go badly on the chief legal officer's "watch," she will be second-guessed and blamed for the wrongdoing even if she had no role in enabling the conduct or capacity to prevent it.

Professor Deborah DeMott has argued that the general counsel is in a strong position "to shape [the corporation's] activities and policies in highly desirable directions, exercising influence that may extend well beyond the bare bones of ensuring legal compliance," including potentially "champion[ing] a transformation of the organizational culture that shapes

26. *Id.* at 5–6.
27. *Id.* at 5.
28. *Id.* at 7.
29. *Id.*

how the corporation addresses its relationships with law and regulation."[30] And the general counsel is in a position to evaluate the entire legal risk portfolio of a company, including its wider consequences, and "'encourage [management] to think of risk in terms other than money.'"[31]

Many general counsel say that the question whether something is legal is often the easiest question that a general counsel gets. As Kim Rucker, Senior Vice President and General Counsel, Avon Products, Inc., says, it is the general counsel's role in "regularly asking . . . whether it is right" that "often takes a lot of curiosity, courage, and drive."[32] The general counsel's role in driving that process, Rucker says, is to "take the businesspeople through questions like: 'What does that decision look like in real life?'" and "'How does that look in front of 'the four M's'—your Maker, your Mother, the Media, and your best Mentor?'"[33] Answering these questions makes an issue "granular, real life, pragmatic. In very few cases, if they still don't get it and you know it's wrong, you have to have the courage to state that and stand firm."[34]

Whether the chief legal officer and other in-house lawyers are able to, and do, counsel the corporate constituents persuasively depends on a range of personal characteristics and other contextual circumstances. Professor Robert Gordon has identified a number of factors that influence the choice and style of compliance advice that may be provided by counsel in a given situation, as follows:

> Which choices are actually made will be a function of the lawyer's situation and convictions, the lawyer's personal courage and confidence, the relations of authority and trust the lawyer has with the managers involved, the lawyer's own position in the hierarchy of the company or outside firm, the importance of the client to the firm, the firm's place in the legal services market, the lawyer's degree of practical knowledge of the business (which will crucially affect the law-yer's ability to suggest alternatives), the form of advice managers prefer to hear from their lawyers, and the general compliance culture of the company (does it

---

30. DeMott, *supra* chapter I, note 24, at 955–56 (footnote omitted).

31. Beardslee, *supra* chapter III, note 18, at 32 (quoting interview with general counsel).

32. Interview with Kim K.W. Rucker, Senior Vice President and General Counsel, Avon Products, Inc. (Jan. 7, 2010).

33. *Id.* Ms. Rucker noted that she once heard someone mention the "4Ms" and that she wishes that she could remember who it was in order to give attribution, but that she often encourages people to think about issues within that framework.

34. *Id.*

walk the line and play hardball with regulators or try to anticipate regulatory problems and initiate its own solutions?).[35]

The general counsel can have a substantial role in shaping many of these factors with respect to both outside and in-house counsel, and thus can significantly influence the ability of all of the client's counsel to function as persuasive counselors. She should also be mindful of factors over which she has less influence or control, but which may also impact her ability to be a strong, persuasive counselor. For example, Professor Sung Hui Kim has hypothesized that situational factors that cause inside counsel to be conformist and obedient are more to blame for in-house counsel's participation in or facilitation of corporate fraud (Kim's "banality hypothesis") than are any conscious or deliberate choices by counsel to follow "the path of greed and depravity" (what Kim terms the conventional "venality hypothesis").[36]

The general counsel has good reason to counsel persuasively and encourage the client to do the right thing. In addition to risks of specific types of liability—some of which are discussed below—a general counsel working in an ethically challenged or otherwise culturally poor corporate environment faces serious reputational risks as well. For an ethical general counsel, those reputational risks can be much more worrisome than any risk of liability she may face.[37]

The good news is that the corporate scandals of the past decade and the current financial crisis have led corporate boards and executives to place greater focus on integrity, ethical corporate culture, and going beyond compliance. The general counsel therefore need not go it alone. Rather than viewing a general counsel who tries to build a culture of ethics and integrity as a troublemaker, most boards will fully support those efforts. Chuck Kalil, Executive Vice President, Law and Government Affairs, General Counsel, and Corporate Secretary, The Dow Chemical Company, stated that the current liability environment creates "peril for the companies [and] peril for individuals," particularly for an individual who is "caught up in a bad culture. But then, a competent GC is going to do everything he or she possibly

---

35. Robert W. Gordon, *The Independence of Lawyers*, 68 B.U.L. Rev. 1, 26–28 (1988).
36. Kim, *supra* chapter V, note 87.
37. *See* Interview with Susan Hackett, Senior Vice President and General Counsel, Association of Corporate Counsel (Sept. 2, 2009) ("I think that the taint of being in an organization that has a cultural or corporate failure problem is a far greater problem in a practical sense for CLOs than the likelihood that they will actually have to walk the perp line themselves.").

can do to modify that culture."[38] And in doing so, she will receive the backing of the board: "The general counsel should be in a safe position in [trying to modify a bad culture] because the directors are going to be 100% behind her for trying to modify that culture. No one on the board would take a different view."[39]

B. REPORTING UP AND REPORTING OUT

As we have discussed above,[40] section 307 of the Sarbanes-Oxley Act directed the SEC to issue rules establishing "minimum standards of professional conduct for attorneys appearing and practicing before the Commission in any way in the representation of issuers"[41]—a very broad group of lawyers to whom the rules might apply.[42] In particular, the Commission was directed to include in its rule-making a rule

(i) requiring an attorney to report evidence of a material violation of securities law or breach of fiduciary duty or similar violation by the company or any agent thereof, to the chief legal counsel or the chief executive officer of the company (or the equivalent thereof); and

(ii) if the counsel or officer does not appropriately respond to the evidence (adopting, as necessary, appropriate remedial measures or sanctions with respect to the violation), requiring the attorney to report the evidence to the audit committee of the board of directors of the issuer or to another committee of the board of directors comprised solely of directors not employed directly or indirectly by the issuer, or to the board of directors.[43]

---

38. Interview with Charles J. Kalil, Executive Vice President, Law and Government Affairs, General Counsel, and Corporate Secretary, The Dow Chemical Company (Nov. 10, 2009).

39. *Id.*

40. *Supra* chapter IV.B.2.

41. 15 U.S.C. § 7245.

42. The rule's definition of "appearing and practicing before the Commission" includes transacting any business or communicating in any way with the SEC, representing an issuer in an SEC administrative proceeding or in connection with any SEC investigation, inquiry, request for information, or subpoena, providing advice regarding the securities laws or the SEC's rules or regulations regarding any document that the attorney has notice will be filed with or submitted to the SEC (or incorporated into any document that will be filed with or submitted to the SEC), and advising an issuer regarding whether information or a statement, opinion, or other writing must be filed with or submitted to the SEC (or incorporated into any document that will be filed with or submitted to the SEC). 17 C.F.R. § 205.2(a)(1).

43. *Id.*

The SEC issued final rules implementing this "up-the-ladder" reporting requirement in February 2003.[44]

The up-the-ladder reporting requirement, which includes an option to report wrongdoing to the SEC,[45] places tension on the general counsel by potentially creating an adversarial atmosphere within the corporation. Where in-house counsel has an obligation to be an internal whistleblower, other constituents within the corporation may become reluctant to bring issues to counsel's attention. In addition, awareness of this codified obligation (which applies to both in-house and outside lawyers) may place management or the board on the defensive when the general counsel does raise an issue because they may automatically view the vetting of issues as out of the ordinary, rather than as appropriate matters of prophylaxis, routine internal control, and management of legal compliance.

As developed previously,[46] the ABA Model Rules of Professional Conduct, in the form finally approved by the ABA House of Delegates in 2003, include comparable provisions. Rule 1.13 contains a presumption that requires the lawyer, as a matter of ethics, to report "up the ladder" within the corporate hierarchy certain law violations that are likely to result in substantial injury to the corporation, unless the lawyer reasonably believes that it is not in

44. 17 C.F.R. pt. 205. The Commission proposed a companion "noisy withdrawal" rule requiring a lawyer to withdraw from representation and notify the Commission about the withdrawal in the event that the lawyer's up-the-ladder reporting does not yield an appropriate response from the board of directors. *See* Proposed Rule: Implementation of Standards of Professional Conduct for Attorneys, 67 Fed. Reg. 1670 (Dec. 2, 2002), *available at* www.sec.gov/rules/proposed/33–8150.htm. That proposal has not been adopted as a final rule, and the SEC's "noisy withdrawal" proposal has effectively been tabled indefinitely.

45. In addition to the "reporting up" provisions, the rules provide that an attorney may report "out" to the SEC:

> An attorney appearing and practicing before the Commission in the representation of an issuer may reveal to the Commission, without the issuer's consent, confidential information related to the representation to the extent the attorney reasonably believes necessary:
> (i) To prevent the issuer from committing a material violation that is likely to cause substantial injury to the financial interest or property of the issuer or investors; (ii) To prevent the issuer, in a Commission investigation or administrative proceeding from committing perjury . . .; suborning perjury . . .; or committing any act proscribed in 18 U.S.C. 1001 that is likely to perpetrate a fraud upon the Commission; or (iii) To rectify the consequences of a material violation by the issuer that caused, or may cause, substantial injury to the financial interest or property of the issuer or investors in the furtherance of which the attorney's services were used.

17 C.F.R. § 205.3(d)(2).

46. *Supra* chapter IV.B.1.

the best interest of the corporate client to do so.[47] The rule contains a further provision that tends to protect the lawyer by requiring that the board be notified if the lawyer is fired or withdraws in connection with reporting up.[48] Model Rules 1.6(b)(2) and 1.6(b)(3) provide counsel with the option of reporting out to prevent, mitigate, or rectify potential, substantial financial harm to the corporation from a crime or fraud, in furtherance of which the lawyer's services were used.[49] Those rules have been adopted in a number of states.[50]

Does the formal up-the-ladder reporting requirement of the SOX and ABA Model Rules tend to undermine the general counsel's position as chief legal advisor to the corporation? Is she instead seen as an enforcer or internal "cop"? In most instances she should not be so viewed, but if the CLO and her in-house lawyers are perceived by other corporate constituents as "cops," that perception does provide counsel with leverage to cause the corporate constituents to "do the right thing." Although that perception could chill communications between other corporate constituents and in-house lawyers, the up-the-ladder reporting requirement may enhance general counsel's ability to exercise judgment, independent of other senior managers. For example, the reporting requirement may provide "some check on the apparent tendency of some general counsel to maintain insufficiently critical detachment from officers and other senior managers, preventing them from giving the board the frank advice it need[s] to perform its own monitoring function."[51] The same considerations would seem to apply to outside counsel in many instances.

As the ABA Task Force on Corporate Responsibility (the Cheek Report) recommended, public corporations should adopt policies that ensure direct contact between the independent members of the board and the general counsel:

> Public corporations should adopt practices in which . . . [g]eneral counsel meets regularly and in executive session with a committee of independent directors to

47. MODEL RULES OF PROF'L CONDUCT R. 1.13(b) (2006).
48. *Id.* R. 1.13(e).
49. *Id.* R. 1.6(b)(2)–(3).
50. *See* ABA Center for Professional Responsibility, Charts Comparing Professional Conduct Rules, *at* http://www.americanbar.org/groups/professional_responsibility/policy/charts.html (providing charts comparing states' ethics rules with the Model Rules); ABA Center for Professional Responsibility, Links of Interest, Ethics 2000 Review Status Chart, *at* http://www.americanbar.org/groups/professional_responsibility/resources/links_of_interest.html (tracking the status of states' review and adoption of the Model Rules).
51. Sargent, *supra* chapter III, note 21, at 38.

communicate concerns regarding legal compliance matters, including potential or ongoing material violations of law by, and breaches of fiduciary duty to, the corporation.[52]

Implementation of such policies may tend to enhance the general counsel's rapport and credibility with the board. It may also facilitate the board's objective and independent evaluation of issues discussed with the general counsel because the general counsel's reports to the board will be perceived as matters to be addressed by the board in the ordinary course of its oversight of the corporation.[53] Whether or not the particular corporation adopts such a formal policy establishing regular contact between the general counsel and the board, the directors should focus on understanding counsel's complex role and the tensions that counsel faces.

Some observers argue that the practice of formally establishing regular contact between the general counsel and the independent directors could put general counsel in an awkward position vis-à-vis the CEO and other members of senior management. There is some risk of that, but such a practice and understanding will help to ensure that the board will be able to identify and address potential pressure points when they arise between general counsel and management.[54] On balance, this would seem to be more for the good than otherwise.

Both Model Rule 1.13 and the SEC part 205 rules permit, but do not require, the lawyer to "report out"—to the SEC, presumably—if the board of directors fails to act after reporting up the ladder. A decision to report out is a tough one, but the ability under the rules to report out empowers the lawyer and gives her some leverage in dealing with a reluctant board.

Even beyond reporting out by lawyers after an internal process of reporting up is followed, the Dodd-Frank Act's whistleblower provisions and the SEC's implementing rules now have further empowered non-management whistleblowers to make reports to the SEC, without first exhausting (or even using) the company's internal reporting system.[55] The general counsel, in conjunction with other company leadership, should ensure that

52. Cheek Report, *supra* chapter III, note 45, at 161.
53. *See Compliance Readiness—General Counsel's Expanded Role, supra* Chapter III, note 25, at 1, 24 (identifying lessons for general counsel learned from the Worldcom scandal, including that the general counsel should have "direct access and frequent and open communication with the board of directors").
54. *Cf.* FOX & MARTYN, *supra* chapter IV, note 60, at 58–59, 71–74, 77 (discussing corporate counsel's responsibilities in the context of splits of authority among constituents of a corporate client, and up-the-ladder reporting obligations).
55. See *supra* chapter I.C.3 for discussion of the whistleblower provisions.

the internal reporting system is structured and implemented to facilitate and encourage internal reporting before external reports are made.[56]

C. UNDERSTANDING THE RISKS: TYPES OF LIABILITY EXPOSURE CONFRONTING IN-HOUSE COUNSEL

1. SEC Enforcement

According to a study undertaken by ACC, the SEC has increasingly focused its attention on in-house counsel as the subjects of enforcement actions following the corporate scandals of 2001–2002 and the passage of the Sarbanes-Oxley Act.[57] The increased activity is likely the result of the SEC's enhanced power, under sections 307 and 602 of Sarbanes-Oxley and the "reporting up" rules of Part 205, to adopt and enforce minimum standards of professional conduct for attorneys appearing and practicing before the Commission.[58] Remarks made by the SEC staff suggest as much. For example, in 2004, then-director of the SEC Division of Enforcement Stephen Cutler remarked in a speech: "We have seen too many examples of lawyers who twisted themselves into pretzels to accommodate the wishes of company management, and failed in their responsibility to insist that the company comply with the law."[59] Cutler went on to delineate how the Commission would use its enforcement power to investigate and pursue actions against in-house and outside corporate counsel who allegedly engaged in various types of malfeasance or misfeasance.

One commentator has suggested that the SEC has substituted its rule-making efforts on "reporting out" or "noisy withdrawal" obligations with

56. *Supra* Chapter I.C.3.d.

57. *See* John K. Villa, *Inside Counsel as Targets: Fact or Fiction?*, ACC Docket, Nov. / Dec. 2005, at 104–05 (discussing the study); *see also* Colleen P. Mahoney, *Recent SEC Enforcement Actions Against Corporate In-House Counsel* 2 (Dec. 14, 2007) (on file with authors) ("Prior to passage of the Sarbanes-Oxley Act . . ., SEC actions against corporate in-house counsel were relatively infrequent. Since the passage of Sarbanes-Oxley in 2002, the SEC has stepped up its pursuit of in-house counsel allegedly involved in purportedly false or misleading financial statements, and the number of actions against lawyers involved in options backdating in particular has dramatically increased.").

58. 15 U.S.C. §§ 7245, 78d-3; 17 C.F.R. pt. 205.

59. Stephen M. Cutler, Director, Division of Enforcement, U.S. Securities and Exchange Commission, Speech at the UCLA School of Law, The Themes of Sarbanes-Oxley as Reflected in the Commission's Enforcement Program (Sept. 20, 2004), http://www.sec.gov/news/speech/spch092004smc.htm.

stepped-up enforcement efforts against in-house counsel.[60] The SEC enforcement activity against general counsel and other in-house counsel seems largely to have tracked widespread corporate scandals, however. For example, of the nine enforcement actions that the SEC filed against or settled with in-house counsel in 2007, six involved stock-option back-dating and pricing issues—a corporate scandal that was very much in the news that year—and one involved Enron.[61] Thus, any increase in enforcement activity against general counsel and other in-house counsel may not be the result of a particular decision by the SEC to target in-house counsel, but rather it correlates to the nature of the corporate compliance issues of the day. Moreover, another of the nine actions involved insider trading allegations—allegations that are not directly tied to the defendant's status as an attorney.[62]

Actions that the SEC can initiate against in-house counsel include civil injunctive actions under § 21(d) of the Exchange Act,[63] administrative actions under § 15(c)(4) of the Exchange Act,[64] cease-and-desist orders under § 21 of the Exchange Act,[65] and proceedings to prevent a lawyer from practicing before the Commission.[66] SEC enforcement actions against lawyers often target the chief legal officer of a company,[67] and most involve situations in which the subject of the action did not rely on the advice of outside counsel.[68] Similarly, in-house counsel appear to be at greater risk

---

60. *See* David B. Bayless, *Recent SEC Enforcement Actions Against In-House Lawyers: Its Impact on Legal and Compliance*, PRACTISING L. INST. CORP. L. & PRAC. COURSE HANDBOOK SERIES PLI ORDER NO. 14035, at 616 (2008) ("Since the initial proposal of 'noisy withdrawal' provisions, the Commission has tabled this rule-making strategy. But, what has emerged in its stead, is the SEC's efforts to obtain through the enforcement process what it could not obtain through rule-making."); *see also* David B. Bayless & Tammy Albarrán, *Recent SEC Enforcement Actions Against In-House Lawyers: An Ominous Trend for the Legal Profession*, 13 ANDREWS LITIG. REPORTER 1, 1–2 (2007).

61. Bayless, *supra* note 60, at 617–21 (summarizing SEC enforcement actions against in-house counsel in 2007).

62. *Id.* at 621.

63. 15 U.S.C. § 78u(d)(1).

64. 15 U.S.C. § 78o(c)(4).

65. 15 U.S.C. § 78u-3(a).

66. 17 C.F.R. § 201.102(e); *see* Villa, *supra* note 57, at 104 (identifying the possible non-criminal actions by the SEC against lawyers).

67. *But cf.* Bayless, *supra* note 60, at 617 ("Historically, the Commission has not pursued enforcement actions against lawyers (much less against general counsels) as aggressively as it did [in 2007].").

68. Villa, *supra* note 57, at 105; *cf. also* Alicia Mundy & Brent Kendall, *U.S. Rebuffed in Glaxo Misconduct Case*, WALL ST. J., May 11, 2011, at B1 (reporting court's directed verdict acquitting in-house counsel of criminal charges for obstruction of justice, where in-house counsel relied on advice of outside counsel).

for SEC enforcement actions against them if they are generalist lawyers who failed to seek out specialized advice when needed.[69]

2. Prosecution

In 2002, the Justice Department established its Corporate Crime Task Force, and a spike in the number of general counsel subject to criminal prosecution for securities-law-related crimes followed.[70] Still, "[g]eneral counsel are not typically primary targets for prosecutors—CEOs, CFOs and board members carry brighter bull's-eyes."[71] But when the general counsel is implicated in a criminal prosecution, "even if the general counsel is innocent, the formal implication of wrongdoing is so toxic the company can rarely allow the lawyer to stay on."[72] And even if the general counsel remains in the position while the charges are pending, real practical problems arise from the need to distance the general counsel—whose roles and functions in the company are multifaceted—from anything related to the investigation or prosecution.[73]

One area in which prosecutorial activity has increased is with respect to obstruction of justice charges.[74] In November 2010, the Department of Justice filed an indictment against Lauren Stevens, a former vice president and associate general counsel at GlaxoSmithKline.[75] Stevens was the point person on an FDA investigation in 2002 of off-label marketing of Wellbutrin SR. The DOJ indictment alleges that Stevens "signed and sent letters denying that Glaxo had marketed Wellbutrin for off-label use despite knowing the company paid physicians to promote the drug in talks that included information on unapproved uses" and that she "withheld documents showing as much despite telling the FDA she had produced all relevant information."[76] The indictment charged Stevens with obstruction of an official proceeding, concealing and falsifying documents to influence a federal agency, and making false statements to the FDA.[77]

---

69. Villa, *supra* note 57, at 106.
70. *Id.* at 105.
71. Steven Andersen, *Nightmare Scenario*, INSIDE COUNSEL, Feb. 2009, at 40.
72. *Id.*
73. *Id.*
74. Melissa Maleske, *Criminal Advocacy*, INSIDE COUNSEL, Jan. 2011, at 18.
75. *Id.* at 16.
76. *Id.* at 17.
77. *Id.* at 18.

The case against Stevens dissolved with a directed verdict of not guilty in May 2011. The judge ordering the acquittal commented ruefully about the "enormous potential for abuse in allowing prosecution of an attorney for giving legal advice."[78] In addition to the concerns articulated by the judge in dismissing the charges, other observers of the case have criticized the Department of Justice for wasting prosecutorial resources by being too aggressive against in-house lawyers.[79] In any event, the case raises important issues about the line between aggressive advocacy and obstruction.[80]

Law enforcement is also employing new methods of uncovering misconduct by corporate executives, including general counsel. In early 2010, media sources reported that an undercover FBI sting operation had led to the indictment, for FCPA violations, of twenty-two corporate executives, including the general counsel of a company that makes military equipment.[81] Observers have noted that "conducting undercover investigations to catch bribery is a dramatic change for the Justice Department," which before this operation had generally only prosecuted FCPA violations after a company or the media reported the violations.[82] In contrast, the type of conduct uncovered by the FBI's sting operation rose to the highest levels of the corporation—it was not a case of internal control failures or inadequate training.[83] The indicted executives had been personally involved in negotiating the bribes[84]—a fact that should give comfort to general counsel who are trying to do the right thing. The charges against many of the indicted

78. Mundy & Kendall, *supra* note 68, at B1.

79. *See Commentary on Court Dismissal of Indictment Against Former VP and Associate General Counsel of GlaxoSmithKline*, WHITE COLLAR CRIME PROF BLOG, http://lawprofessors.typepad.com/whitecollarcrime_blog/page/7/ (Mar. 25, 2011) ("But what is more questionable here is that the government thinks that specific intent should not be required here. Should you really prosecute someone who may not have had the specific intent to do these alleged acts? Will this achieve the deterrence from criminality that we desire? Irrespective of whether one accepts the government's claim that advice of counsel is an affirmative defense or the defense and court position that it negates the mens rea, is prosecution of this alleged conduct the way we want to spend valuable tax dollars?").

80. *Id.*; *see also* Sue Reisinger, *New Docs in Case of Ex-Glaxo In-House Counsel Lauren Stevens Reveal Other Lawyers' Roles*, CORP. COUNSEL, Mar. 18 2011, http://www.law.com/jsp/cc/PubArticleCC.jsp?id=1202486806785; Tom Schoenberg, *Ex-Glaxo Lawyer "Went Too Far," U.S Says at Opening of Obstruction Trial*, bloomberg.com, at http://www.bloomberg.com/news/2011–04–27/ex-glaxo-lawyer-went-too-far-u-s-says-at-opening-of-obstruction-trial.html (Apr. 27, 2011).

81. Amy Miller, *Top Lawyer Nabbed in Undercover FBI Bribery Sting*, CORP. COUNSEL, Jan. 21, 2010, http://www.corpcounsel.com.

82. *Id.* (reporting observations of Alexandra Wrage, president of Trace International, a nonprofit association that tracks FCPA violations).

83. *Id.*

84. *Id.*

executives are proceeding to trial, while four of them have pleaded guilty.[85]

There is some concern that certain prosecutions of general counsel have lowered the bar relating to what conduct by in-house counsel will be determined to have been criminal. In 2007, a Chicago jury convicted an in-house lawyer at Hollinger International Inc. of fraud in conjunction with former chairman Conrad Black's conviction for fraud.[86] The lawyer, Mark Kipnis, had drafted non-compete documents in connection with the sale of Hollinger publications that channeled millions of dollars to Black and others. Kipnis was charged as a participant in the fraud, but not with helping conceive the fraud or receiving any benefit from the payments. "Essentially, Kipnis . . . was charged as an enabler of deals he knew were crooked."[87]

In 2005, the SEC charged Google, Inc. and its general counsel, David Drummond, with failure to register the issuance of over $80 million in stock option grants to employees or make associated financial disclosures required by the securities laws in the two years preceding Google's initial public offering.[88] The SEC's order found that Drummond "was aware that the registration and related financial disclosure obligations had been triggered, but believed that Google could avoid providing the information to its employees by relying on an exemption from the law. According to the Commission, Drummond advised Google's Board that it could continue to issue options, but failed to inform the Board that the registration and disclosure obligations had been triggered or that there were risks in relying on the exemption, which was in fact inapplicable."[89] To settle the charges, Google and Drummond agreed to a cease-and-desist order.[90] Commentators have argued that the charges against Drummond make securities-law claims out of "what arguably amounts to providing incorrect legal advice."[91]

85. Nedra Pickler, *Jurors Weigh First Undercover Sting Case to Enforce Foreign Bribe Law as US Enforcement Rises*, NEWSER (June 28, 2011), http://www.newser.com/article/d9o4ntu82/jurors-weigh-first-undercover-sting-case-to-enforce-foreign-bribe-law-as-us-enforcement-rises.html.

86. Michael Orey, *In-House Attorneys, Watch Your Step*, BUS. WEEK, Aug. 6, 2007.

87. *Id.*

88. SEC Charges Google and Its General Counsel David C. Drummond with Failure to Register over $80 Million in Employee Stock Options Prior to IPO, Release No. 2005-6 (SEC Jan. 13, 2005).

89. *Id.*

90. *Id.*

91. Mikulka, *supra* chapter II, note 13, at 73.

Such charges may signal targeting of lawyers who are more tangentially involved than those who typically have been prosecuted.[92] Some commentators believe that this "sets disturbingly high expectations for in-house attorneys when it comes to recognizing when transactions are being used for corrupt purposes," particularly because transactions like the special-purpose entities used by Enron and the non-compete deals at issue in the Hollinger case "can serve legitimate ends."[93] Thus, prosecution of a lawyer for drafting documents that effectuated such transactions may criminalize mere negligence "for failing to ask questions" of the client.[94] Michele Coleman Mayes, General Counsel of The Allstate Corporation, has said that the current environment establishes nearly a strict liability regime for general counsel: "If you are a GC, you may now be held accountable for failing to stop the misconduct even if you had no role in the wrongdoing."[95]

As with SEC enforcement actions, the involvement of outside counsel appears to mitigate the risk of criminal prosecution.[96] But it is not an absolute shield. In the case of the indictment of Lauren Stevens at GlaxoSmithKline, discussed above, Ms. Stevens had vetted the situation with outside counsel, who had reviewed the relevant documents and advised with respect to the decision.[97]

Aside from worrying about personal exposure to an increased risk of criminal prosecution, the spike in criminal prosecutions against corporations and their officers means that general counsel need to be more familiar with criminal law and procedure than in the past. "If a general counsel is not familiar with criminal procedure and criminal law and how it affects business nowadays, they are behind the eight-ball because so many of our laws today have a criminal component. There is more emphasis by the government on using that side of the law than the civil side than there was even five years ago. As to things that used to be handled as a civil issue, you have a lot of people now wanting to make them criminal. That is an unfortunate development for general counsel, but something that general counsel must make sure that they are well versed in, because it is a critical part of what they have to advise management and the board about."[98]

---

92. Orey, *supra* note 86.
93. *Id.*
94. *Id.*
95. Mikulka, *supra* Chapter II, note 13, at 73 (quoting Michele Mayes).
96. Villa, *supra* note 57, at 106.
97. Maleske, *supra* note 74, at 18.
98. Interview with Charles Matthews, General Counsel, Exxon Mobil Corporation (Sept. 1, 2009).

3. Fiduciary Duty Liability

The general counsel, like all corporate officers, owes fiduciary duties to the corporation.[99] As a general matter, those fiduciary duties are the same as the duties owed by directors,[100] although there have not been a large number of decisions of the Delaware courts explicating the parameters of officers' fiduciary duties.[101] Just as for other types of liability and enforcement actions, nothing about the economic crisis should inherently have heightened general counsel's risk of liability for breaches of fiduciary duty. But because the crisis has increased scrutiny and public attention on corporations and corporate executives, general counsel may be more likely than before to be targeted in fiduciary duty litigation.

Under Delaware law, fiduciary duties include the duties of due care and loyalty. Other duties, such as the obligations of candor and good faith, are subsets of the duties of loyalty and care.[102] The duty of care requires that, in managing the corporation's affairs, officers act with due care, in good faith, in a manner they honestly believe to be in the best interests of the corporation.[103] It is important to note that Delaware and many other states that have exoneration statutes like section 102(b)(7) of the DGCL do not provide for exoneration of officers, although some states do so provide.[104]

The duty of care also includes the duty to monitor, or the duty of oversight. Directors (and presumably officers) have a duty to monitor the

---

99. Guth v. Loft, 5 A. 2d 503, 510 (Del. 1939) (officers and directors owe fiduciary duties to the corporations they serve).

100. Gantler v. Stephens, 965 A. 2d 695, 709 (Del. 2009) ("[T]he fiduciary duties of officers are the same as those of directors."); Hampshire Group, Ltd. v. Kuttner, 2010 WL 2739995, at *11 (Del. Ch. July 12, 2010) ("As a general matter, our Supreme Court has found that the duties of corporate officers are similar to those of corporate directors. Generally, like directors, [officers are] expected to pursue the best interests of the company in good faith (i.e., to fulfill their duty of loyalty) and to use the amount of care that a reasonably prudent person would use in similar circumstances (i.e., to fulfill their duty of care).").

101. Lyman P.Q. Johnson & Robert V. Ricca, *(Not) Advising Corporate Officers About Fiduciary Duties*, 42 WAKE FOREST L. REV. 663, 665–66 (2007).

102. *See* Pfeffer v. Redstone, 965 A.2d 676, 684 (Del. 2009) ("'[T]he duty of disclosure is not an independent duty, but derives from the duties of care and loyalty.'"); Stone v. Ritter, 911 A. 2d 362, 370 (Del. 2006) (holding that the duty of good faith is a subset of the duty of loyalty).

103. *See* Brehm v. Eisner, 746 A.2d 244 (Del. 2000); Cede & Co. v. Technicolor, Inc., 634 A.2d 345, 361 (Del. 1993); Smith v. Van Gorkom, 488 A.2d 858 (Del. 1985); *see also* 2 MODEL BUS. CORP. ACT ANN. § 8.30 (a)-(b) (4th ed. 2008, Supp. 2009); 3A FLETCHER CYCLOPEDIA OF THE LAW OF PRIVATE CORP. § 1036 (2002 and 2008–2009 Cum. Supp.); RADIN, *supra* chapter V, note 5, at 431–43.

104. See discussion of Delaware's section 102(b)(7), *supra* chapter V.A.4. Louisiana is one state that does provide for officer exoneration. LA. REV. STAT. ANN. § 12:24(C)(4).

---

corporation and investigate possible wrongdoing within the corporation.[105] As explained in *In re Caremark International Derivative Litigation*[106] and *Stone v. Ritter*,[107] this duty of oversight includes "a duty to attempt in good faith to assure that a corporate information and reporting system, which the board concludes is adequate, exists."[108] The utter failure to have and to monitor such a system can result in liability of a director or officer.[109] Any director who has actual knowledge of facts suggesting a material problem in the company must promptly initiate board or management consideration of the issue.[110] On one hand, if through exercise of the oversight function a director suspects, or should have suspected, wrongdoing, the director must act reasonably in light of the information gained.[111] On the other hand, directors generally do not have a duty to "ferret out" wrongdoing, to uncover "hard-core" fraud by officers or directors, or to "predict the future" or correctly evaluate business risk—so long as the proper monitoring systems are in place.[112]

---

105. *See* E. Norman Veasey, *Counseling Directors in the New Corporate Culture*, 59 Bus. Law. 1447 (2004); *see also* 15 U.S.C. § 7262 (requiring a company's annual report to describe and assess the company's internal controls); Stone v. Ritter, 911 A.2d 362 (Del. 2006) (affirming dismissal where complaint alleged that directors had failed in their oversight duty); ATR-Kim Eng. Fin. Corp. v. Araneta, 2006 Del. Ch. LEXIS 215, at *70–77 (Del. Ch. Dec. 21, 2006) (directors breached fiduciary duties where they "did nothing to make themselves aware of this blatant misconduct or to stop it"); Saito v. McCall, 2004 WL 3129876 (Del. Ch. Dec. 20, 2004) (denying motions to dismiss where directors allegedly failed to monitor the company's accounting practices and failed to implement sufficient internal controls to guard against wrongful accounting practices).

106. 698 A.2d 959 (Del. Ch. 1996). Former Chancellor Allen in *Caremark* cited the federal sentencing guidelines as crediting companies with effective compliance programs.

107. 911 A.2d 362 (Del. 2006).

108. *Caremark*, 698 A.2d at 970.

109. *Id.*; *see also Stone*, 911 A.2d at 370 (holding that director oversight liability requires showing that directors "utterly failed to implement any reporting or information system or controls" or, if such controls were in place, consciously failed to oversee their operation); *In re* Citigroup Inc. S'holder Deriv. Litig., 964 A.2d 106, 122 (Del. Ch. 2009) (same).

110. *See Caremark*, 698 A.2d at 970; *see also Stone*, 911 A.2d at 369 (holding that bad faith may be shown where a "fiduciary intentionally fails to act in the face of a known duty to act, demonstrating a conscious disregard for his duties").

111. *See* Graham v. Allis-Chambers Mfg. Co., 188 A.2d 125, 130 (Del. 1963) (director who ignores either willfully or through inattention obvious signs of wrongdoing will be held liable); *cf. Stone*, 911 A.2d at 373 ("In the absence of red flags, good faith in the context of oversight must be measured by the directors' actions 'to assure a reasonable information and reporting system exists . . . .'"); *In re* Dow Chem. Co. Deriv. Litig., 2010 WL 66769, at *13 (Del. Ch. Jan. 11, 2010) (rejecting oversight claims where plaintiffs failed to sufficiently allege "red flags" that would give the directors reason to suspect misconduct).

112. *Citigroup*, 964 A.2d at 131; *Caremark*, 698 A. 2d at 968–70; *Stone*, 911 A.2d at 373. In a similar context, former SEC Commissioner Harvey J. Goldschmid has stated:

In *World Health Alternatives, Inc. v. McDonald*,[113] the United States Bankruptcy Court for the District of Delaware held that the duty of oversight as articulated with respect to directors in *Caremark, Stone,* and *ATR-Kim Eng Financial Corp. v. Araneta*[114] also applies to officers who are not directors.[115] In *World Health*, the bankruptcy trustee of World Health Alternatives, Inc. alleged that a number of former officers and directors of World Health had breached their fiduciary duties and committed fraud and other misconduct in connection with accounting abnormalities, related-party loans, misrepresentations in World Health's SEC filings, and other problems at World Health. One of the defendants was Brian Licastro, who was World Health's vice president of operations and general counsel.[116] The trustee alleged that "as the vice president of operation and in-house general counsel to World health, Licastro was responsible for failing to implement any internal monitoring system and/or failing to utilize such system."[117] Pointing to the up-the-ladder reporting requirements of the SEC rules implementing Section 307 of the Sarbanes-Oxley Act,[118] the court noted that "a general counsel has an affirmative duty to inspect the truthfulness of the SEC filings" made by a company.[119] The court therefore agreed with

Some who champion the idea of an active audit committee [of the board of directors] say it will stop venal, hard-core fraud. That I do not consider realistic. An active audit committee will not, when acting alone, be able to catch thieves in most circumstances. Even the most active and effective auditors will have some trouble when hard-core fraud is involved. There are techniques being developed today to try to reach hard-core misconduct, including forensic auditing and other techniques. But when no red flags are flying, even when an audit committee acts reasonably, it will be difficult to spot fraud that is concealed and hard-core. The dangers of hard-core fraud, in short, will only be somewhat deterred or mitigated by an active audit committee.

Post-Enron America: An SEC Perspective (Dec. 2, 2002), www.sec.gov/news/speech/spch120202hjg.htm.

113. 385 B.R. 576 (Bankr. D. Del. 2008).

114. 2006 Del. Ch. LEXIS 215 (Del. Ch. Dec. 21, 2006). In *Araneta*, the Delaware Court of Chancery held two defendants who were officers and directors of a company liable for breach of fiduciary duty for failing to stop the company's majority stockholders and fellow director from making self-interested transfers of the company's assets. *Id.* at *3–4.

115. *World Health*, 385 B.R. at 591–92. The court in *World Health* was applying Florida law, but it referred extensively to Delaware law because "the Florida courts have relied upon Delaware corporate law to establish their own corporate doctrines." *Id.* at 590 (internal quotations omitted).

116. *See id.* at 581 & n. 2 (acknowledging some uncertainty regarding whether Licastro was general counsel on a formal or a de facto basis, but accepting the allegation that he was general counsel as true in the context of a motion to dismiss).

117. *Id.* at 591.

118. 17 C.F.R pt. 205 (Jan. 29, 2007).

119. *World Health*, 385 B.R. at 591.

the trustee that Licastro, "as the in-house general counsel and the only lawyer in top management of World Health during the relevant period, had a duty to know or should have known of these corporate wrongdoings and reported such breaches of fiduciary duties by the management."[120] After reviewing Delaware law and concluding that officers owe the same fiduciary duty of oversight as directors (and that the Florida law would reach the same result), the court refused Licastro's motion to dismiss the breach of fiduciary duty allegations against him.[121]

The court similarly rejected Licastro's motion to dismiss breach of fiduciary duty claims arising out of allegations that officers of World Health committed corporate waste by causing World Health to lease time on private jets, to pay the monthly lease payments of certain officers' luxury automobiles, and to pay another officer a large bonus in cash and stock, at times when World Health had negative net income and extremely limited cash available.[122] Licastro sought dismissal of these claims because he received no personal benefit from the transactions and "he was not involved."[123] Although the court noted that "[t]he call on this count is a close one," it rejected Licastro's motion to dismiss.[124] It wrote:

> There is no allegation that Licastro personally benefited from the alleged expenditures. Licastro's role was vice president of operations and general counsel. Because he was not a financial officer his knowledge of the alleged wasteful spending for personal benefit to other officers and directors would seem not to be readily discernible. However, given the fact that we must view the allegation in the light most favorable to the Trustee, I believe the motion should be denied with respect to this count.
>
> While Licastro may not have been actively engaged in these alleged wasteful expenditures, the Complaint alleges that "Defendants actively engaged in and/or allowed routine waste of the Company's limited resources," and the "directors, officers and other senior management[s] knew or should have known about the above referenced mismanagement and waste and they exhibited a substantial and systematic failure to control and monitor the accrual of unnecessary expenses." Because the Complaint alleges that Defendants, including Licastro, "allowed" and "knew or should have known" the corporate waste, it follows that the Complaint is asserting that Defendants, including Licastro, were aware of

120. *Id.*
121. *Id.* at 592–93.
122. *Id.* at 593.
123. *Id.*
124. *Id.*

the alleged corporate waste and took no action, as fiduciaries, to prevent such conduct. Also, it is conceivable that no person acting in good faith in pursuit of World Health's interest would approve chartering expensive flights, leasing luxury automobiles, and granting large bonuses to certain directors and officers while World Health was experiencing negative net income. Thus, the motion to dismiss will be denied as to the corporate waste count.[125]

Similarly, with respect to claims for aiding and abetting the corporate waste described above, the court held that the complaint sufficiently alleged that

> Licastro had knowledge of the wasting of assets and took no action to correct it or to establish guidelines for corporate expenditures. In his role as general counsel, it seems highly likely that he would have been consulted as to guidelines for out of the ordinary expenditures. To the extent other officers directly caused those expenditures to be made, one can infer, and the Complaint so alleges, that Licastro was aware of them.[126]

The claims were ultimately settled.[127]

With respect to the corporate waste and the aiding and abetting corporate waste claims, the *World Health* court seems to have given plaintiffs substantial leeway with respect to the specificity with which they must allege an officer's failure to fulfill his duty of oversight. If *World Health* correctly states the pleading standards applicable to oversight claims for officers, there seems to follow a substantial duty—and associated risk of liability for failure to fulfill that duty—of general counsel to "ferret out" wrongdoing, even where the executives or employees directly committing and benefiting from the wrongdoing have every motivation to conceal their misconduct.

D. KEY TAKEAWAYS FOR MITIGATING THE RISK OF LIABILITY AND SANCTIONS[128]

Although general counsel and other in-house counsel are subject to the same state ethical, professional conduct, and disciplinary rules as other

---

125. *Id.* at 593–94 (record citation omitted).

126. *Id.* at 594.

127. Sheri Qualters, *Top Lawyers Discuss Risks of Landing in the Hot Seat*, CORPORATE COUNSEL (Oct. 2009), http://www.law.com/jsp/cc/PubArticleFriendlyCC. jsp?id=1202434889052#.

128. These practice tips are drawn from the authors' interviews with general counsel, as well as other sources, *e.g.*, Mikulka, *supra* chapter II, note 13, at 74.

lawyers admitted to the bar of a particular state, the current risks of liability for corporate counsel for ethical misconduct most likely originate primarily with the SEC. State disciplinary counsel tend to focus their resources on preventing and sanctioning lawyers locally. Some state disciplinary counsel tell us they must focus their time and resources on lawyers who are "lyin,' cheatin,' and stealin'" from local folks.

There has been a recent perceived increase in liability risk for general counsel. Of course, most general counsel conduct themselves ethically and with integrity, while encouraging others throughout their organizations to do the same. Even so, there are a number of steps that general counsel can take to further manage and mitigate their risk of liability:

Strengthen relationships and earn trust. The general counsel works hard to establish credibility and build relationships with both senior management and the board. This effort increases the tendency of the board and management to keep her "in the loop," to ensure that she receives the information she needs when she needs it, and to take her advice seriously.

Work regularly with good outside counsel. Even the best (and most sleepless) general counsel cannot possibly develop in-depth expertise on all the myriad legal and related issues facing the corporation. Experienced outside counsel with strong knowledge of the business can provide wise and specialized guidance and enhance the general counsel's credibility with the board and management.

Create meaningful internal processes. Proactively anticipating problems, establishing risk assessment and compliance programs, and following up on their usefulness demonstrate an intent and effort to do the right thing. Even if something goes wrong, a court or other body charged with conducting the post mortem will likely take those efforts into consideration when assessing liability and any penalties.

Provide value. "Yes" and "no" answers often are not enough—if the answer were that clear, it probably would have been given before bubbling up to the general counsel. And the general counsel will be expected to coach subordinate in-house counsel to do the same. Developing practical and creative solutions (the "yes, if," or "no, but" responses)[129] that add value to a situation while keeping the company on the right path strengthens internal relationships. Thus, it helps to ensure that management and the board will continue to seek the advice of the general counsel and her department.

---

129. *See* the approach articulated by Douglas M. Hagerman, Senior Vice President, General Counsel, and Secretary, Rockwell Automation, Inc. (Sept. 16, 2010), discussed *supra* text accompanying chapter III note 53.

Follow up. If the general counsel or other lawyer said "no," or "no, but," was that advice followed? Finding out can become part of an internal risk and compliance review program, and can help the lawyer help the client and avoid a red-flag, or "you should have known," scenario upon hindsight review. If the lawyers said "yes," or "yes, if," what was the result? Finding out can guide future advice, as well as allowing the creative lawyer to be recognized for her contributions, which encourages future value-driven lawyering.

Trust your gut. Is instinct telling you that something just isn't right? A real problem may underlie that feeling. Look into it. Keep looking until satisfied. And encourage others to similarly heed red flags, and to bring their concerns to your attention.[130]

Go up the ladder, and be prepared to leave if necessary. If management fails to remedy improper conduct, the general counsel should be prepared to report the conduct to the board, and to resign if necessary. These measures may be nerve-wracking, and it is easier for us to preach those steps than it is for the general counsel to actually "pull the trigger." But the risks of irreparable damage to reputation and career probably would outweigh the costs. And how far one is willing to go may open other eyes to the severity of the situation and prompt a corrective response.

---

130. *See, e.g.*, Interview with Deirdre Stanley, Executive Vice President and General Counsel, Thomson Reuters Corporation (Jan. 25, 2010) ("Even outside of knowing the specific law, engaged, well-trained lawyers have a certain expectation that there's probably something wrong about X. It just doesn't sound right or feel right.").

Conclusion

In the Preface, we said that we would "endeavor to conclude with some of our own opinions about best practices." Rather than write one final conclusion that undertakes to summarize all those best practices, we have tried to summarize some specific best practices in our "key takeaways" at the end of each chapter.

Importantly, these takeaways come more from the minds and experiences of general counsel than out of our heads and experiences. Our opinions of best practices are, however, laced throughout the book and juxtaposed with the views of general counsel.

Nevertheless, we believe that the cardinal, overarching value of this work is our marshaling of the wisdom of the chief legal officers on whom we have relied heavily and quoted liberally. Again, we express to them our deepest gratitude.

APPENDIX A

Table of Contents of THE CORPORATE DIRECTOR'S GUIDEBOOK (6th ed. 2011)*

CONTENTS

APPENDIX B

Table of Contents of Stephen A. Radin, The Business Judgment Rule (6th ed. 2009)*

VOLUME I

VOLUME II

VOLUME IV

INDEX

CROs (chief risk officers), 151
CROs (corporate responsibility
   officers), 117–18n75
CSR (corporate social responsibility).
   See Corporate citizenship
Culture of corporations. *See* Corporate
   culture
Cutler, Stephen, 204

D&O insurance, 157
Decentralization of legal
   departments, 159–64, 189
de Cunha, Maria, 181
Delaware General Corporation Law
   (DGCL), 78–79, 84, 98n5, 133,
   139n29, 143, 210. *See also*
   Delaware law
Delaware law
   business judgment rule in, 141–42,
      143, 144
   conduct and liability, standards
      of, 138
   corporate citizenship and, 120
   corporate governance under, 17
   corporate law and, 133–35,
      134n6, 139–41
   fiduciary duties and, 210
   majority voting under, 18–19n40
   oversight, duty of, 213
   proxy access rules
      under, 18–19, 19n41
Delaware Supreme Court, 136, 140, 145
DeMott, Deborah A., 60, 197–98
Denniston, Brackett, 4n5, 30n17, 97
Derivative suits, stockholder, 136
Desjardins, Daniel, 40, 73–74, 101,
   103, 167
de Wolf, Buckmaster, 185
DGCL. *See* Delaware General
   Corporation Law
Di Guglielmo, Christine T., xv, xix–xx, xxi
Directors. *See* Boards of directors
Diversity programs, 122–28,
   122n98, 130
Document retention policies, 172–73
Document review, 183
Dodd-Frank Wall Street Reform and
   Consumer Protection Act of 2010
   conflict minerals and, 121
   corporate governance and, 15–20

executive compensation and, 81
   impact of, 12
   new reality and, 1–2, 15, 25, 26
   self regulatory organizations and, 141
   whistleblower provisions in, 16, 17,
      20–24, 43, 154–55, 156, 203–4
DOJ. *See* Justice Department
Drucker, Peter, 9
Drummond, David, 208
DuPont, 126–27, 176, 187n128
DuPont Legal Model, 176, 176n60, 184
Duty of care. *See* Care, duty of
Duty of confidentiality. *See*
   Confidentiality
Duty of loyalty. *See* Loyalty, duty of
Duty of oversight. *See* Oversight, duty of

Educators, general counsel as, 44, 44n31
Enablers, general counsel as, 34, 45
Enhanced scrutiny, 145–46
Enron
   compartmentalization
      and decentralization at, 160,
      160n3, 162
   liability of general counsel
      and, 192
   Model Rules of Professional Conduct
      and, 105n30
   new reality and, 14
   outside counsel and, 50
   prosecutions and, 209
   Sarbanes-Oxley Act and, 11
   scandal, 193, 194
   SEC enforcement actions and, 205
Entire fairness test, 142, 146
Entity theory, 64n101
Environmental practices, standards
   on, 117, 121
Ethical considerations, 97–130
   creating ethical culture, 97–105
   key takeaways for, 129–30
   openness and community
      involvement and, 117–29
   corporate citizenship and,
      117–18n75, 117–22, 130
   diversity and, 122–28, 122n98, 130
   pro bono programs
      and, 128–29, 130
   professional conduct rules
      and, 105–17

Investors, 90–91, 96. *See also*
    Stockholders
Israel, offshoring in, 183

Jacobs, Jack, 138*n*24
Job security, 12–13, 12*n*24, 37,
    56–57, 88
Johnson, Christina, 14*n*30
Judicial independence, 165–66*n*18
Judicial selection debates, 92
Justice Department (DOJ), 155,
    156, 206–7

Kalil, Chuck, 10*n*15, 199–200
Kaplan, Lewis, 156
Kennedy, Gary, 62–63, 128*n*119,149*n*71
Khodorkovsky, Mikhail, 165–66*n*18
Kim, Sung Hui, 199
Kipnis, Mark, 208
KPMG case (*United States v. Stein*
    (2006)), 156, 156*n*100

Labor conditions, standards on, 117
Labor Department, 21*n*52, 22
Lalla, Thomas, 127–28
Lambeth, E. Julia (Judy), 54
"Lawyer exceptionalism," 195*n*18
Lawyer-statesman concept, xv,
    xvii–xviii, 9, 196–97
Leadership, perspectives on, 9
"Legal but stupid" concept, 8, 32, 63, 161
Legal departments, 159–90
    budget issues for, 169–87, 189
        alternative fee arrangements,
            173–74, 176, 179–82
        convergence, 173–74*n*50, 177–79
        fee structure models, 177–82, 190
        in-house work, 171–73
        litigation financing, 186–87,
            186*n*124, 186*n*126, 187*n*128
        outside costs, 173–84
        outsourcing and
            offshoring, 173, 182–84
        revenue generation, 184–85
    compartmentalization and
        decentralization of, 159–64, 189
    diversity in, 127–28, 128*n*116
    ethical culture and, 100
    global challenges for, 164–69, 189
    hiring considerations for, 93

key takeaways for, 189–90
    management of, 40–41
    outside counsel and, 173, 187–88,
        187–88*n*131, 189–90
    pro bono programs and, 129
    resources for, 159, 189
    structuring of, 73–74
Legal fees. *See* Fee arrangements
Legal Leaders for Diversity, 125
Legal services organizations, 129
Leitch, David, 48*n*49, 103, 103*n*25,
    150, 163
Liability. *See also* Personal liability;
    Sanctions, prosecution, and
    liability
    exposure to, 204–14
    standards of, 137–41
Licastro, Brian, 212–14
Litigation avoidance programs, 178
Litigation financing, 186–87,
    186*n*124, 186*n*126, 187*n*128
Lobbying, 44, 164
Loyalty, duty of, 132–33, 137, 138,
    143, 145, 210
Lytton, William, 32*n*25

Majority voting, 18–19*n*40
Management teams, 59–68
Marijuana production, 120
Martyn, Susan R., 111–12
Matthews, Charles, 162*n*9,
    171–72, 189*n*134, 209*n*98
Mayes, Michele Coleman, 46, 209
MBCA (Model Business
    Corporation Act), 138
McLean, Rhonda, 123–24
McNulty Memorandum, 155
Media relations, 93–94, 96
Mediators, general counsel
    as, 42, 42*n*23
Metropolitan Corporate Counsel on
    diversity, 123
Mexico, farmers in, 119
Michelin, 185
Microsoft, 122
Millstein, Ira M., xix, xxi, 33
Minutes, corporate, 45, 78–86, 95, 96
Missouri, judicial selection in, 92
Model Business Corporation Act
    (MBCA), 138

implementation of, 201
legal departments and, 75
liability and, 200–204, 201n45, 216
Model Rules of Professional Conduct
    and, 110, 110–11nn57–58
SEC requirements and, 110–11

Valihura, Karen, 65
Value-billing concept, 176–77
Values and ethical
    standards, 41–42, 41n19
Veasey, E. Norman, xv, xix–xx, xxi,
    105n30, 156n101, 196n24

Walt Disney Co. Deriv. Litig., In re (2006),
    79, 83, 84, 136, 140
Waste, corporate, 213–14
Water cooler phenomenon, 72. *See also*
    Back-channel information
Weil Gotshal & Manges LLP,
    xxiv, 83–84, 118

Weinberger v. UOP, Inc. (1983), 146
Wellbutrin SR, 206
Whistleblower Press Release,
    SEC, 24n65
Whistleblowers
    compliance programs and, 43
    Dodd-Frank Act and, 16, 17, 20–24
    implications for, 22–24
    incentives and, 20–21
    internal investigations
        and, 153, 154–55
    retaliation, protection from, 21–22
    up-the-ladder reporting and, 201
Work-product doctrine, 65, 155,
    166, 186
Worldcom, 11, 192, 193, 194
*World Health Alternatives, Inc. v.
    McDonald* (2008), 212–14

Zero-tolerance approach to ethics,
    101–2